# EZ IRS HELP

## EASY FIXES TO YOUR IRS PROBLEMS

**Use the IRS Fresh Start Program or bankruptcy and save up to 100 percent on your IRS tax debt.**

Retired IRS agent, fraud coordinator, instructor and group manager tells how to take advantage of tax tips and loopholes in a forty-seven-chapter tax reference manual. Learn how to navigate the IRS.

# GEORGE J. CAMBERIS,
## Enrolled Agent

PAGE PUBLISHING, INC.
New York, NY

First originally published by Page Publishing, Inc. 2017

The publication is designed to provide accurate and authoritative information in regard to the subject matter covered. It is sold with the understanding that neither the author nor the publisher is engaged in rendering legal, accounting, or other professional services. If legal advice or expert assistance is required, the services of a competent professional should be sought.

ISBN 978-1-68348-687-9 (Paperback)
ISBN 978-1-68348-688-6 (Digital)

Printed in the United States of America

# E Z IRS HELP

This book may save you hundreds or even thousands of dollars on IRS taxes, accounting, and legal fees.

Here are some of the forty-seven chapters to help answer your questions and help solve most IRS problems:

- The IRS Fresh Start Program
- Can Bankruptcy Help Many Taxpayers Eliminate Their IRS Tax Debt? Yes.
- Criminal Fraud and Your Chances of Going to Jail: How IRS Catches Tax Cheats
- Failure to File Cases: What to Do, How to Avoid Penalties and Jail
- Benefits of Filing a Joint Return Versus Separate Returns: Married and Not Living Together, You May Be Able to File as Head of Household
- How to Qualify for Innocent Spouse or Injured Spouse
- What to Do When You Receive a Notice or Letter from the IRS
- Know When You Need a Representative and How to Choose an Accountant
- Tax Filing Options for Same-Sex Couples Lawfully Married
- How to Handle an IRS Tax Audit
- How to Notify IRS if Your Identity and Tax Refund Are Stolen
- How to Deal with the IRS Collection Division
- How to Contact the IRS
- How and Where to Get Free Tax Help
- A List of Fourteen Free E-file Companies on IRS.GOV, Easy Steps to Get There

George worked in the Examination Division of the Internal Revenue Service for over thirty-nine years. During that time, he was involved in the examination of all types of federal tax returns and held various positions, including supervisory positions, instructor, and reviewer.

# WHY YOU SHOULD READ

# THIS BOOK

This might be the most important money-saving book that you can buy. This book should pay for itself many times over. After reading this book, you will have a basic understanding on how to deal with the IRS and a reference guide to answer most of your IRS questions. There are numerous books regarding how to handle a tax audit. Unfortunately, the vast majority of these books were written by CPAs or lawyers who never worked at IRS or worked there for a few years. How can they be an expert on the IRS? Two retired grade 15 IRS managers/revenue agents and one grade 14 large case revenue agent reviewed my book, and they made many valuable suggestions.

**Peace of Mind**

This book will give most of you peace of mind and erase some of your fears of the IRS. Unlike most tax books, this one will be interesting and so easy to understand. Most (not all) of your tax problems can be solved reading this book. The chapters in this book will give you step-by-step instructions on what to do and how to handle your IRS problems. Look at the chapter titles, and you will see that I cover most common problems.

I provide guidance on time-saving and less costly ways to navigate and avoid IRS problems. Many taxpayers are unaware of the free time-saving services that the IRS provides. There is an abundance of information readily available on the IRS Web, IRS tax tips, and publications.

After reading this book, the average person will be able to avail themselves of these IRS services.

My book is the quick-and-easy reference guide. Here are just a few examples to possibly save you time and money:

1. How to legally avoid paying IRS tax on cancelled debt.
2. CPAs, lawyers, and enrolled agents can pay as little as $64.90 instead of $394 for twenty-six hours (including two hours of ethics training) of continuing professional education (CPE).
3. You file your delinquent 1040 returns and do not pay your self-employment taxes. You will get Social Security credit whether or not you pay the taxes. IRS should fix this loophole.
4. When a married person can file as Head of Household instead of Married Filing Separately.
5. How to lower or avoid needless accounting and legal fees.
6. How your marital status can affect your Obama Care Premium Tax Credit.
7. A list of fourteen free e-file companies on IRS.gov. Easy steps to get there.
8. Three easy ways to reconstruct auto mileage when you kept no auto mileage records.
9. A handy weekly travel and entertainment document to keep track of your expenses.
10. How to notify the IRS if your identity and tax refund are stolen.

## Save Research Time

I have been told that anyone can research the topics in this book. That is true. However, how can you research the Web if you don't know what topic to look for? Many of the chapters cover my experience and knowledge and can't be found on the Web. I originally had sixty pages on the Fresh Start Program. I cut it down to twenty pages and made the chapter easy to understand using my IRS instructor skills. You can read over thirty Obama Care tax tips or my chapter summary.

## My Valuable Experience

The book will have many interesting stories regarding my experience dealing with taxpayers and representatives. I will show examples of how we caught tax cheats and your chances of going to jail. Also, what to do if you haven't filed your 1040 tax returns.

Most of the information in the book can be considered accurate and reliable because 60 percent or more of the book material is from the IRS manual, government websites, IRS tax tips, and IRS materials I accumulated over the years. My comments will start and end with a dash or be obvious when the letter "I" is used. Everything else comes from IRS. Therefore, there will be only be a few quotations in this book. Government publications that are prepared by government officers or employees as part of their official duties are not subject to copyright protection. See 17 USC 105.

Each taxpayer has different facts and circumstances in regard to income and deductions. Therefore, none of the information in this book should be considered tax advice or relied upon. Check the information on the internet if phone numbers have been changed or for current version of IRS Tax Tips, tax law or IRS tax forms.

# ACKNOWLEDGMENTS

I wanted this book to be special and easy to understand. I wrote this book for the average taxpayer. My only previous experience at writing was a Fraud Audit Technique hand book for Revenue Agents in the Chicago District. At a recent retirement luncheon, my friend Tom showed an advance copy of the book to 25 IRS Revenue Agents. The majority were interested in buying the book.

As you can see on the last page of this book, my qualifications are in many different areas. Few Revenue Agents have the diversity of experience I had in many different functions of IRS. Yet, when I researched the book, I was surprised to learn about many tax tips I was not aware of. Most taxpayers, Revenue Agents, accountants and lawyers will also find tax tips they were not aware of. For example: the First Time Penalty Abatement and 40 % acceptance rate of Offers in Compromise in the IRS Fresh Start Program.

The following people and my life partner, Eva Powers, were supportive of my book and made many valuable suggestions:

A special thanks to Tom Jurinek who edited the whole book twice and let me know areas of the book that should be explained better for the average person. What a great friend!

John Vest was very helpful to me in regard to dealing with the IRS Collection Division and the Taxpayer Advocate.

John Leaver made some excellent suggestions.

All three (retired) were grade 15 Chicago managers who held important IRS positions.

Bobby Greenspan (Senior Large Case Team Coordinator GS-14) who challenged me to do a better job explaining areas of the book.

Michael Dickler, a health club friend, suggested that I put a small jail cell with hands sticking out of the jail cell on the book cover. I forwarded the suggestion to Page Publishing and they did a fantastic job on the book cover. The jail cell ties into the back cover which covers criminal fraud and your chances of going to jail. Thank you Michael.

# CONTENTS

# CHAPTER 1

# The IRS Fresh Start Program

There is only one difficult chapter in the book, and I have set it up similar to classes I taught at the IRS. Ability to pay and effective tax administration will be covered. My comments will be started and ended with a dash. The rest came from the IRS.

**Chapter Objectives**

- Overview of offer in compromise (OIC).
- The three grounds for OIC acceptance.
- Pertinent IRS Web OIC information.
- OIC acceptance rate.
- My six steps that are needed for IRS acceptance.
- My OIC examples.
- My check sheet for allowable monthly expenses.
- Assets that must be included in reasonable collection potential.
- Future income taken into account computing reasonable collection potential (RCP).
- *Effective tax administration used to accept OICs.*
- Preparing and submitting the offer in compromise.

- Low-income certification chart. If eligible, the $150 fee and 20 percent down payment are waived. Also, no payments are due while OIC is being considered.
- National standards for monthly expenses.

## IR-2012-53, May 21, 2012

Washington-The Internal Revenue Service today announced another expansion of its "Fresh Start Initiative" by offering more flexible terms to its Offer in Compromise (OIC) program that will enable some of the most financially stressed taxpayers who are struggling to clear up their tax problems and in many cases more quickly than in the past.

The objective of this chapter is to give the average person an easy-to-understand guide to see if an offer in compromise (OIC) will help eliminate your IRS tax debt. You don't have to read the whole chapter to make an initial determination.

When I first heard the claims of many accountants on television and radio by tax resolution firms, I did not believe their claims of saving up to 85 percent on settling your IRS tax debt. I took a CPE course with "Professional Education Services, LP" (PES). The title of the course was "Settling Tax Debt with the IRS." The excellent course covered offers in compromise, installment agreements, bankruptcy, liens, and levies.

I learned that the tax-saving claims were possible for many taxpayers who could not pay the full amount of their IRS debt in full in the remaining months left on the collection statute of limitations. However, asset equity will affect the OIC.

There are some highly rated tax resolution firms. Be careful when hiring a tax resolution firm. Check with the Better Business Bureau. There are some rich individuals who made a fortune charging people up front using credit cards. They are being sued because they did not provide the services promised. You would get a salesman on the phone and end up paying $4,500 up front on your charge card. Then you would not receive the promised services. You should never pay more than $3,750 unless you have a payroll tax problem or a complex audit. Payroll tax cases can range from $1,000 to $5,000.

There is a higher charge if your representative is fighting to keep your business going. If the business is closed, the fee may be only $1,000 to $3,500 to protect you from liability.

I would personally want to deal in person with a CPA, lawyer, or enrolled agent with collection experience rather than a salesman on the phone. Your first consultation should be free. Then you should find out what your fees are up front in an engagement letter.

## My Quiz

*Question 1*

You owe IRS less than $10,000. Should you contact a tax resolution firm?

No. A simple installment agreement should solve your problem. Request the IRS installment agreement on the Internet. It is easy to fill out, and it takes five minutes. Read my chapter on installment agreements. I would charge $300 to handle the installment agreement. There are some accountants or firms that would try to charge you $1,000 to $1,500.

*Question 2*

You *owe* IRS less than $10,000, and you lost your job or retired on Social Security. Should I hire an accountant? Maybe. What if you cannot pay the tax? You may also not be able to afford an accountant. If your living expenses exceed your income, you probably do not need an accountant because of the small amount of tax. If your accountant will charge you less than $1,000 or $1,500 and you do not want to deal with the IRS, hire an accountant. If you owe IRS a large amount of tax, I would strongly recommend you hire a representative who has experience dealing with the Collection Division of the IRS. If you do not hire an accountant, fill out form 433-A or have the revenue officer help you fill out the form 433-A. The revenue officer may 53 your account (treat it as currently not collectible). You will have to file a form 433-F every year if your account is treated as uncollectable. If you get a job, your account may become current again. Then an installment agreement should be considered.-

*The IRS may accept an OIC based on three grounds:*

- *First, acceptance is permitted if there is doubt as to liability.* This ground is only met when there is a genuine dispute as to the existence or amount of the correct tax debt under the law.

- *Second, acceptance is permitted if there is doubt that the amount owed is fully collectible.* Doubt as to collectability exists in any case where the taxpayer's assets and income are less than the full amount of the tax liability.

- *Third, acceptance is permitted based on effective tax administration.* An offer may be accepted based on effective tax administration when there is no doubt that the tax is legally owed and that the full amount owed can be collected, but requiring payment in full would either create an economic hardship or would be unfair and inequitable.

We will be covering the second and third grounds for acceptance. The second is the most common. The only part you have to remember is the ability to pay monthly income, monthly expenses, and asset equity. These items will be explained with examples. Effective tax administration acceptance will be covered in the second half of the chapter.

## Per IRS Web-Offer in Compromise

An offer in compromise allows you to settle your tax debt for less than the full amount you owe. It may be a legitimate option if you can't pay your full tax liability, or doing so creates a financial hardship. We consider your unique set of facts and circumstances:

- ability to pay
- income
- expenses
- asset equity

We generally approve an offer in compromise when the amount offered represents the most we can expect to collect within a reasonable period of time. Explore all other payment options before submitting an offer in compromise. The offer in compromise program is not for everyone. If you hire a tax professional to help you file an offer, be sure to check his or her qualifications.

The IRS accepted approximately 40 percent of the offers in 2014.

Offers in Compromise Per 2012–2014 IRS Data Books

|  | 2012 | 2013 | 2014 |
| --- | --- | --- | --- |
| Offers Submitted | 64,000 | 74,000 | 68,000 |
| Offers Accepted | 24,000 | 31,000 | 27,000 |
| Offer Dollar Amount | $196,652,000 | $195,379,000 | $179,354,000 |

*How would I handle an OIC?*

Don't let the chapter intimidate you. I will explain the following six items and give examples that are easy to understand.

*I will explain how to compute the following to see if you qualify for an OIC.*

1. Make sure you are eligible.
2. Compute monthly income and expenses using form 433-A.
3. Compute how many months are left on the statute of limitation.
4. Compute asset equity.
5. Compute reasonable collection potential (RCP).
6. Are there any dissipated assets? Don't worry, most taxpayers won't have dissipated assets. IRS examples will explain dissipated assets in detail.

## Step 1
*Make sure you are eligible.*

Per form 433-A, "Before you submit your offer, you must (1) file all tax returns you are legally required to file, (2) make all required estimated tax payments or withholding for the current year, and (3) make all required federal tax deposits for the current year if you are a business owner with employees."

If you do not qualify for the current year because you haven't made the required estimated tax payments or withholding for the current year, then pay the required estimated taxes or withholding the next year.-

## Step 2
*Compute the remaining months left on the ten-year (120 months) statute of limitations.*

If you can add or subtract, you can easily compute the remaining years on the collection statute. Start with the date the tax return is due. If filed late or on extension, use that date. For example, a 2010 return is due on April 15, 2011. If the return was filed on September 12, 2011, then use that date. If the current date is June 12, 2015, you are three months short of four years (48 months - 3 months = 45 months). Thus, 120 months - 45 months = 75 months left on the collection statute. If you file on March 13, 2008, and the due date is April 15, 2008, you will use April 15, 2008. Then add ten years to 2008, and the ten-year statute expires on April 15, 2018. You will see how important this is shortly. You must compute the remaining months on the statute for each year. A tax return filed on April 15, 2006 will have the collection statute expire on April 15, 2016. If you haven't filed a return, you will have a ten-year statute of limitations after you file the return. A collection substitute for return (SFR) will not start the statute of limitations.

## Step 3
*Compute your monthly net income for the last three months.*

You must show your monthly income less your monthly expenses. If your net monthly income will not be sufficient to pay off your debt in the remaining months, you may be entitled to a large write-off of your IRS debt. The most important or critical part of the IRS Fresh Start Initiative is the computation of your monthly income minus your allowable expenses (use form 433-A Revised January 2015). See the National Standards for living expenses chart I prepared after step 6. I also transferred pages from form 433-A, which list monthly income and monthly expenses. Fill in your income and expenses.

Enter your household's gross monthly income. The entire household income includes spouse, significant other, children, and others who contribute to the household. This is necessary for the IRS to accurately evaluate your offer.

## Step 4
*Compute your asset equity.*

This will be covered in detail later in the asset section and in examples below. Let us assume you can come up with $7,000. Items that have to be taken into account are cash, savings accounts, securities, stock, cash surrender of insurance policies, IRA and Roth accounts, retirement accounts you can borrow on or liquidate, and other valuable items (artwork, collections, jewelry, collectibles).

## Step 5
*Compute reasonable collection potential (RCP).*

This would be your net monthly income times remaining months on the statute plus asset equity. Paying off your car will increase your future monthly income. Buying a new car with payments over seventy-two months will also decrease your RCP. See examples below:

## Step 6
*Are there any dissipated assets?*

## IRM 5.8.5.18 (09-30-2013)
## Dissipation of Assets

Inclusion of dissipated assets in the calculation of the reasonable collection potential (RCP) is no longer applicable, except in situations where it can be shown the taxpayer has sold, transferred, encumbered, or otherwise disposed of assets in an attempt to avoid the payment of the tax liability or used the assets or proceeds (other than wages, salary, or other income) for other than the payment of items necessary for the production of income or the health and welfare of the taxpayer or their family, after the tax has been assessed or within six months prior to the tax assessment.

Generally, a three-year time frame will be used to determine if it is appropriate to include a dissipated asset in RCP. Include the year of submission as a complete year in the calculation.

You can skip dissipated assets if you haven't sold assets in the last three years and used the funds for expenses other than living expenses.

The following examples will be helpful if you disposed of assets in the three-year period. The dissipation information above and below are IRM (Internal Revenue Manual) guidelines.

*Assets That Should Be Included in RCP*

The taxpayer dissolved an IRA or other investment account to pay for specific nonpriority items, i.e., child's wedding, child's university tuition, extravagant vacation, etc.

The taxpayer inherited funds and used the funds for nonpriority items (other than health/welfare of the family or production of income).

The taxpayer closed bank/investment accounts and will not disclose how the funds were spent or if any funds remain. Examples of situations in which the value of an asset should *not* be included in RCP and are not limited to the following:

Dissolving an IRA during unemployment or underemployment-review of available internal sources verified the taxpayer's income was insufficient to meet necessary living expenses. In this case, do not include the funds up to the amount needed to meet allowable expenses in the reasonable collection potential calculation.

Substantial amount withdrawn from bank accounts-taxpayer provided supporting documentation that funds were used to pay for medical or other necessary living expenses. This amount will not be included in the RCP calculation.

## My Offer in Compromise Examples

- The taxpayer's tax debt is $44,000. The taxpayer's monthly gross income is $6,200. His/her monthly expenses are $6,000. There are eighty months left on the ten-year collection statute of limitations. The taxpayer has $7,000 in realizable assets (cash in bank). The taxpayer can only pay back $6,200 - $6,000, or $200 a month net monthly income for eighty months, which equals only $16,000. Add the $7,000, and the total reasonable collection potential (RCP) is $23,000. The taxpayer qualifies for an offer in compromise because the debt ($44,000) is greater than the reasonable collection potential ($23,000). However, the law has been changed, and we can offer twelve months of net monthly income instead of forty-eight months, or remaining months on the statute if shorter. We would take twelve months of net monthly income ($200 × 12 months) or $2,400 plus $7,000 and offer $9,400 if paid in five months. If paid within twenty-four months, we would offer twenty-four months × $200, or $4,800 plus the $7,000, for a total of $11,800. If paid within twenty-four months, the taxpayer could save $32,200.

Same facts as above, except the taxpayer has an IRA account in the amount of $60,000.

Equity is the cash value less any tax consequences for liquidating the account and early withdrawal penalty. In this example, the taxpayer would get credit for the 10 percent early withdrawal tax penalty ($6,000) and the 25 percent tax bracket on the IRA ($15,000) or $21,000 offset against the $60,000. The reasonable collection potential is $39,000 plus $2,400 plus $7,000, or $48,400. Since the reasonable collection potential ($48,400) is greater than the tax owed ($44,000), the OIC will be rejected. Generally, the IRS will not accept an offer if you can pay your tax debt in full through an installment agreement or a lump sum. There are exceptions regarding effective tax administration that will be covered later. Also, later in the book, you will learn that the 10 percent early withdrawal penalty may be waived if the funds were used to pay IRS taxes and a levy has been issued.

Later in the chapter, you will see that future income can affect your monthly income computation. The most common are retirement, loss of job, etc. In some cases, income is expected to rise, and a collateral agreement will be considered. This will be covered in detail.

- The taxpayer owes $25,000 and $26,000 respectively for the timely filed 2005 and 2006 1040 tax returns. The ten-year statute will expire on April 15, 2016 and April 15, 2017 respectively. The IRS is taking out 15 percent of his/her social security, and he/she is not working. After two years, the tax debt will be wiped out by the ten-year statute, and he/she will be receiving the full Social Security. If he/she cannot afford to pay necessary living expenses, he/she may try to have his/her account treated as currently not collectible. If IRS collection currently writes off your account, your 15 percent Social Security offset should be removed. On April 15, 2017, the IRS collection statute will expire.

It is very important to take every allowable expense when computing your net monthly income. I prepared the following check sheet to make you aware of the expenses you can deduct when computing your net monthly income. How to look up the amounts allowed will be covered at the end of the chapter.

# IRS Collection Financial Standards-My Check Sheet

## NATIONAL STANDARDS

### FOOD, CLOTHING AND OTHER ITEMS
FAMILY SIZE GENERALLY BASED ON EXEMPTIONS
ON MOST RECENT 1040 RETURN.
Effective 03/15/2015

| EXPENSES PER FAMILY MEMBER | ONE | TWO | THREE | FOUR |
|---|---|---|---|---|
| FOOD, CLOTHING, OTHER ITEMS | 315 | 588 | 660 | 821 |
| HOUSEKEEPING SUPPLIES | 32 | 66 | 65 | 78 |
| APPAREL & SERVICES | 88 | 182 | 209 | 244 |
| PERSONAL CARE PRODUCTS | 34 | 61 | 64 | 70 |
| MISCELLANEOUS | 116 | 215 | 251 | 300 |
| TOTAL | 585 | 1,092 | 1,249 | 1,513 |

MORE THAN FOUR PERSONS- ADD 378 FOR EACH PERSON
TO TOTAL ALLOWANCE
"National standards for food, clothing and other items applied nationwide. Taxpayers are allowed total National Standards amounts for family size, without questioning the amount spent." If you can substantiate a higher amount for an item (example food) you can receive the larger amount for food.

### HOUSING AND UTILITIES-LOCAL STANDARDS          LOOK UP YOUR COUNTY
CHICAGO-COOK COUNTY                                1824   2142   2257   2517

FIVE OR MORE PERSONS 2,557. It also appears that the housing and utilities standard can easily be exceeded and IRS would probably allow you your basic living expenses. Look up your county in your state.

### NATIONAL PUBLIC TRANSPORTATION
184 PER HOUSEHOLD                          NO CAR

### NATIONAL CAR OWNERSHIP COSTS

| | ONE CAR | TWO CAR |
|---|---|---|
| | 517 | 1034 |

### CAR OPERATING COSTS
| | | |
|---|---|---|
| CHICAGO | 262 | 524 |
| NEW YORK | 342 | 684 |

Add 200 if car is six years old or has over 75,000 miles. It would appear that car operating costs can exceed the standard amount, especially if your drive is a long distance to work. Look up your geographic area for deduction.

### OUT OF POCKET HEALTH CARE.    60 PER PERSON.  144 PER PERSON OVER 65.
Add health insurance costs and out of pocket medical expenses which include prescriptions, medical supplies, eyeglasses, and contact lenses.

## INCLUDE

Minimum credit card payments, bank fees and term life insurance. _____
Delinquent state and local taxes. _____
Estimated taxes- divide quarterly payments by three. _____
Student loans-minimum payment and must
    be guaranteed by federal government. _____
Child/dependent care for 1040 dependents. _____
Court ordered payments-submit copy of court order. _____

**Monthly Household Income-Form 433-A**
Round to the nearest whole dollar.

**Primary taxpayer**
Wages _____
Social Security _____
Pension(s) _____
Other Income *(e.g. unemployment)* _____
Total primary taxpayer income = (30) $_____

**Spouse**
Wages _____
Social Security
Pension(s) _____
Other Income *(e.g. unemployment)* _____
Total spouse income = (31) $_____

Additional sources of income used to support the household (e.g., non-liable spouse, or
    anyone else who may contribute to the household income, etc.) (32) $_____
Interest and dividends (33) $_____
Distributions *(e.g., income from partnerships, sub-S Corporations, etc.)* (34) $_____
Net rental income (35) $_____
Net business income from Box C (36) $_____
Child support received (37) $_____
Alimony received (38) $_____

Round to the nearest whole dollar. Do not enter a negative number. If any line item is a
negative, enter "0" on that line. **Add lines 30 through 38, and enter the amount in Box D**
**Box D** Total Household Income_____

**Monthly Household Expenses** Enter your average monthly expenses.
Food, clothing, and miscellaneous *(e.g., housekeeping supplies, personal*
    *care products, minimum payment on credit card). A reasonable*
    *estimate of these expenses may be used.* (39) $_____
Housing and utilities *(e.g., rent or mortgage payment and average monthly cost of*
    *property taxes, home insurance, maintenance, dues, fees, and utilities including electricity,*
    *gas, other fuels, trash collection, water, cable television and Internet, telephone, and*
    *cell phone).* (40) $_____
Vehicle loan and/or lease payment(s). (41) $_____

Vehicle operating costs *(e.g., average monthly cost of maintenance, repairs,*
*insurance, fuel, registrations, licenses, inspections, parking, tolls, etc.).*
A reasonable estimate of these expenses may be used. (42) $_____
Public transportation costs *(e.g., average monthly cost of fares for mass transit, such as bus,*
*train, ferry, taxi, etc.). A reasonable estimate of these expenses may be used.* (43) $_____
Health insurance premiums. (44) $_____
Out-of-pocket health-care costs (e.g. average monthly cost of prescription drugs, medical
services and medical supplies, like eye glasses, hearing aids, etc.). (45) $_____
Court-ordered payments, e.g., monthly cost of any alimony,
child support, etc. (46) $_____
Child/dependent care payments, e.g., day care, etc. (47) $_____
Life insurance premiums. (48) $_____
Current taxes (e.g. monthly cost of federal, state, local tax, personal
property tax, etc.). (49) $_____

**Section 7** (Continued)
Other secured debts (e.g. any loan where you pledged an asset as collateral not
previously listed, government guaranteed student loan). (50) $_____

| | |
|---|---|
| Delinquent state and local taxes | (51) $_____ |
| Total monthly household expenses | Box E _____ |
| Remaining monthly income | Box F _____ |

A more detailed explanation of expenses will come at the end of
the chapter. So far, you can see if you are eligible for an OIC based on
monthly income times remaining months on the collection statute.
The next step is to see which assets have to be included in the reasonable collection potential (RCP). If you don't qualify because you have
the ability to pay the full amount of tax owed, then we will see if you
are eligible under effective tax administration.

## IRM 5.8.5.4 (09-30-2013)
### Equity in Assets

-An IRS employee may or may not decide to request the following documents. The following are guidelines for IRS employees. It doesn't mean they will read them and follow them. However, we can cite them when it is to our advantage-

Proper asset valuation is essential to determine reasonable collection potential. In some cases, it may be necessary to review the following documents to determine undisclosed assets or income and assist in valuing the property:

A.  Divorce decrees or separation agreements to determine the disposition of assets in the property settlements;

B.  Homeowners or renters insurance policies and riders to identify high value personal items such as jewelry, antiques, or artwork;

C.  Financial statements recently provided to lending institutions or others to identify assets.

## IRM 5.8.5.4.1 (09-30-2013)
### Net Realizable Equity

Normally, quick sale value (QSV) is calculated at 80 percent of FMV. A higher or lower percentage may be applied in determining QSV when appropriate, depending on the type of asset and current market conditions.

Revenue officers currently seize less than a thousand homes a year.

## IRM 5.8.5.7 (09-30-2013)
### Cash

These are important examples regarding how to report cash. This includes your savings, checking, and money market funds. Reduce the total amount listed by $1,000.

Exception is the following:

> If the total amount listed on the form 433-A (OIC) is over $1,000 and you have reason to believe the money will be used to pay for the taxpayer's monthly allowable living expenses, do not include it as an asset.

Example,

1.  The taxpayer lists $10,000 on form 433-A (OIC). The taxpayer's allowable living expenses is $3,000. Include $6,000 ($10,000 less $1,000 less $3,000) as an asset value.

Example,

2.  The taxpayer lists $3,000 on the form 433-A (OIC), and his allowable living expenses is $2,700. Do not include any amount as an asset since the $300 difference is less than $1,000.

## IRM 5.8.5.8 (09-30-2013)
## Securities and Stocks of Closely Held Entities

1.  Financial securities are considered an asset, and their value should be determined and included in the RCP when investigating an offer.
2.  When the taxpayer will liquidate the investment to fund the offer, allow associated fees in addition to any penalty for early withdrawal and the current year tax consequence.

## IRM 5.8.5.9 (09-30-2013)
## Life Insurance

Term insurance is OK.

1.  Identify the type, conditions for borrowing or cancellation, and the current loan and cash values.

2.  Life insurance as an investment (e.g., whole life) is not considered necessary.

## IRM 5.8.5.10 (09-30-2013)
### Retirement or Profit Sharing Plans

1.  Funds held in a retirement or profit-sharing plan are considered an asset and must be valued for offer purposes.
2.  Contributions to voluntary retirement plans are not a necessary expense.
3.  It may be necessary to secure a copy of the plan to determine the taxpayer's vested interest and ability to borrow. Equity is the cash value less any tax consequences for liquidating the account and early withdrawal penalty, if applicable.

My comment-it would appear that if you cannot withdraw the funds or borrow on the funds, you don't have to include the funds in the RCP.

## IRM 5.8.5.11 (10-22-2010)
### Furniture, Fixtures, and Personal Effects

1.  The taxpayer's declared value of household goods is usually acceptable unless there are articles of extraordinary value, such as antiques, artwork, jewelry, or collector's items. Exercise discretion in determining whether the assets warrant personal inspection.
2.  There is a statutory exemption from levy that applies to the taxpayer's furniture and personal effects. This exemption amount is updated on an annual basis.

If we look at form 433-A, there are no spaces to list your furniture and household goods as an asset on form 433-A. Therefore, I would ignore furniture, clothing, and personal affects except for those other valuable items listed below.

**Section 3** *(Continued)*
**Personal Asset Information**

Other valuable items (artwork, collections, jewelry, items of value in safe deposit boxes, interest in a company or business that is not publicly traded, etc.).

**IRM 5.8.5.12 (09-30-2013)**
**Motor Vehicles, Airplanes, and Boats**

1. Equity in motor vehicles, airplanes, and boats must be determined and included in the RCP. Unusual assets such as airplanes and boats may require an appraisal to determine FMV, unless the items can be located in a trade association guide.
2. It is not necessary to personally inspect automobiles used for personal transportation. When it appears reasonable, accept the taxpayer's stated value.
3. Exclude $3,450 per car from the QSV of vehicles owned by the taxpayer(s) and used for work, the production of income, and/or the welfare of the taxpayer's family (two cars for joint taxpayers and one vehicle for a single taxpayer).

You would multiply the fair market of each auto by 80 percent.

Item 2 is very important, and I don't think IRS will force you to sell your car. However, if you have a classic corvette worth a lot of money, they will probably go after that.

**IRM 5.8.11.1 (09-23-2008)**
**Overview**

1. As part of the IRS Restructuring and Reform Act of 1998 (RRA 98), Congress added section 7122(c) to the Internal Revenue Code. That section provides that the Service shall set forth guidelines for determining when an OIC should be accepted. Congress explained that these guide-

lines should allow the Service to consider: hardship, public policy, and equity.

Treasury Regulation 301.7122-1 authorizes the Service to consider OIC's raising these issues. These offers are called effective tax administration (ETA) offers.

## IRM 5.8.11.2.1 (09-23-2008)
### Economic Hardship

1. When a taxpayer's liability can be collected in full but collection would create an economic hardship, an ETA offer based on economic hardship can be considered.
2. The definition of economic hardship as it applies to effective tax administration (ETA) offers is derived from Treasury Regulations 301.6343-1. Economic hardship occurs when a taxpayer is unable to pay reasonable basic living expenses.

   For individuals (including sole proprietorship entities)-compromise on economic hardship grounds is not available to corporations, partnerships, or other nonindividual entities.
3. The taxpayer's financial information and special circumstances must be examined to determine if they qualify for an ETA offer based on economic hardship. Financial analysis includes reviewing basic living expenses as well as other considerations.
4. The taxpayer's income and basic living expenses must be considered to determine if the claim for economic hardship should be accepted. Basic living expenses are those expenses that provide for health welfare and production of income of the taxpayer and the taxpayer's family.
5. In addition to the basic living expenses, other factors to consider that impact upon the taxpayer's financial condition include the following:

   • The taxpayer's age and employment status

- Number, age, and health of the taxpayer's dependents
- Cost of living in the area the taxpayer resides
- Any extraordinary circumstances such as special education expenses, a medical catastrophe, or natural disaster.

This list is not all-inclusive. Other factors may be considered in making an economic hardship determination.

**Factors that support an economic hardship determination may include the following:**

A. The taxpayer is incapable of earning a living because of a long-term illness, medical condition, or disability, and it is reasonably foreseeable that the financial resources will be exhausted providing for care and support during the course of the condition.

B. The taxpayer may have a set monthly income and no other means of support and the income is exhausted each month in providing for the care of dependents.

C. The taxpayer has assets but is unable to borrow against the equity in those assets, and liquidation to pay the outstanding tax liability(s) would render the taxpayer unable to meet basic living expenses.

**Note**

These factors are representative of situations the Service regularly encounters when working with taxpayers to resolve delinquent accounts. They are not intended to provide an exhaustive list of the types of cases that can be compromised based on economic hardship.

6. The following examples illustrate the types of cases that may be compromised under the economic hardship standard:

The taxpayer has assets sufficient to satisfy the tax liability and provides full-time care and assistance to a dependent child, who has a serious long-term illness. It is expected that the taxpayer will need to use the equity in assets to provide for adequate basic living expenses and medical care for the child. The taxpayer's overall compliance history does not weigh against compromise.

The taxpayer is retired, and the only income is from a pension. The only asset is a retirement account, and the funds in the account are sufficient to satisfy the liability. Liquidation of the retirement account would leave the taxpayer without adequate means to provide for basic living expenses. The taxpayer's overall compliance history does not weigh against compromise.

## IRM 5.8.5.20 (09-30-2013)
## Future Income

1.  Future income is defined as an estimate of the taxpayer's ability to pay based on an analysis of gross income, less necessary living expenses, for a specific number of months into the future.

2.  As a general rule, the taxpayer's current income should be used in the analysis of future ability to pay.

    Note-this may include situations where the taxpayer's income is recently reduced based on a change in occupation or employment status.

3.  Consideration should be given to the taxpayer's overall general situation, including such facts as age, health, marital status, number and age of dependents, level of education or occupational training, and work experience.

Examples,

1.  Taxpayer's spouse has not worked for over two and a half years and has no expectations of returning to work. Do not average income for the spouse's past employment.

2.  Taxpayer has been unemployed for over one year and provided proof that Social Security Disability is the sole source of income. Do not apply income averaging in this case, but use current income to determine the taxpayer's future ability to pay.

4.  The taxpayer recently began working after several months of unemployment. Use the most recent three month pay statements to determine future income. Since the taxpayer is a wage earner, the use of income averaging over the prior three years of income is not appropriate. [Yes, I skipped 3.]

5.  The taxpayer has been receiving gifts from their parents to meet current living expenses for the past six months. The taxpayer has no guaranteed right to the funds in the future, and the amount does not appear to be based on the transfer of assets to the parents. The gift amount should not be included as income.

Taken from future income tables,

1.  The taxpayer is sixty-five years of age and has indicated he will retire at the age of sixty-six. He provided copies of documents that have been submitted to his employer discussing his retirement date. Use the taxpayer's current income until the taxpayer's anticipated retirement date, then adjust the taxpayer's income to reflect the amount expected in retirement.

2.  The taxpayer is sixty-two years of age, the taxpayer is in good health, and his income has remained stable for the past three years. The taxpayer states he would like to retire at age sixty-five. Use the taxpayer's current income, and if the RCP exceeds the offer amount, discuss the option of securing an installment agreement until the taxpayer actually retires, at which time an offer may be appropriate.

## IRM 5.8.6.2.1 (07-31-2014)
## Future Income-Collateral Agreement

1. It is appropriate to consider future income collateral agreements for individuals, limited liability companies, and corporations when the investigation reveals that a substantial increase in the taxpayer's future income is expected.

2. The use of a future income collateral agreement may be an option when the calculation of the taxpayer's future income for reasonable collection potential (RCP) purposes does not reasonably reflect the taxpayer's earnings potential. Scenarios where the taxpayer's future income may be substantially higher include the following:

    A. The taxpayer's past income does not provide an accurate analysis for what may be earned in the future based on their earnings potential due to their training or education.

    Example,

    The taxpayer is a student and is expected to graduate soon and begin earning a significant annual income.

    B. The taxpayer's current income is minimal or considerably less than what the taxpayer has earned in the past, and a reasonable expectation exists that the taxpayer's earnings will be increasing substantially prior to the expiration.

    Example,

    The taxpayer is an engineer but is currently employed as a salesman, earning less than half of his prior salary due to difficulty he has had in obtaining a job in the engineering field at the present time.

3.   Future income collateral agreements must be monitored annually for the life of the agreement.

*Consult area counsel relative to the wording of unique collateral agreement situations.* You will not find form 2261 on IRS.gov. Your representative should ask IRS to prepare it. Few people are aware of the form.

Download the national standards for food, clothing and other items in PDF format for printing. Please note that the standard amounts change, so if you elect to print them, check back periodically to assure you have the latest version.

## IRM 5.8.5.22.1 (10-22-2010)
## Necessary Expenses

1.   National and local expense standards are guidelines. If it is determined a standard amount is inadequate to provide for a specific taxpayer's basic living expenses, allow a deviation. Require the taxpayer to provide reasonable substantiation and document the case file.

Example,

National Standard Expense amount is $1,100. The taxpayer's actual expenditures are housekeeping supplies, $100; clothing, $100; food, $700; personal care products, $100; and miscellaneous, $200 (total expenses, $1,200). The taxpayer is allowed the national standard amount of $1,100, unless the higher amount is justified as necessary. In this example, the taxpayer has claimed a higher food expense than allowed. Justification would be based on prescribed or required dietary needs. The taxpayer must substantiate and verify only the food expense. The taxpayer is not required to verify expenses for all five categories if a higher expense is claimed for one category. The standard amounts will be allowed for the remaining categories.

2.  Generally, the total number of persons allowed for national standard expenses should be the same as those allowed as dependents on the taxpayer's current year income tax return. There may be reasonable exceptions.

Examples,

Foster children or children for whom adoption is pending.
Custodial parent released the dependency exemption to ex-spouse.

Go to Local Standards: Housing and Utilities-Internal Revenue Service on the Internet. Choose your state to get your local standards.

## IRM 5.8.5.22.2 (10-22-2010)
## Housing and Utilities

1.  When determining a taxpayer's housing and utility expense, use an amount sufficient to provide for basic living expenses. Use the amount shown in the expense standard schedules as a guideline unless such use results in the taxpayer not having adequate means to provide for basic living expenses. If it is determined that a standard amount is inadequate to provide for a basic living expenses, allow a deviation.

Local Standards: Transportation-Internal Revenue Service, look up on Internet.

## IRM 5.8.5.22.3 (09-30-2013)
## Transportation Expenses

1.  Transportation expenses are considered necessary when they are used by taxpayers and their families to provide for their health and welfare and/or the production of income. Employees investigating OICs are expected to exercise appropriate judgment in determining whether claimed transportation expenses meet these standards.

2.  The transportation standards consist of nationwide figures for loan or lease payments referred to as ownership costs and additional amounts for operating costs broken down by Census Region and Metropolitan Statistical Area. Operating costs include maintenance, repairs, insurance, fuel, registrations, licenses, inspections, parking, and tolls.

3.  Ownership Expenses-expenses are allowed for purchase or lease of a vehicle. Taxpayers will be allowed the local standard or the amount actually paid, whichever is less, unless the taxpayer provides documentation to verify and substantiate that the higher expenses are necessary.

4.  Operating Expenses-allow the full operating costs portion of the local transportation standard, or the amount actually claimed by the taxpayer, whichever is less. Substantiation for this allowance is not required unless the amount claimed is more than the total allowed by any of the transportation standards.

5.  If a taxpayer claims higher amounts of operating costs because he commutes long distances to reach his place of employment, he may be allowed greater than the standard.

6.  In situations where the taxpayer has a vehicle that is currently over six years old or has reported mileage of 75,000 miles or more, an additional monthly operating expense of $200 will generally be allowed per vehicle (up to two vehicles when a joint offer is submitted).

## IRM 5.8.5.22.4 (09-30-2013)
## Other Expenses

Other expenses may be allowed in determining the value of future income for offer purposes. The expense must meet the necessary expense test by providing for the health and welfare of the taxpayer and/or his or her family or must be for the production of income.

1.  Repayment of loans incurred to fund the offer and secured by the taxpayer's assets will be allowed, if the asset is nec-

essary for the health and welfare of the taxpayer and/or their family, i.e. taxpayer's residence, and the repayment amount is reasonable.

2. The taxpayer has secured a second mortgage against their residence, which will be paid toward the offer amount upon acceptance. The payment is reasonable based on the amount borrowed and terms of repayment. The payment should be allowed as an expense on the Income/Expense Table.

3. A taxpayer may have a liability for a court-ordered judgment. Unless the taxpayer is actually making payments on that liability, it is not considered as an allowable monthly expense.

When a taxpayer owes both delinquent federal and state or local taxes, and does not have the ability to full pay the liabilities, monthly payments to state taxing authorities will be allowed in certain circumstances.

Example,

The taxpayer owes the state $20,000 and owes the IRS $100,000, a total of $120,000 ($20,000 / $120,000 = 17 percent; $100,000 / $120,000 = 83 percent). The taxpayer has disposable income of $300 per month. A monthly payment to the State Taxing Authority of $51 may be allowed until the debt is retired. See the If/Then table below for examples. I did not include the table.

- Seventeen percent (17%) of $300 = $51
- Eighty-three percent (83%) of $300 = $249

## Should You Prepare the Offer in Compromise?

You should be able to prepare the form 433-A and gather the necessary documents after reading the chapter. However, you should consider hiring a professional with offer in compromise (OIC) and collection experience for the following reasons:

- There are many procedural requirements necessary for OIC approval. One defect can cause rejection. Many OIC offers fail because of procedural deficiencies.
- You will be no match for the IRS personnel reviewing your offer. Their job is to get the best deal for IRS, not you. The IRS personnel are very formidable.
- You are not familiar with IRS guidelines, procedures, and have no idea on what is the lowest possible offer IRS will accept.

## Submit Your Offer-Offer in Compromise Booklet

You'll find step-by-step instructions and all the forms for submitting an offer in the Offer in Compromise Booklet, form 656-B (PDF). Your completed offer package will include the following:

- Form 433-A (OIC) (individuals) or 433-B (OIC) (businesses) and all required documentation as specified on the forms
- Form 656(s)-individual and business tax debt (corporation/LLC/partnership) must be submitted on separate form 656
- $150 application fee (nonrefundable)
- Initial payment (nonrefundable) for each form 656.

## Select a Payment Option

Your initial payment will vary based on your offer and the payment option you choose:

| Check here if you qualify for Low Income Certification based on the monthly income guidelines below. Size of family unit | 48 Contiguous States and D.C. | Hawaii | Alaska |
|---|---|---|---|
| 1 | $2,431 | $2,796 | $3,038 |
| 2 | $3,277 | $3,769 | $4,096 |
| 3 | $4,123 | $4,742 | $5,154 |
| 4 | $4,969 | $5,715 | $6,213 |
| 5 | $5,815 | $6,688 | $7,271 |
| 6 | $6,660 | $7,660 | $8,329 |
| 7 | $7,506 | $8,633 | $9,388 |
| 8 | $8,352 | $9,606 | $10,446 |
| For each additional person, add | $ 846 | $ 973 | $1,058 |

- **Lump Sum Cash**-submit an initial payment of 20 percent of the total offer amount with your application. Wait for written acceptance. Then pay the remaining balance of the offer in five or fewer payments.
- **Periodic Payment**-submit your initial payment with your application. Continue to pay the remaining balance in monthly installments while the IRS considers your offer. If accepted, continue to pay monthly until it is paid in full.

If you meet the Low Income Certification guidelines, you do not have to send the $150 application fee or the initial payment and you will not need to make monthly installments during the evaluation of your offer. See your application package for details.

**Understand the Process: Form 656-Offer in Compromise Booklet**

While your offer is being evaluated,

- Your nonrefundable payments and fees will be applied to the tax liability (you may designate payments to a specific tax year and tax debt);
- A Notice of Federal Tax Lien may be filed;
- Other collection activities are suspended;
- The legal assessment and collection period is extended;
- Make all required payments associated with your offer;
- You are not required to make payments on an existing installment agreement; and
- Your offer is automatically accepted if the IRS does not make a determination within two years of the IRS receipt date.

| If your offer is accepted | If your offer is rejected |
|---|---|
| • You must meet all the **Offer Terms** listed in **Section 8** of form 656, including filing all required tax returns and making all payments;<br>• Any refunds due within the calendar year in which your offer is accepted will be applied to your tax debt;<br>• Federal tax liens are not released until your offer terms are satisfied. | • You may appeal a rejection within thirty days using Request for Appeal of Offer in Compromise, form 13711 (PDF). |

# CHAPTER 2

---

# How to Qualify as an
# Innocent Spouse

**Innocent Spouse Relief**

Innocent spouse cases are quite common in civil fraud and criminal cases, and I have been involved with many of these cases as part of my duties as Civil Fraud Coordinator. In many of those cases, the spouse was not aware of the unreported income. However, an important criteria is whether the spouse received a substantial benefit from the funds. At the end of this chapter, there are forty-one questions and answers covering all your concerns.

If you have been the victim of spousal abuse, intimidation, or domestic violence, you may not need to file for innocent spouse relief. You may not be jointly and severally liable for any income tax liabilities arising from that return because it is not a valid return. You will still need to file form 8857. You may also be required to file a separate return. See if the following applies to your circumstances.

**Part 111 Form 8857**

**12. Did you sign the return(s)?** If the answers are *not* the same for all tax years, explain.

**Yes.** If you were forced to sign under duress (threat of harm or other form of coercion), check here. See instructions.

**No.** Your signature was forged. See instructions.

IRS Publication 971

By law, if a person's name is signed to a return, it is presumed to be signed by that person, unless that person proves otherwise. If you believe your signature was forged, or you signed under duress, explain in the space provided. If you sign a joint return under duress or your signature was forged, the election to file jointly is not valid and you have no valid return. You are not jointly and severally liable for any income tax liabilities arising from that return. In that case, innocent spouse relief does not apply and is not necessary for obtaining relief. If you file form 8857, but also maintain that there is no valid joint return due to duress or forgery, the IRS will first make a determination as to the validity of the joint return and may accordingly deny the request for innocent spouse relief based on the fact that no joint return was filed (and thus, relief is not necessary). If it is ultimately determined that a valid joint return was filed, the IRS will then consider whether you would be entitled to innocent spouse relief on the merits.

**Forged Signature**

Your signature on the joint return is considered to be forged if it was not signed by you and you did not authorize (give tacit consent) the signing of your name to the return.

## *Tacit Consent*

*Tacit consent* means that, "based on your actions at the time the joint return was filed, you agreed to the filing of the joint return even if you now claim the signature on the return is not yours." Whether you have tacitly consented to the filing of the joint return is based on an examination of all the facts of your case. Factors that may support a finding that you consented to the filing of the joint return include the following. You gave tax information (such as forms W-2 and 1099) to your spouse. You did not object to the filing.

## Part VI

## Complete this part if you were (or are now) a victim of domestic violence or spousal abuse

Also, were you or other members of your family a victim of spousal abuse, or domestic violence, or suffering the effects of such abuse during any of the tax years you want relief or when any of the returns were filed for those years? Complete questions 24a and b.

## Factors supporting actual knowledge

The IRS may rely on all facts and circumstances in determining whether you actually knew about erroneous item at the time you sign the return.

    **Attach a statement** to explain the situation and **when** it started. Provide photocopies of any documentation, such as police reports, a restraining order, a doctor's report or letter, or a notarized statement from someone (neighbor, relative, or friend) who was aware of the situation.

    (-Can neighbors substantiate frequent police visits when there were no police reports? Yes.)

    If you can show any of the above exceptions, you can just fill out form 8857. See questions 4 and 5 on where to send form 8857 and if you have any questions.

Go to your computer and put in "Form 8857" on the Internet (Google). Click on Form 8857 (Rev. January 2014)-Internal Revenue Service.

Also put in "Form 8857 Instructions." Click on Instructions for Form 8857-Internal Revenue Service. Make sure it has the following words underneath. www.irs.gov/pub/irs-pdf/i8857.pdf - Cached - Similar pages

> Jan 30, 2014...8857 and its **instructions**, such as legislation enacted after they were published

You should be able to complete form 8857 by yourself. Read the following information and the forty-one questions before preparing form 8857.

The following are my own observations (boldface) of important parts of form 8857:

**See Part ll Form 8857:-**

**6. What is the current marital status between you and the person on line 5?**

Married and still living together
Married and living apart since          MM DD YYYY

Widowed since          MM DD YYYY
Attach a photocopy of the death certificate and will (if one exists).

Legally separated since          MM DD YYYY
Attach a photocopy of your entire separation agreement.

Divorced since          MM DD YYYY
Attach a photocopy of your entire divorce decree.

**Note**-a divorce decree stating that your former spouse must pay all taxes does not necessarily mean you qualify for relief.

**Married and still living together is the only unfavorable answer for Separation of Liability Relief.** See Married Filing Separately chapter.

**7. What was the highest level of education you had completed when the return(s) were filed? If the answers are not the same for all tax years, explain.**

- High school diploma, equivalent, or less.
- Some college.
- College degree or higher. List any degrees you have.
- List any college-level business or tax-related courses you completed.

**Completion of tax related courses would be unfavorable.**

Part 11 Form 8857

**9. When any of the returns were signed, did you have a mental or physical health problem, or do you have a mental or physical health problem now? If the answers are not the same for all tax years, explain.**

**Yes. Attach a statement** to explain the problem and **when** it started. Provide photocopies of any documentation, such as medical bills or a doctor's report or letter.

**No.**

**13. Tell us if and how you were involved with finances and preparing returns for those tax years.**

**(If you were involved with finances or preparing the return, that is unfavorable.)**

**19 Did you (or the person on line 5) incur any large expenses, such as trips, home improvements, or private schooling, or make any large purchases, such as automobiles, appliances, or jewelry, during any of the years you want relief or any later years?**

**Yes.** Attach a statement describing (a) the types and amounts of the expenses and purchases and (b) the years they were incurred or made.

**No.**

**A substantial benefit from the spouse's unreported income will hurt your chances.** However, if the return was signed under duress, or you were not living together, that would be very favorable. See part VI: **Exception for spousal abuse or domestic violence**. Even if you had actual knowledge, you may still qualify for **Separation of Liability Relief.**

The following is taken from publication 971. I have summarized the twenty-five pages to save you time. Also, the forty-one questions enclosed cover a lot of the same information.

## Types of Relief

### Four types of relief are available:

1. Innocent spouse relief
2. Separation of liability relief
3. Equitable relief
4. Relief from liability for tax attributable to an item of community income.

## Innocent Spouse Relief

By requesting innocent spouse relief, you can be relieved of responsibility for paying tax, interest, and penalties if your spouse (or former spouse) improperly reported items or omitted income on your tax return. Generally the tax, interest, and penalties that qualify for relief can only be collected from your spouse (or former spouse). However, you are jointly and individually responsible for any tax, interest, and penalties that do not qualify for relief. The IRS can collect these amounts from either you or your spouse (or former spouse). You must meet all of the following conditions to qualify for innocent spouse relief.

1. You filed a joint return.
2. There is an understated tax on the return that is due to erroneous items (defined later) of your spouse (or former spouse).
3. You can show that when you signed the joint return, you did not know, and have no reason to know, that the under-

stated tax existed (or to the extent to which the understated tax existed).

4. Taking into account all the facts and circumstances, it would be unfair to hold you liable for the understated tax.

## Actual Knowledge or Reason to Know

You knew or had reason to know tax was understated if you actually knew of the understated tax, or a reasonable person in similar circumstances would have known of the under stated tax.

**Partial relief when a portion of erroneous item is unknown**. You may qualify for partial relief if at the time you filed the return, you had no knowledge or reason to know, of only a portion of the erroneous item. You will be relieved of the understated tax due to that portion of that of the item if all other requirements are met for that portion.

Example,

The time you filed your return, you knew that your spouse did not report $5000 in lottery winnings. You establish that you did not know about the actual winnings totaling $25,000. The understated tax due to $20,000 will qualify for innocent spouse relief.

## There are three types of relief from joint and several liability for spouses who filed joint returns:

(However, if the wife benefited from the unreported income as in a family room addition, lavish vacations, in ground pool, a new Mercedes, she would be aware or should be aware of where this extra money came from.)

## Separation of Liability Relief

To qualify for **"separation of liability relief,"** you must have filed a joint return and must meet **one** of the following requirements at the time you request relief: you are divorced or legally separated from the spouse with whom you filed the joint return. You are widowed, or you have not been a member of the same household as the spouse with whom you filed the joint return at any time during the twelve-month period ending on the date you request relief. If, at the time you signed the joint return, you had actual knowledge of the item that gave rise to the understatement of tax, you do not qualify for separation of liability relief.

**Burden of proof** must be able to prove that you meet all of the requirements for Separation of Liability Relief except actual knowledge and that you did not transfer property to avoid tax.

### Conditions for getting equitable relief- IRS Publication 971:

- You may qualify for equitable relief if you meet all of the following conditions.
- You did not pay the tax. However, for situations in which you are entitled to a refund of payments you made.
- Establish that, taking into account all the facts and circumstances, it would be unfair to hold you liable for the understated or underpaid tax.
- You and your spouse (or former spouse) did not transfer assets to one another as part of a fraudulent scheme.
- Your spouse or former spouse did not transfer property to you for the main purpose of avoiding tax or the payment of tax.
- The income tax liability from which you seek relief must be attributable to an item of the spouse or former spouse with whom you filed a joint return, unless one of the following exceptions applies.
- The item is attributable or partially attributable to you solely due to the operation of community property law. If you meet this exception, that item will be considered attributable to your spouse or former spouse for purposes of equitable relief.

- If the item is titled in your name, the item is presumed to be attributable to you. However, you can rebut this presumption based on the facts and circumstances.

## Do You Qualify for Innocent Spouse Relief, Separation of Liability Relief, Equitable Relief?

See Publication 971, pages 16–18 for three flow charts.

## Innocent Spouse Questions and Answers

### 1. How do I request relief?

File form 8857, Request for Innocent Spouse Relief, to ask the IRS for relief. You need not file multiple forms. One form can cover multiple years.

### 2. Should I include a letter when filing form 8857?

You may include a letter and any other information you would like IRS to consider.

### 3. When should I file form 8857?

You should file form 8857 as soon as you become aware of a tax liability for which you believe only your spouse or former spouse should be held. The following are some of the ways you may become aware of such a liability.

- The IRS is examining your tax return and proposing to increase your tax liability.
- The IRS sends you a notice.

However, you generally must file form 8857 no later than two years after the first IRS attempt to collect the tax from you that occurs after July 22, 1998, **exception for equitable relief.**

On July 25, 2011, the IRS issued Notice 2011-70 expanding the amount of time to request equitable relief. The amount of time to request equitable relief depends on whether you are seeking relief from a balance due, seeking a credit or refund, or both:

- Balance Due

  Generally, you must file your request within the period the IRS has to collect the tax. Generally, the IRS has ten years from the date the tax liability was assessed to collect the tax. In certain cases, the ten-year period is suspended.

- Credit or Refund

  Generally, you must file your request within three years after the date the original return was filed or within two years after the date the tax was paid, whichever is later. But you may have more time to file if you live in a federally declared disaster area or you are physically or mentally unable to manage your financial affairs. See Pub 556 for details.

**4. Where should I file my innocent spouse claim?**

If you use the U.S. Postal Service, please mail the form 8857, Request for Innocent Spouse Relief, to

Internal Revenue Service, P.O. Box 120053,
Covington, KY 41012

Or if using a private delivery service, please mail the form 8857, Request for Innocent Spouse Relief, to

Internal Revenue Service, 201 W. River center Blvd.
Stop 840F, Covington, KY 41011

Or you may fax the form 8857 and attachments to the IRS at 855-233-8558. Please write your name and social security number on any attachments.

Note-please do not file the form 8857 with your tax return.

**5. Is there a toll free number to call if I have questions regarding an innocent spouse claim or how to complete the form 8857, Request for Innocent Spouse Relief?**

If you need additional information on your innocent spouse claim or on the form 8857, Request for Innocent Spouse Relief, the toll free number is 1-855-851-2009.

## 6. What type of documents do I need to submit with the form 8857, Request for Innocent Spouse Relief?

You should carefully review the form 8857, Request for Innocent Spouse Relief, and it will guide you on what documents to submit. For comprehensive information on innocent spouse, Publication 971, Innocent Spouse Relief, explains each type of relief, who may qualify, and how to request relief.

## 7. I want to file, but I am afraid of what my ex-spouse will do, should I still file?

By law, the IRS must contact your spouse or former spouse. There are no exceptions, even for victims of spousal abuse or domestic violence. Therefore, you should consider all options including an offer in compromise doubt as to liability.

We will inform your spouse or former spouse that you filed form 8857 and will allow him or her to participate in the process. We must also inform him or her of its preliminary and final determinations regarding your request for relief.

However, to protect your privacy, the IRS will not disclose your personal information, for example, your current name, address, phone number(s), information about your employer, your income or assets, or any other information that does not relate to making a determination about your request for relief from liability.

Caution-if you petition the tax court, your spouse or former spouse may see your personal information.

## 8. How long will the process take?

When a form 8857, Request for Innocent Spouse Relief, is filed with the IRS, it may take up to six months before a determination is made. During the processing time, the Service is requesting your tax information and contacting the nonrequesting spouse. By law, the IRS must contact your spouse or former spouse. There are no exceptions, even for victims of spousal abuse or domestic violence.

**9. Should I wait to file my current year tax return pending the outcome of my claim?**

No, you should file your current return, and we will not hold any refund you are due.

**10. I filed a joint tax return with my spouse, and the entire refund was applied to my spouse's back child support, should I file a form 8857, Request for Innocent Spouse Relief, to receive my portion of the refund?**

This issue is generally not related to innocent spouse relief. You may be eligible for injured spouse provisions if you file a joint tax return and all or part of your portion of the overpayment was applied or offset to your spouse's legally enforceable past-due federal tax, state income tax, child or spousal support, or a federal nontax debt, such as a student loan. You should review the information on injured spouse and form 8379, Injured Spouse Allocation.

**11. I received an Automated Under-reporter Notice, or CP 2000 Notice, and the unreported income belongs to my former spouse. What should I do?**

If you filed a joint tax return, you are jointly and individually responsible for the tax and any interest and penalty due on the joint return. This is true even if a divorce decree states that a former spouse will be responsible for any amounts due on a previously filed joint return.

In some cases, a spouse may be relieved of the tax, interest, and penalties on a joint tax return. You can ask for relief no matter how small the liability.

Three types of relief are available:

- Innocent Spouse Relief
- Separation of Liability
- Equitable Relief

You must file form 8857, Request for Innocent Spouse Relief, to request any of the methods of relief.

## 12. My innocent spouse claim was previously denied, and I now have new additional information, can I file a claim again?

Yes, you can file a second claim, provide the new additional information, and it will be reconsidered. However, you will not have tax court rights on this reconsideration.

## 13. What is the effective date of the new innocent spouse rules under Internal Revenue Code 6015?

Internal Revenue Code 6015 innocent spouse rules are effective for unpaid balances as of July 22, 1998 and liabilities arising after July 22, 1998.

## 14. What is joint and several liability?

Many married taxpayers choose to file a joint tax return because of certain benefits this filing status allows. Both taxpayers are jointly and individually responsible for the tax and any interest or penalty due on the joint return even if they later divorce. This is true even if a divorce decree states that a former spouse will be responsible for any amounts due on previously filed joint returns. One spouse may be held responsible for all the tax due.

## 15. How can I get relief from joint and several liability?

Relief now falls into three categories: innocent spouse relief, separation of liability, and equitable relief. Each of these kinds of relief has different requirements. They are explained separately below:

## 16. Can both spouses request relief?

Yes, each spouse can file a form 8857 to request relief from liability from tax, interest, and penalties.

## 17. Does the nonrequesting spouse have any appeal rights?

Per Rev. Proc. 2003-19, the nonrequesting spouse has the right to appeal the preliminary determination to grant partial or full relief to the requesting spouse when the preliminary determination letter is issued April 1, 2003 or later. However, the nonrequesting spouse may not petition the tax court from the final determination letter.

**18. Will the other spouse be notified that I filed a claim for innocent spouse relief?**

The IRS is required to notify the nonrequesting spouse to allow them to participate. They will also be notified of the determination on your election and have the opportunity to appeal IRS's preliminary determination to grant you full or partial relief.

**19. What are the rules for innocent spouse relief?**

To qualify for innocent spouse relief, you must meet all of the following conditions:

- You must have filed a joint return, which has an understatement of tax.
- The understatement of tax must be due to erroneous items of your spouse.
- You must establish that at the time you signed the joint return, you did not know, and had no reason to know, that there was an understatement of tax.
- Taking into account all of the facts and circumstances, it would be unfair to hold you liable for the understatement of tax.
- You must request relief within two years after the date on which the IRS first began collection activity against you after July 22, 1998.

**20. What are erroneous items?**

Erroneous items are any deductions, credits, or bases incorrectly stated on the return, and any income not reported on the return.

**21. What is an understatement of tax?**

An understatement of tax is generally the difference between the total amount of tax that should have been shown on your return and the amount of tax that was actually shown on your return. For example, you reported total tax on your 2009 return of $2,500. IRS determined in an audit of your 2009 return that the total tax should be $3,000. You have a $500 understatement of tax.

## 22. Will I qualify for innocent spouse relief in any situation where there is an understatement of tax?

No. There are many situations in which you may owe tax that is related to your spouse but not be eligible for innocent spouse relief. For example, you and your spouse file a joint return that reports $10,000 of income and deductions, but you knew or had reason to know that your spouse was not reporting $5,000 of dividends. You are not eligible for innocent spouse relief when you have knowledge or reason to know of the understatement.

## 23. What are the rules for separation of liability?

Under this type of relief, you divide (separate) the understatement of tax (plus interest and penalties) on your joint return between you and your spouse. The understatement of tax allocated to you is generally the amount of income and deductions attributable to your earnings and assets. To qualify for separate liability, you must have filed a joint return and meet either of the following requirements at the time you file form 8857:

- You are no longer married to, or are legally separated from, the spouse with whom you filed the joint return for which you are requesting relief. (Under this rule, you are no longer married if you are widowed.)
- You were not a member of the same household as the spouse with whom you filed the joint return at any time during the twelve-month period ending on the date you file form 8857.

## 24. Why would a request for separate liability be denied?

Even if you meet the requirements listed above, a request for separate liability will not be granted in the following situations:

- The IRS proves that you and your spouse transferred assets for the main purpose of avoiding payment of tax.
- The IRS proves that at the time you signed your joint return, you had actual knowledge that any items giving rise to the deficiency and allocable to your spouse were incorrect.

**25. If a husband and wife are still married but separated for twelve months, prior to filing a claim for relief due to an involuntary reason, such as incarceration or military duty, can separation of liability relief be granted?**

Separation of liability applies to taxpayers who are (1) no longer married, (2) legally separated, or (3) living apart for the twelve months prior to the filing of a claim. Under this rule, you are no longer married if you are widowed.

Living apart does not include a spouse who is temporarily absent from the household. A temporary absence exists if it is reasonable to assume that the absent spouse will return to the household or a substantially equivalent household is maintained in anticipation of such a return. A temporary absence may include absence due to incarceration, illness, business, vacation, military service, or education.

A claim can be filed if any of the three statutory requirements are met.

**26. What are the rules for equitable relief?**

Equitable relief is only available if you meet all of the following conditions:

- You do not qualify for innocent spouse relief or the separation of liability election.
- The IRS determines that it is unfair to hold you liable for the understatement of tax, taking into account all the facts and circumstances.

Note-unlike innocent spouse relief or separation of liability, if you qualify for equitable relief, you can get relief from an understatement of tax or an underpayment of tax. (An underpayment of tax is an amount properly shown on the return but not paid).

**27. What factors are considered in determining whether or not to grant equitable relief?**

The following factors may be considered, but the list is not all-inclusive:

- Current marital status

- Reasonable belief of the requesting spouse, at the time he or she signed the return, that the tax was going to be paid; or in the case of an understatement, whether the requesting spouse had knowledge or reason to know of the understatement
- Current financial hardship/inability to pay basic living expenses
- Spouse's legal obligation to pay the tax liability pursuant to a divorce decree or agreement to pay the liability
- To whom the liability is attributable
- Significant benefit received by the requesting spouse
- Mental or physical health of the requesting spouse on the date the requesting spouse signed the return or at the time the requesting spouse requested the relief
- Compliance with income tax laws following the taxable year or years to which the request for relief relates
- Abuse experienced during the marriage. The IRS understands and is sensitive to the effects of domestic violence and spousal abuse and encourages victims of domestic violence to call 911 if they are in immediate danger. **If you have concerns about your safety,** please consider contacting the twenty-four-hour (confidential) National Domestic Violence Hotline at 1-800-799-SAFE (7233), or 1-800-787-3224 (TTY), or 206-787-3224 (Video Phone Only for Deaf Callers) before you file this form.

## 28. How do state community property laws affect my ability to qualify for relief?

Community property states are Arizona, California, Idaho, Louisiana, Nevada, New Mexico, Texas, Washington, and Wisconsin. Generally, community property laws require you to allocate community income and expenses equally between both spouses. However, community property laws are not taken into account in determining whether an item belongs to you or your spouse (or former spouse) for purposes of requesting any relief from liability.

**29. If I am denied innocent spouse relief, must I reapply if I believe I might qualify under one of the other two provisions?**

No. The IRS will automatically consider whether any of the other provisions would apply. If you requested innocent spouse relief or separation of liability, IRS will automatically consider equitable relief.

The only time you can reapply for relief is if you were denied relief because you were considered still married at the time the request for relief was filed and you now satisfy the marital status requirements to elect to separate the liability.

**30. Will the IRS deny me relief if I do not provide them with the information they request?**

IRS will base their decision upon all the information available to them. If enough information is not available, it could adversely affect a request for relief.

**31. I filed a form 656, Offer in Compromise, under doubt as to liability. The IRS accepted the offer in compromise. Can I still apply for innocent spouse relief?**

No. We cannot consider your claim for any year in which an offer in compromise was accepted. Acceptance of an offer in compromise conclusively closes the tax year(s) compromised from any redetermination of the tax liability.

**32. I signed a closing agreement, can I still apply for innocent spouse relief?**

It depends on the type of closing agreement you signed.

If you signed form 866, Agreement as to Final Determination of the Tax Liability, the tax year is closed with finality and you cannot apply for innocent spouse relief.

If you signed form 906, Closing Agreement on Final Determination Covering Specific Matters, only those matters covered in the closing agreement are conclusively closed. Innocent spouse relief may be requested for matters not covered in the closing agreement.

**33. I am currently undergoing an examination of my return. How do I request innocent spouse relief?**

Prepare form 8857, Request for Innocent Spouse Relief, and mail it to the address shown in question 4.

**34. What if the IRS has levied my account for the tax liability and I decide to request relief?**

Upon receipt of your request for relief, all collection activity against you will be suspended unless the liability is in jeopardy or the statute of limitation on collection will expire shortly.

**35. What constitutes a collection activity for purposes of starting the two-year statute of limitations that cover the filing of form 8857?**

The following are examples of collection activity: when the IRS (1) sends a notice under section 6330 of the Service's intent to levy and of the taxpayer's right to a collection due process (CDP) hearing, (2) offsets a refund from another tax year and you received a notice advising you of your rights under Section 6015, or (3) files a judicial suit or claim that puts the requesting spouse on notice the IRS intends to collect the joint tax liability from specific property belonging to that spouse. For further information on collection activity, see Treas. Reg. 1.6015-5(b) (2).

**36. I filed a valid joint return with my spouse and have an installment agreement to pay the taxes. Can I still apply for relief?**

The innocent spouse rules may apply in your situation. However, regarding the installment agreement, there are some important considerations:

If you do not continue to make payments while we consider your request for relief, your installment agreement will default and full payment will be due immediately if your request for relief is denied.

**37. My spouse forged my signature to a joint return. Am I eligible for innocent spouse relief? Should I file form 8857?**

You may be eligible for relief, but relief does not fall under the innocent spouse rules. If you can establish your signature was forged, and there was not tacit (implied) consent, the joint election is invalid, and you will only be liable for your separate tax liability.

## 38. What is the meaning of "economic hardship" for purposes of equitable relief of an underpayment of tax liability shown on a tax return?

"Economic hardship" means that you are unable to pay your basic living expenses, e.g. food, clothing, housing, utilities, medical expenses (including health insurance), transportation, childcare, child support, etc.

## 39. Will I receive a refund of all amounts I paid, if relief is granted?

It depends upon the provision under which relief is granted.

- If innocent spouse relief is granted under section 6015(b), refunds are allowable for amounts paid on or after July 22, 1998.
- If separation of liability is granted under section 6015(c), no refunds are allowable.
- If equitable relief is granted under section 6015(f), refunds are allowed for payments made after July 22, 1998 unless the payments were made jointly with the nonrequesting spouse, payments were made with the return or payments were made by the nonrequesting spouse.

## 40. Will I be granted innocent relief with respect to unreported income if I feel it is my accountant's fault that the income was not reported on the return?

Innocent spouse relief is in no way meant to transfer the liability to an accountant. If the income was yours (rather than your spouse's), or was your spouse's but you knew about it, you will probably not be relieved of liability.

## 41. If an understatement is the result of signing an examination report that lists omissions of income, does this indicate there was knowledge of items giving rise to the deficiency?

No, innocent spouse provisions clearly state the knowledge has to do with what was known at the time the return was signed.

CHAPTER 3

# How to Qualify as an Injured Spouse

-Can the current spouse prevent his/her share of their income tax refund from being offset? Yes, by filing form 8379. Many taxpayers are not aware of this tax benefit. A married couple can also file separate returns to avoid offset. You can avoid the offset by having a balance due on your return by eliminating some of or all of your withholding or estimated tax.-

**Seven Facts about Injured Spouse Relief**

Tax Tip 2011-60, March 25, 2011

If you file a joint return and all or part of your refund is applied against your spouse's past-due federal tax, state income tax, child or spousal support, or federal nontax debt, such as a student loan, you may be entitled to injured spouse relief.

**Here are seven facts the IRS wants you to know about claiming injured spouse relief:**

1. To be considered an injured spouse, you must have made and reported tax payments, such as federal income tax withheld from wages or estimated tax payments, or claimed a refundable tax credit, such as the earned income credit or additional child tax credit on the joint return, and not be legally obligated to pay the past-due amounts.

2. If you live in a community property state, special rules apply. For more information about the factors used to determine whether you are subject to community property laws, see IRS Publication 555, Community Property.

3. If you filed a joint return, and you're not responsible for the debt, but you are entitled to a portion of the refund, you may request your portion of the refund by filing form 8379, Injured Spouse Allocation.

4. You may file form 8379 along with your original tax return, or you may file it by itself after you are notified of an offset.

5. You can file the form 8379 electronically. If you file a paper tax return, you can include form 8379 with your return, write "Injured Spouse" at the top left corner of the form 1040, 1040A, or 1040EZ. IRS will process your allocation request before an offset occurs.

6. If you are filing form 8379 by itself, it must show both spouses' Social Security numbers in the same order as they appeared on your income tax return. You, the "injured" spouse, must sign the form.

7. Do not use form 8379 if you are claiming innocent spouse relief. Instead, file form 8857, Request for Innocent Spouse Relief. This relief from a joint liability applies only in certain limited circumstances. IRS Publication 971, Innocent Spouse Relief, explains who may qualify, and how to request this relief.

Go to the Internet, and put in "form 8379" for the actual form. Fill out the form 8857.-

## When to File Per IRS

File form 8379 when you become aware that all or part of your share of an overpayment was, or is expected to be, applied (offset) against your spouse's legally enforceable past-due obligations. You must file form 8379 for each year if you meet this condition and want your portion of any offset refunded.

A notice of offset for federal tax debts is issued by the IRS. A notice of offset for past-due state income tax, state unemployment compensation debt, child or spousal support, or federal nontax debts (such as a student loan) is issued by the U.S. Treasury Department's Financial Management Service (FMS).

## Time Needed to Process Form 8379

Generally, if you file form 8379 with a joint return on paper, the time needed to process it is about fourteen weeks (eleven weeks if filed electronically). If you file form 8379 by itself after a joint return has been processed, the time needed is about eight weeks.

## Specific Instructions
## Avoid Common Mistakes

Mistakes may delay your refund or result in notices being sent to you. If you file form 8379 separately, do not include a copy of your joint tax return. This will prevent delays in processing your allocation. Make sure to enclose copies of all forms W-2 and W-2G for both spouses and any forms 1099 showing income tax withheld. If you file form 8379 with your joint tax return or amended joint tax return, enter "Injured Spouse" in the upper left corner of page 1 of your joint return. Any dependency exemptions must be entered in whole numbers. Items of income, expenses, credits, and deductions must be allocated to the spouse who would have entered the item on his or her separate return. Make sure the debt is subject to offset (for example, a legally enforceable past-due federal tax, state income tax, child or spousal support, state unemployment compensation debts, or other federal nontax debt, such as a student loan).

## Where to File Form 8379

*If you file form 8379 with your joint return,* then mail form 8379 and your joint return to the Internal Revenue Service Center for the area where you live.

*If you file form 8379 by itself after you filed your original joint return on paper,* send form 8379 to the same Internal Revenue Service Center where you filed your original return.

*If you file form 8379 by itself after you filed your original return electronically,* then mail form 8379 and your joint return to the Internal Revenue Service Center for the area where you live.

*If you filed form 8379 with an amended return (form 1040X or other subsequent return),* then mail form 8379 and your joint return to the Internal Revenue Service Center for the area where you live.

# CHAPTER 4

# Installment Agreements

## Streamlined Installment Agreements

IRS changed its rules because of the Fresh Start Program. The dollar amount criteria were changed from $25,000 to $50,000, and the maximum term was extended to seventy-two months instead of sixty months.

If you owe more than $50,000, you may want to pay down the amount owed to less than $50,000. For example, you owe $54,000. If you pay down the amount owed to less than $50,000, you will generally not need a financial statement (form 433-F). You can also apply on line instead of filing form 9465. The number of months you choose is flexible and cannot exceed the remaining months on the collection statute of limitations.

## Installment Agreement Fees

| Payment Method | Application Fee |
|---|---|
| Check, money order, or credit card | $105 |
| Payroll deduction installment agreement | $105 |

| Electronic funds withdrawal | $52 |
| Income below a certain level | $43 |

## Where to File: Form 9465 Instructions

Attach form 9465 to the front of your return, and send it to the address shown in your tax return booklet. If you already filed your return or you are filing this form in response to a notice, file form 9465 by itself with the Internal Revenue Service Center using the address in the table below that applies to you.

For all taxpayers, except those filing form 1040 with schedules(s) C, E, or F for any tax year for which the installment agreement is being requested.

| **If you live in...** | **Then use this address...** |
| --- | --- |
| Alabama, Florida, Georgia, Kentucky, Louisiana, Mississippi, North Carolina, South Carolina, Texas, Virginia | Department of the Treasury Internal Revenue Service P.O. Box 47421 Stop 74 Doraville, GA 30362 |
| Alaska, Arizona, Colorado, Connecticut, Delaware, District of Columbia, Hawaii, Idaho, Illinois, Maine, Maryland, Massachusetts, Montana, Nevada, New Hampshire, New Jersey, New Mexico, North Dakota, Oregon, Rhode Island, South Dakota, Tennessee, Utah, Vermont, Washington, Wisconsin, Wyoming | Department of the Treasury Internal Revenue Service 310 Lowell St. Stop 830 Andover, MA 01810 |

| Arkansas, California, Indiana, Iowa, Kansas, Michigan, Minnesota, Missouri, Nebraska, New York, Ohio, Oklahoma, Pennsylvania, West Virginia | Department of the Treasury Internal Revenue Service Stop P-4 5000 Kansas City, MO 64999–0250 |

## Payment Plans, Installment Agreements

If you're financially unable to pay your tax debt immediately, you can make **monthly payments** through an installment agreement. As long as you pay your tax debt in full, you can reduce or eliminate your payment of penalties or interest and avoid the fee associated with setting up the agreement. If you miss a payment, it should not be cause for worry. Just call IRS and explain your situation.

Before applying for any payment agreement, **you must file all required tax returns.**

**You may be eligible to apply for an online payment agreement through the following:**

- Individuals must owe $50,000 or less in combined individual income tax, penalties and interest, and have filed all required returns.
- Businesses must owe $25,000 or less in payroll taxes and have filed all required returns.
- If you meet these requirements, you can apply for an online payment agreement.
- Please note, if you file joint tax returns with your spouse, you may be unable to complete your installment agreement request using this application.

**Even if you're ineligible for an online payment agreement, you can still pay in installments:**

- Complete and mail form 9465, Installment Agreement Request (PDF), and form 433-F, Collection Information Statement (PDF).

- Call 800-829-1040 or the phone number on your bill or notice.

**Small businesses can apply for an in-business trust fund express installment agreement:**

- Call the IRS business and specialty tax assistance line 800-829-4933.
- Call the phone number on your bill or notice.

**Understand your agreement and avoid default:**

- Your future refunds will be applied to your tax debt until it is paid in full.
- Pay at least your minimum monthly payment when it's due.
- Include your name, address, SSN, daytime phone number, tax year, and return type on your payment.
- File all required tax returns on time and pay all taxes in full and on time (contact us to change your existing agreement if you cannot).
- Make all scheduled payments even if we apply your refund to your account balance.
- Ensure your statement is sent to the correct address, contact us if you move or complete and mail form 8822, Change of Address (PDF).

If you don't receive your statement, send your payment to the address listed in your agreement.

There may be a reinstatement fee if your agreement goes into default. Penalties and interest continue to accrue until your balance is paid in full. If you are in danger of defaulting on your payment agreement for any reason, contact us immediately. We will generally not take enforced collection actions:

- When an installment agreement is being considered;
- While an agreement is in effect;

- For thirty days after a request is rejected; or
- During the period the IRS evaluates an appeal of a rejected or terminated agreement.

*Page Last Reviewed or Updated: 10-Dec-2014*

# CHAPTER 5

# What to Do When You Receive a Notice or Letter from the IRS

-You receive a notice from the IRS and are afraid to open it. Don't panic. Each year, the IRS sends millions of letters and notices to taxpayers, requesting payment of taxes, notifying them of changes to their account, or requesting additional information. The notice you receive normally covers a specific issue about your account or tax return. Each letter and notice offers specific instructions to satisfy the inquiry. Most notices also give you a phone number to call. Quite often, a correction of an error by IRS can greatly reduce your chances of an audit. It may be put in the completed category and be taken out of the audit stream.

Many of these letters can easily be handled with little effort. For example, you forgot to send in a 1099, which had income tax withheld. The IRS will include the income in its calculations but not the withholding. You forget to include the form 1098-T Tuition Statement to substantiate your education expense. Sending in the forms will resolve your problem. You may have had a calculation error or are subject to an estimated tax penalty on your return. You could have forgotten a SSN number or not signed your return. Missing forms, no enclosed payment, etc., are also a problem. The envelope may have a refund check. Don't throw the envelope away. Correct postage is very important. A taxpayer had his tax return sent back to him by the post office for an additional seven cents. The IRS charged him over $500 for filing late. I told him to call the number on the notice and explain the delay. The returned envelope was proof of the date mailed. The IRS official abated the $500 and said, "We usually allow you at least one mistake." When in doubt, weigh the envelope or put on an extra stamp.-

**Math Errors on Individual 2013 Returns, Source-2014 IRS Data Book**

| | |
|---|---|
| Total math errors | 2,266,024 |
| Tax calculation/other taxes | 588,175 |
| Exemption number/amount | 324,507 |
| Standard/itemized deductions | 278,188 |
| Earned income tax credit | 256,312 |
| First-time home buyer credit repayment | 211,621 |
| Adjusted gross/taxable income amount | 106,818 |
| Other credits | 89,806 |
| Child tax credits | 89,116 |
| Refund/amount due | 88,156 |
| Education credit | 65,441 |
| Adjustments to income | 51,195 |
| Filing status | 44,135 |
| Withholding or excess Social Security | 40,689 |
| Other | 31,865 |

-I included the table to show common errors and why you should not fear a notice from the IRS.

A friend's son received a notice that asserted a $166 estimated tax penalty. I told my friend to go to TurboTax and fill out form 2210. The correct estimated tax turned out to be only $68. I instructed my friend to send in the form 2210 along with a check for $68 payable to the United States Treasury. My friend called IRS twelve days later and wasted two hours on the phone. Sometimes, it takes thirty days for your reply to get to the right person. Therefore, be patient when dealing with the IRS. IRS accepted the $68 after receiving my friend's response.

Most correspondence can be handled without calling or visiting an IRS office. Follow instructions in the letter or notice. However, if you have any questions, call the number in the right-hand corner of the notice. Have a copy of your tax return and the correspondence available when you call so your account can be easily accessed.

Before contacting the IRS, review the correspondence and compare it with the information on your return. If you agree with the correction to your account, no reply is necessary unless a payment is due. In that case, send in a payment. However, if you do not agree with the correction the IRS made, it is important that you respond. Provide a detailed explanation why you disagree. Include any documents and information you want the IRS to consider. Mail your reply with the bottom tear-off portion of the notice. Mail the information to the IRS address shown in the upper left-hand corner of the notice. Allow at least thirty days for a response.

Sometimes, the IRS will send a second letter or notice requesting additional information. Be sure to keep copies of any correspondence and documents provided for your own records. You may have to send in the same documents a second or third time.

If you are unsure as to what to do, promptly take the correspondence to your CPA or tax preparer. It is not worth worrying about. A phone call to the number on the notice may be very helpful. Don't ignore IRS notices. By so doing, you can cause more problems, which could cause hefty legal expenses. The IRS can garnish your wages, put liens on your property, and go after your bank account. If IRS attempts to take most of your check, you will be wise to obtain an installment agreement.

The IRS sends letters and notices by mail. IRS does not contact people by e-mail or social media to ask for personal or financial information.

Generally, the IRS will send a notice if it believes you owe additional tax, are due a larger refund, or a need for additional information.

The first thing you should do is go to Google or the Internet and put in "Understanding Your IRS Notice or Letter." Look for "Understanding Your IRS Notice or Letter-Internal Revenue Service." You will find about 260 notices or letters. "The notice number is on the top right-hand side of each page of all notices and the lower right-hand side of the tear-off stub included with most of them. That number identifies the message we deliver in every notice. While the contents vary somewhat, every notice with the same number has the same basic purpose." Next, go to the notice or letter number in blue listed on your notice. For example, your letter lists notice number CP23. Click on CP23 notice, and a new page comes up-which states, "We made changes to your return because we found a difference between the amount of estimated tax payments on your return and the amount we posted to your account. You have a balance due because of these changes." Then see what you need to do in red letters.-

- Read your notice carefully-it will explain how much money you owe on your taxes.
- Check the list of payments we applied to your account to see if we applied all the payments you made.
- Correct the copy of your tax that you kept for your records.
- Pay the amount you owe by the date on the notice's payment coupon if you agree with the notice.
- If you disagree with the notice, please contact us on the toll free number listed on its top right-hand corner (within sixty days of the notice's date).
- Make payment arrangements if you can't pay the full amount.

There are over 260 (I did not count them) notices. Look for the notice number on your letter or notice, and click on the notice number in the left-hand column. Here are some of the notices.

## Redesigned Notices

| | | |
|---|---|---|
| CP01S | We received your form 14039 or similar statement for your identity theft claim. We'll contact you when we finish processing your case or if we need additional information. | |
| CP02H | You owe a balance due as a result of amending your tax return to show receipt of a grant received as a result of Hurricane Katrina, Rita, or Wilma. | Balance Due |
| CP03C | You received a tax credit (called the First-Time Homebuyer Credit) for a house you purchased. You may need to file a form to report a change in ownership to the house you purchased. | |
| CP04 | Our records show that you or your spouse served in a combat zone, a qualified contingency operation, or a hazardous duty station during the tax year specified on your notice. As a result, you may be eligible for tax deferment. | |
| CP05 | We're reviewing your tax return. | |
| CP05A | We are examining your return, and we need documentation. | |
| CP07 | We received your tax return and are holding your refund until we complete a more thorough review of the benefits you claimed under a treaty and/or the deductions claimed on schedule A. | |
| CP08 | You may qualify for the Additional Child Tax Credit and be entitled to some additional money. | Additional Child Tax Credit |

# CHAPTER 6

---

# Failure to File Cases, What to Do, How to Avoid Penalties and Jail

-Not filing returns for many years can have a devastating effect on your ability to collect social security. If that is the case, hopefully, you will have been married for at least ten years and then you could collect Social Security computed on your spouse's social security income.

Example,

> Taxpayer A filed six delinquent 1040 returns and never paid the self-employment tax. The collection division treated the account as uncollectible. Will Taxpayer A get Social Security credit for the self-employment tax shown on the return? The answer is yes. Social Security and IRS should fix this loophole. So file all your returns timely even though you don't have the funds to pay the tax.

Failure to file is a misdemeanor, and you could receive a year in jail for each year not filed. You can receive five years in jail for each fraudulent return filed. Normally, IRS does not go criminally on failure to file cases unless the taxpayer is a high-profile person involving a lot of money. IRS does not go after poor people. Normally, the revenue officer will accept the returns you file unless there appear to be discrepancies. Revenue officers don't audit returns. They normally accept the returns as filed unless the expenses are out of line or the income does not reflect the taxpayer's standard of living. For example, income reported on the return is $40,000, and the interest and taxes for a Barrington, Illinois, home on schedule A is over $60,000. The R/O would ask an office auditor or revenue agent to look at the return and possibly submit a referral for audit.

If you stopped filing returns, received a 1099 or W-2, IRS knows about it. Some taxpayers would have received refunds. The first thing you should do is contact IRS if they have not contacted you. If you contact them first, they will not go after you criminally unless you later file a false return. There is an exception for rich or famous people. IRS may go after them. Either way, I suggest you hire someone to prepare the returns and represent you. As an enrolled agent, I would get a power of attorney for all possible tax years. The less you deal with IRS, the better. An accountant or attorney would insulate you from incriminating yourself. I would go into the IRS office or online and request a transcript of account for all possible tax years. The transcripts will show income you should have reported and for which years. If they have records for two or three years, then only file for those years. A schedule C or small business might not have a 1099 or W-2. However, bank deposits could reflect the correct income. I don't know how long banks keep bank statements anymore, but they may keep them for seven years. Ask your accountant for advice regarding number of years to file.

Don't file a fraudulent return. However, if you spent the money, deduct the expense. If the records were destroyed by fire or flood, try to recreate the records. Under the Cohan Rule, if you had a business, you paid for rent, utilities, phone, etc., the IRS has to allow some expenses. The Cohan Rule does apply to business expenses but does not apply to travel and entertainment. A little bit of trivia-James Cagney played George Cohan in the movie *Yankee Doodle Dandy*. Cohan would deduct travel and entertainment expenses and had poor or no records. Usually, 50 percent was allowed. Cohan kept on increasing his deductions hoping to get the 50 percent allowance. Keep current monthly records so you can show IRS what your normal monthly business expenses are. Then the tax auditor or revenue agent would have a basis to allow expenses for the audit years.

When I was the Chicago District Civil Fraud Coordinator, many representatives would agree to 52.5 percent rather than the 50 percent fraud penalty, 5 percent per month for five months (25 percent) late filing, failure to pay, 5 percent per month or 22.5 percent, and a 5 percent negligence penalty. They felt the fraud penalty had a bad connotation. The current fraud penalty is 75 percent.

Sometimes it is difficult to locate a taxpayer because of many factors. The taxpayer may have moved and lived in different places during the year. The taxpayers may be snow birds living on the east coast and Florida during the winter. These taxpayers are easily located with a minimum amount of effort. However, there are some taxpayers who don't want to be found. It could be to escape from an abusive spouse, debts, legal and family problems, etc. These taxpayers are more difficult to find.

When you stop filing returns, IRS computers will notify IRS of your last known address. I could list a hundred places to research and look for a taxpayer. Everything is now computerized and easier for IRS to find you through numerous sources. I am going to list a few sources of information. You can check out the Internal Revenue Manual if you are curious to learn about more sources:-

Federal Sources

- IRS
- Military
- Post office
- Social Security administration
- Federal agencies

State Sources

- Auto registration
- Driver's license

- Professional licensing boards
- Retirement plans
- Unemployment compensation
- Welfare

County Sources

- City sources
- Credit cards
- Banks
- Dentists and doctors
- Return preparer

-When I was working at IRS, all revenue agents had access to Choice Point, which at that time had seventeen billion pieces of domestic information, eight billion overseas. I could pull up a list of a corporations' law suits and most state and county records-for example, bankruptcy, divorce records, estate records, property ownership and sales, birth, SSN, age records, etc. I was looking for a taxpayer (corporate officer), who had a very common last name who worked for a corporation. When I listed the common name and corporation on Choice Point, I found the right taxpayer and was now able to see if he filed tax returns. Your next question is why I would need to do this. IRS agents are required on their audits to check to see that certain high officers of the corporation have filed their returns. Yes, I found a few nonfilers.

I had a CPA ask me for advice regarding an estate tax return. The deceased had not filed for ten years. The executor filed estimated 1040 returns for the ten years based on the last return filed. The tax and penalties wiped out the entire estate. If there are no records to accurately show the income from a cash business and IRS has no records showing 1099s or w-2s, then why file returns for ten years? Maybe three years? And then only if there were records to prepare the returns, bank deposits might go back seven years. Did the taxpayer's net worth increase or decrease? If I were an agent auditing this taxpayer, a bank deposit and net worth approach would have been utilized. The executor may have or should have requested a transcript of account from IRS. The taxpayer may have had losses. I asked the CPA, did the executor take into account all the expenses? I told the CPA to consider filing amended returns and the possibility of filing a malpractice lawsuit against the executor. I did not see the returns that were filed and was not aware of all the facts.

Revenue officers (R/A) sometimes will canvas city blocks to see if the businesses filed tax returns. The Revenue officer will ask to see copies of tax returns filed. If none filed, the R/O will request returns to be filed.

When you let employers treat you as an independent contractor instead of an employee, it is a big mistake. For example, an individual earning $20,000 and receiving a 1099 will have to pay $3,060 in self-employment taxes. Add $765 (25 percent) for late filing. Add another thousand dollars in state income tax where applicable. In Illinois, an additional thousand dollars would be due. When April 15 comes around, the average taxpayer is hard-pressed to come up with $5,000 or more. If the individual was treated as an employee, his/her federal income taxes would be $1,530 less, and withholding of $300 a month would cover the federal income taxes. It is quite difficult for a person earning $20,000 a year to come up with over $5000 on April 15. What do a lot of people do if they do not have to funds to pay the tax? They make another big mistake. They don't file a federal income tax or state tax return. After five months, a taxpayer would owe another thousand dollars or 25 percent more in tax. It is important to file a tax return timely even if you don't have the money to pay the tax. You can see that $4000 in tax plus late payment fee and interest can add up to a lot of tax in three or four years. You will not get any sympathy from a revenue officer. Obviously, your employer may not give you a choice in how you are to be treated. I would recommend that you look for another job where you are treated as an employee or pay in estimated taxes. If you are close to retirement, IRS can only withhold 15 percent of your Social Security.-

# CHAPTER 7

# Criminal Fraud and Your Chances of Going to Jail, How IRS Catches Tax Cheats

The following chart covers your chances of going to jail.

**INTERNAL REVENUE SERVICE DATA BOOK FISCAL YEAR 2014**

|  | Total | Legal Sources Tax Crimes | Legal Sources Financial Crimes | Narcotics Related Financial Crimes |
|---|---|---|---|---|
| Investigations initiated | 4297 | 1976 | 1475 | 846 |
| Investigations completed | 4606 | 2249 | 1502 | 855 |
| Referrals for prosecution | 3478 | 1621 | 1123 | 734 |
| Indictments and informations | 3272 | 1513 | 1071 | 688 |
| Convictions | 3110 | 1388 | 1116 | 596 |
| Sentenced | 3268 | 1373 | 1188 | 707 |
| Incarcerated | 2601 | 1102 | 908 | 591 |
| % of those sentenced incarcerated | 79.6 | 80.3 | 76.4 | 83.6 |

-You don't want IRS coming after you for criminal fraud. When I was a newer agent, I referred a case to CID now called CI. When I confronted the accountant with the wrongdoing, he said, "Who told you?" A special agent accompanied me on my next visit to the taxpayer. It is pretty scary when a special agent reads you your rights. The accountant turned white, red, and then white again. Criminal audits can greatly affect your health, and I have heard it has caused heart attacks and some suicides.

You would be surprised how many investigations and prosecutions are caused by informants'-spouses, relatives, lovers, and immediate family members-turning on each other. Bragging can also get you into trouble. If you let relatives know you have a million dollars on the side from a business, it spurs on requests for loans of thousands of dollars, which will never be repaid. If you brag about unreported cash in a public place or at your club, there is good chance you will be reported to the IRS.

For those of you who don't report all your income, I give this valuable advice. I have seen many cases of unreported income in many professions. Let us use restaurants as an example.

Going back thirty years, it was easy to steal 10 percent off the top or more because it was a cash business. What did some of the restaurant owners do with the extra money? They couldn't show it in their checking accounts, so they spent it on travel, cars, gambling, or women. Now what have they to show for all that extra money they spent? Just think if they would have reported and invested that money in the stock market, retirement plans, property, or more restaurants, how much better off financially they would be? Accountants could have found legal ways to avoid much of the taxes on these funds. Now, it is more difficult to under report restaurant receipts because most people pay with a credit card. Also, think about how much sleep you will lose if you are worried about going to jail. After you file a false tax return, then the nightly worry begins.

There were some restaurant owners who under reported their food purchases so they could under report their income. That was foolish. We could go to their suppliers to verify purchases. It was especially easy to check hot dog sales. We also know gross profit percentages in food and liquor, which might indicate personal use of the food and liquor. Thirty-five years ago, I heard of a restaurant owner who couldn't sell his restaurant because he reported very little gross receipts on his tax returns. The owner had two sets of books and under reported his income.

IRS loves to prosecute high-profile figures, such as politicians, lawyers, accountants, sports figures, movie stars. We also prosecute doctors for Medicare fraud. We usually don't put poor people in jail for cheating a little. But when people get greedy and under report their income by a certain dollar amount, we may go after them. Normally, CI likes to see a three-year pattern of under reporting income. I had one taxpayer double deduct and in a few instances triple deduct the same expenses. He recorded the expense when it was an accounts payable and then when he paid it.-

## Hiding Money or Income Offshore among the "Dirty Dozen" List of Tax Scams for the 2015 Filing Season

### Per IRS

Washington-The Internal Revenue Service today said avoiding taxes by hiding money or assets in unreported offshore accounts remains on its annual list of tax scams known as the "Dirty Dozen" for the 2015 filing season.

"The recent string of successful enforcement actions against offshore tax cheats and the financial organizations that help them shows that it's a bad bet to hide money and income offshore," said IRS Commissioner John Koskinen. "Taxpayers are best served by coming in voluntarily and getting their taxes and filing requirements in order."

Since the first Offshore Voluntary Disclosure Program (OVDP) opened in 2009, there have been more than fifty thousand disclosures, and we have collected more than $7 billion from this initiative alone. The IRS conducted thousands of offshore-related civil audits that have produced tens of millions of dollars. The IRS has also pursued criminal charges leading to billions of dollars in criminal fines and restitutions.

Through the years, offshore accounts have been used to lure taxpayers into scams and schemes.

Illegal scams can lead to significant penalties and interest and possible criminal prosecution. IRS criminal investigation works closely with the Department of Justice (DOJ) to shut down scams and prosecute the criminals behind them.

## Hiding Income Offshore

Over the years, numerous individuals have been identified as evading U.S. taxes by hiding income in offshore banks, brokerage accounts, or nominee entities and then using debit cards, credit cards, or wire transfers to access the funds. Others have employed foreign trusts, employee-leasing schemes, private annuities, or insurance plans for the same purpose.

The IRS uses information gained from its investigations to pursue taxpayers with undeclared accounts, as well as the banks and bankers suspected of helping clients hide their assets overseas. The IRS works closely with the Department of Justice (DOJ) to prosecute tax evasion cases.

-In the past, it was estimated that at least twelve million people fail to file tax returns. Did we put them in jail? Rarely, unless it's a high-profile person or a large amount of tax. If a 1099 has been sent to the IRS, we know about you and will catch up to you sooner or later. Later could involve a reduction of your Social Security. However, you probably won't go to jail.

However, if you are a lawyer, politician, sports figure, movie star, doctor, or haven't paid a lot of taxes, IRS is more likely to prosecute you. In the following chapters, I will help you get your taxes under control.

A good accountant will normally require a taxpayer to show enough income to support the taxpayer's standard of living if he thinks the taxpayer isn't reporting all his income.

Be careful what you put on Facebook. You may be showing IRS all your hidden wealth and assets from your posted pictures-your expensive vacations, expensive boat, classic corvette, or summer or winter vacation home.

Organized crime figures would report race track or other winnings rather than show the real income to support their standard of living. IRS has so many tools at its disposal. In the past, R/Os would check small businesses a block at a time and request copies of current filed returns. So if you had a store front in Chicago, you might get a visit.

I list some examples of tax preparers going to jail for preparing false tax returns.-

**Per IRS**

Return preparer fraud involves the preparation and filing of false income tax returns by preparers who claim inflated personal or business expenses, false deductions, unallowable credits, or excessive exemptions on returns prepared for their clients. Preparers may, for example, manipulate income figures to fraudulently obtain tax credits, such as the Earned Income Tax Credit. In some situations, the client, or taxpayer, may not know of the false expenses, deductions, exemptions, and/or credits shown on his or her tax return.

However, when the IRS detects a fraudulent return, the taxpayer, not the return preparer, must pay the additional taxes and interest and may be subject to penalties.

The IRS Return Preparer Program focuses on enhancing compliance in the return-preparer community by investigating and referring criminal activity by return preparers to the Department of Justice for prosecution. The IRS can also assert appropriate civil penalties against unscrupulous return preparers. As a manager, I was involved in preparer projects. We would audit every return prepared by the return-preparer. So it is wise to stay clear of preparers who make outrageous claims and promise big refunds.

**-I know these are old years.**

## Criminal Investigation Statistical Information on Return Preparer Fraud

|  | FY 2006 | FY 2005 | FY 2004 |
|---|---|---|---|
| Investigations Initiated | 197 | 248 | 206 |
| Prosecution Recommendations | 153 | 140 | 167 |
| Indictments/Information | 135 | 119 | 121 |
| Sentenced | 109 | 118 | 90 |
| Incarceration Rate* | 89.0% | 85.6% | 84.4% |
| Avg. Months to Serve | 18 | 18 | 19 |

*Incarceration may include prison time, home confinement, electronic monitoring, or a combination.

## Criminal and Civil Legal Actions

Additionally, the courts have issued 175 permanent injunctions against abusive tax scheme promoters and abusive return preparers since 2003. The following case summaries are excerpts from public record documents on file in the court records in the judicial district in which the legal actions were filed.

Here are a few examples:

## California Tax Preparers Sentenced to Prison Terms for Operating Tax Fraud Schemes

On October 6, 2006, in California,—a professional tax preparer who operated "The—Group," was sentenced to ten years and five months in prison and ordered to pay $113,179 in restitution. She was convicted on May 2, 2006, for tax evasion, defrauding the United States and aiding and assisting in the filing of fraudulent tax returns.

Codefendants were also sentenced to prison terms of seventy-eight and twenty-four months, respectively.

### Minnesota Tax Preparer Sentenced for Filing False Tax Returns

On March 23, 2006, in Minneapolis, Minnesota,—was sentenced to forty-one months in prison for aiding and assisting in the preparation of eighty-four false tax returns.—was also ordered to pay a $7,500 criminal fine and $198,958 in back taxes.

### Tax Preparer Who Used Bogus Business Losses to Wipe Out Clients' Income Taxes Sentenced to Eleven Years in Prison

On February 21, 2006, in Los Angeles, California,—was sentenced to eleven years in federal prison following his April 22, 2005, conviction of twenty-four counts of aiding and advising in the preparation of false income tax returns.

### Rockford Tax Preparer Sentenced to Fifty-Six Months in Federal Prison for Preparing False Tax Returns

On February 13, 2006, in Rockford, Illinois,—was sentenced to fifty-six months in prison, followed by one year supervised release, for preparing false federal income tax returns for others and for filing a false federal income tax return for himself.

-I was the group manager of the Information Gathering Program (IGP). We had numerous projects. We did compliance checks to see if certain groups were correctly reporting their income. For example, we would go to a nurses' registry where a nurse would pay 7 percent of her income to the registry. We then would check transcripts to see if the nurses reported the other 93 percent they earned. If not, we picked up the income and asserted a 5 percent negligence penalty. IRS stopped these projects a very long time ago. Normally, we did not go criminal because judges and IRS don't normally like to go after low-income people like barbers, waiters, waitresses, hairdressers, etc. However, there are some waiters and waitresses who earn over $300 a night.

We found people with Swiss bank accounts by looking at the outside of the mail envelope they received in New York. For example, the post marks were indications of a possible unreported amount of income.

People had offshore accounts that issued charges with numbered accounts. However, when they bought a plane ticket, a name had to be provided. The penalties are very stiff. Not declaring offshore accounts on your tax return is committing perjury.

We would also look at checks cashed at currency exchanges to see the number of checks cashed by individuals, which in many cases was unreported income. Also, form 8300 has to be filed by banks and car dealers when more than $10,000 in cash is deposited or used to purchase a car.

I have seen many checks for contributions altered to reflect a larger amount. For example, a $14 check would be changed to $1400. How stupid. The magnetic ink on the bottom right would show a $14 amount. I instructed the review staff to send these cases back to the field to assert the 50 percent fraud penalty. The penalty has been increased to 75 percent.

On a corporate audit, analyzing cancelled checks and endorsements can lead to corporate fraud. So the next time you think you can put one over on IRS, think twice.-

**The following are from the Fraud Awareness Handbook for Revenue Agents that I prepared:**

**Types of Deductions Having High Potential for Unusual Endorsements**

Outside research expense
Professional and consultant fees
Outside commissions and finder's fee
Accounts representing travel and entertainment expenses
Purchase shown through cash disbursements books
Trade and cash discounts or rebates paid in cash by the seller
Payments made for services to self-employed individuals

Payments to proprietors or principal corporate officers
Miscellaneous expense

## Unusual Forms of Endorsements (Not All-Inclusive)

- No endorsement by payee
- Longhand endorsement, rather than by stamp (in the case of a business)
- Several endorsements before bank clearing
- Absence of a clearing stamp generally indicates check was negotiated at bank on which drawn
- Bank stamp of note teller, bond teller, trust department (this may indicate purchase of bonds, payment of a loan, or payment to a trust of investment account)
- A bank clearance date preceding the check date (possible alteration)

## Unusual Check Negotiations

- Cashing it (bank tellers stamp)
- Cashing it as a check casher
- Using it to purchase cashier's checks, bank checks, or money orders
- Depositing in the personal checking or savings account of the payee or spouse
- Negotiating it to a foreign bank
- Negotiating it to an out-of-town (in proximity to the payee's address) bank
- Endorsing it to corporations, travel agencies, religious or other charitable organizations, department stores, supermarkets, or any other third party
- Negotiating it to a stock brokerage firm
- Endorsing it back to or cashing by the drawer

-IRS has a whole list of badges of fraud that indicate the possibility of fraud. The net worth approach has also been successfully used in proving fraud. Normally, you would list assets when you apply for a loan. Years later, your accumulation of assets vastly exceeded your reported income.

Some schedule C taxpayers who do home improvements or repairs think they are safe because they cash the check at the bank rather than deposit it. Most R/As who do a bank deposit analysis look at the check endorsement on the back of the check. If the payee does not deposit the check, it is very likely the income is not being reported.

Don't lie to an R/A. Never attempt to bribe an Internal Revenue agent (IRA) or revenue officer (R/O). I would never consider taking a bribe because I could go to jail for ten years. If you came up with a bribe overture, the R/A would pretend to consider it or hold it in abeyance to the next visit. The R/A would then be wired up by the Criminal Investigation Division on the next visit.-

## IRM 25.1.2.3 (04-24-2014)
### Indicators of Fraud

Listed below are categories of fraud indicators. Each category list is not intended to be all-inclusive; instead, citing examples of actions taxpayers may take to deceive or defraud. Look up IRM on Google or Internet for fraud items.

1. **Indicators of Fraud-Income**
   There are thirteen items listed.
2. **Indicators of Fraud-Expenses or Deductions**
   There are four items listed.
3. **Indicators of Fraud-Books and Records**
   There are twelve items listed.

# CHAPTER 8

# Can Chapter 7 Bankruptcy Wipe Out Your IRS Tax Debt? Yes.

-Originally, I had sixty pages on this subject and then I realized that I wanted to make the book nontechnical. Since you will be hiring a bankruptcy attorney, let him guide you on what you will need to file for bankruptcy. I will try to give you the basics on what to expect and if you qualify.

Chapter 7 bankruptcy can wipe out federal taxes. Bankruptcy can wipe out state taxes in three states (Illinois, Pennsylvania, and California). Check with your state. Obviously, with California's 12 percent state income tax, state income taxes can be very important. There are some exceptions-such as student loans, payroll taxes, and liens on property before the bankruptcy. If there was a lien on your home, bankruptcy will not eliminate the lien, which you will have to pay when you sell your house.

The good news is that your 401 and 403 retirement plans are safe. Your IRA has an exemption of 1.1 to 1.3 million in most states. The states have different amounts for exemptions on auto (three to four thousand), furniture (twelve thousand), and life insurance cash value (twelve thousand).-

## Step 1

You can discharge (wipe out) debts for federal income taxes in chapter 7 bankruptcy only if all of the following conditions are true:

- **The taxes are income taxes**-taxes other than income, such as payroll taxes or fraud penalties, can never be eliminated in bankruptcy.
- **You did not commit fraud or willful evasion**-if you filed a fraudulent tax return or otherwise willfully attempted to evade paying taxes, such as using a false Social Security number on your tax return, bankruptcy can't help.
- **The debt is at least three years old**-to eliminate a tax debt, the tax return must have been originally due at least three years before you filed for bankruptcy.
- **You filed a tax return**-you must have filed a tax return for the debt if you wish to discharge at least two years before filing for bankruptcy. IRS filing a substitute for return (SFR) is not considered a filed return.
- **You pass the "240-day rule"**-the income tax debt must have been assessed by the IRS at least 240 days before you file your bankruptcy petition, or must not have been assessed yet. (This time limit may be extended if the IRS suspended collection activity because of an offer in compromise or a previous bankruptcy filing.) Add sixty days for California.

## Step 2 (Medium-Income Comparison)

Compare your income to the median income in your state for a family the same size as yours.

| (Each state may have large differences in the median income for your family size.) State | 1 Earner | 2 People | 3 People | 4 People |
|---|---|---|---|---|
| Alabama | $41,370 | $49,806 | $55,289 | $65,381 |
| Alaska | $60,079 | $82,156 | $85,867 | $95,010 |
| Arizona | $43,749 | $54,236 | $57,927 | $67,800 |
| Arkansas | $38,530 | $47,017 | $51,773 | $58,149 |
| California | $49,185 | $63,745 | $67,817 | $78,150 |
| Colorado | $51,552 | $67,129 | $70,827 | $84,998 |
| Connecticut | $59,582 | $72,352 | $87,071 | $107,360 |
| Delaware | $51,686 | $61,849 | $74,300 | $84,179 |
| District of Columbia | $48,638 | $77,117 | $77,117 | $77,117 |
| Florida | $42,036 | $51,584 | $57,052 | $66,461 |
| Georgia | $40,985 | $52,827 | $57,858 | $68,066 |
| Hawaii | $61,107 | $67,463 | $80,681 | $88,217 |
| Idaho | $42,918 | $51,791 | $55,949 | $61,353 |
| Illinois | $47,469 | $61,443 | $72,342 | $83,546 |
| Indiana | $42,716 | $53,074 | $61,056 | $73,020 |
| Iowa | $43,792 | $61,104 | $67,062 | $81,219 |
| Kansas | $45,246 | $59,610 | $65,010 | $74,804 |
| Kentucky | $41,330 | $48,355 | $57,617 | $68,680 |
| Louisiana | $41,016 | $49,279 | $57,289 | $72,828 |
| Maine | $41,908 | $54,267 | $61,527 | $75,290 |
| Maryland | $59,475 | $76,489 | $88,221 | $105,382 |
| Massachusetts | $55,356 | $69,673 | $85,637 | $106,812 |
| Michigan | $44,504 | $53,640 | $62,973 | $76,622 |
| Minnesota | $50,121 | $65,503 | $79,750 | $93,294 |
| Mississippi | $35,213 | $44,116 | $46,583 | $58,182 |
| Missouri | $41,700 | $51,940 | $61,119 | $71,550 |
| Montana | $44,074 | $54,839 | $61,043 | $67,614 |
| Nebraska | $42,446 | $60,389 | $65,804 | $78,363 |
| Nevada | $42,988 | $55,467 | $58,399 | $68,560 |

| | | | | |
|---|---|---|---|---|
| New Hampshire | $55,804 | $67,659 | $81,709 | $94,432 |
| New Jersey | $60,265 | $70,845 | $89,413 | $105,737 |
| New Mexico | $40,722 | $53,385 | $53,385 | $61,837 |
| New York | $48,840 | $60,743 | $71,706 | $88,156 |
| North Carolina | $40,412 | $51,857 | $56,782 | $69,370 |
| North Dakota | $47,629 | $67,024 | $76,620 | $88,887 |
| Ohio | $43,276 | $53,551 | $62,134 | $77,367 |
| Oklahoma | $41,544 | $52,995 | $57,087 | $63,419 |
| Oregon | $46,304 | $57,182 | $64,107 | $71,508 |
| Pennsylvania | $48,200 | $56,946 | $71,703 | $84,396 |
| Rhode island | $47,742 | $62,190 | $71,977 | $88,389 |
| South Carolina | $39,983 | $50,679 | $54,028 | $66,561 |
| South Dakota | $40,427 | $57,383 | $57,383 | $73,089 |
| Tennessee | $40,977 | $50,169 | $56,091 | $66,846 |
| Texas | $42,223 | $57,730 | $60,520 | $70,824 |
| Utah | $52,021 | $58,595 | $66,552 | $72,274 |
| Vermont | $46,494 | $61,671 | $72,558 | $82,047 |
| Virginia | $52,436 | $67,021 | $75,044 | $91,859 |
| Washington | $52,384 | $65,802 | $74,428 | $84,786 |
| West Virginia | $43,554 | $46,658 | $54,097 | $66,009 |
| Wisconsin | $42,969 | $58,786 | $68,489 | $82,350 |
| Wyoming | $49,721 | $64,086 | $75,456 | $80,477 |

*Add $8,100 for each individual in excess of four.*

If your income is higher than the median income, it doesn't necessarily mean that you can't file for chapter 7 bankruptcy; it just triggers the second step in the test.

### Step 3 (Calculate disposable income and unsecured debts.)

Certain allowable expenses (determined by IRS guidelines) are subtracted from your income to find your "disposable income." If your projected disposable income over the next five years equals less than

$6,000 ($100/month), you will likely "pass" and become eligible to file under chapter 7.

If your disposable income is greater than $10,000 ($166/month) over the next five years, a presumption arises that you do not really need to file for chapter 7 bankruptcy. Check with your attorney for special circumstances.

## Step 4 (Homestead Exemption)

**The federal homestead exemption is $29,750 and roughly half the states can use it.**

If your home value is less than your mortgage before or after your homestead exemption, filing for bankruptcy to eliminate federal taxes and credit card debt may be a good choice. Check to see what the home homestead is for your state regarding how much equity in your home can be protected.

Florida, Iowa, Kansas, Oklahoma, South Dakota and Texas have some of the broadest homestead protections in the U.S., in terms of the value of property that can be protected. Your home is probably safe in these states.

California protects up to $75,000 for single people; $100,000 for married couples; and $175,000 for people over sixty-five or legally disabled. Illinois has a $15,000 homestead exemption and $30,000 if you are married. Massachusetts has a $500,000 homestead if you are sixty-two years of age.

If you live in one of the listed states, you can choose to use the federal bankruptcy exemptions ($29,750). If not, then you are limited to your state's exemptions. These states include Alaska, Arkansas, Connecticut, District of Columbia, Hawaii, Kentucky, Massachusetts, Michigan, Minnesota, New Hampshire, New Jersey, New Mexico, New York, Oregon, Pennsylvania, Rhode Island, Texas, Vermont, Washington, and Wisconsin.

If you have equity in your home after taking into account the homestead exemption, creditors may be able to force the sale of your home. If you are in that situation, your attorney can advise you. He/

she knows more than I do. You might have to file chapter 13 to save your home.

**Step 5**

*Credit counseling requirement* must be approved 180 days before bankruptcy filing and also must be approved by the U.S. Trustee's Office. Ask your attorney which credit counseling agency he/she recommends. Counseling will explain the need to proceed to filing for bankruptcy or a repayment plan.

You must also complete Debtor Education Course before a discharge in bankruptcy. You can handle on the Internet or in person. The cost must be reasonable (around $30 to$60).

**United States Courts**
**Federal Courts**
*How Chapter 7 Works*

A chapter 7 case begins with the debtor filing a petition with the bankruptcy court serving the area where the individual lives or where the business debtor is organized or has its principal place of business or principal assets. In addition to the petition, the debtor must also file with the court (1) schedules of assets and liabilities; (2) a schedule of current income and expenditures; (3) a statement of financial affairs; and (4) a schedule of executory contracts and unexpired leases (Fed. R. Bankruptcy, P. 1007[b]). Debtors must also provide the assigned case trustee with a copy of the tax return or transcripts for the most recent tax year as well as tax returns filed during the case (including tax returns for prior years that had not been filed when the case began) (11 USC 521). Individual debtors with primarily consumer debts have additional document filing requirements. They must file a certificate of credit counseling and a copy of any debt repayment plan developed through credit counseling; evidence of payment from employers, if any, received sixty days before filing; a statement of monthly net income and any anticipated increase in income or expenses after filing; and a record of any interest the debtor has in federal or state qualified education or tuition accounts. A husband and wife may file a joint petition or individual petitions (11 USC 302[a]).

If the debtor's income is less than 150 percent of the poverty level (as defined in the Bankruptcy Code) and the debtor is unable to pay the chapter 7 fees even in installments, the court may waive the requirement that the fees be paid (28 USC 1930[f]). In order to complete the official bankruptcy forms that make up the petition, statement of financial affairs, and schedules, the debtor must provide the following information:

- A list of all creditors and the amount and nature of their claims
- The source, amount, and frequency of the debtor's income
- A list of all of the debtor's property and a detailed list of the debtor's monthly living expenses, i.e., food, clothing, shelter, utilities, taxes, transportation, medicine, etc.

Married individuals must gather this information for their spouse regardless of whether they are filing a joint petition, separate individual petitions, or even if only one spouse is filing. In a situation where only one spouse files, the income and expenses of the nonfiling spouse are required so that the court, the trustee and creditors can evaluate the household's financial position. Among the schedules that an individual debtor will file is a schedule of "exempt" property. The Bankruptcy Code allows an individual debtor to protect some property from the claims of creditors because it is exempt under federal bankruptcy law or under the laws of the debtor's home state (11 USC 522[b]). Many states have taken advantage of a provision in the Bankruptcy Code that permits each state to adopt its own exemption law in place of the federal exemptions. In other jurisdictions, the individual debtor has the option of choosing between a federal package of exemptions or the exemptions available under state law. Thus, whether certain property is exempt and may be kept by the debtor is often a question of state law. The debtor should consult an attorney to determine the exemptions available in the state where the debtor lives.

Filing a petition under chapter 7 "automatically stays" (stops) most collection actions against the debtor or the debtor's property (11 USC 362). But filing the petition does not stay certain types of actions listed under 11 USC 362(b), and the stay may be effective only for a short time in some situations. The stay arises by operation of law and requires no judicial action. As long as the stay is in effect, creditors generally may not initiate or continue lawsuits, wage garnishments, or even telephone calls, demanding payments. The bankruptcy clerk gives notice of the bankruptcy case to all creditors whose names and addresses are provided by the debtor.

## Credit Card Debt

-If your main reason for filing bankruptcy is credit card debt, think again. In most cases, you can negotiate with the credit card companies for pennies on the dollar. Credit card companies usually receive around 10 percent when they sell your debt. Your credit is lousy, but chapter 7 will make it worse. Stop paying on the credit cards. Contact them and tell them that you can't afford to pay the credit card after paying rent, food, utilities, etc. A lot of people may have great reasons for not paying because they have been laid off or fired. In many cases, if you owe $5,000, the credit card company may accept a $1,500 payment in settlement. Some credit card companies will settle for 40 percent of the debt.

I recently prepared a return involving a home foreclosure and discharge of credit card indebtedness for a friend. I filed form 982 and attached letters from the credit card companies (showing cancellation of the debts) and a copy of the chapter 7 bankruptcy. This resulted in no additional tax. Without the bankruptcy, the credit card cancellation of income would have been taxable unless she was insolvent at the time.-

## *You Can't Discharge a Federal Tax Lien*

If your taxes qualify for discharge in a chapter 7 bankruptcy case, your victory may be bittersweet. This is because bankruptcy will not wipe out prior recorded tax liens. A chapter 7 bankruptcy will wipe out your personal obligation to pay the debt and prevent the IRS from going after your bank account or wages.

Note-individual debtors should use their home address when filing form 1040 with the IRS. Returns should *not* be filed "in care of" the trustee's address.

## Tax Returns Due after the Bankruptcy Filing

For debtors filing bankruptcy under all chapters (chapters 7, 11, 12, or 13), the Bankruptcy Code provides that if the debtor does not file a tax return that becomes due after the commencement of the bankruptcy case, or obtain an extension for filing the return before the due date-the taxing authority may request that the bankruptcy court either dismiss the case or convert the case to a case under another chapter of the Bankruptcy Code. If the debtor does not file the required return or obtain an extension within ninety days after the request is made, the bankruptcy court *must* dismiss or convert the case.

## Debt Cancellation

If a debt is canceled or forgiven, other than as a gift or bequest, the debtor generally must include the canceled amount in gross income for tax purposes. A debt includes any indebtedness for which the debtor is liable or that attaches to property the debtor holds. In the event that the amount forgiven is $600 or more, the debtor should receive a form 1099-C, Cancellation of Debt, from the lender. See form 1099-C and the separate instructions. The debtor may not have to report the entire amount of canceled debt as income as certain exclusions may apply.

## *Exclusions*

Do not include a canceled debt in gross income if:

- the cancellation takes place in a bankruptcy case under the Bankruptcy Code,
- the cancellation takes place when the debtor is insolvent, and the amount excluded is not more than the amount by which the debtor is insolvent, or
- the canceled debt is qualified farm debt (debt incurred in operating a farm).

# CHAPTER 9

# Benefits of Filling a Joint Return Versus Separate Returns: Not Living Together, You May Be Able to File as Head of Household

*Should you file separate, jointly, or single?*

-Filing as head of household is much better than married filing separately. If you are married and do not live together the last six months of the year, the custodial parent may be able to claim head of household. The non-custodial parent cannot claim head of household just because the spouse signs over the exemption for a child.

The perfect situation would be a married couple living in a two- or three-flat building. If they lived in separate apartments (households) and each had one or more children living with them, they both may be able to claim head of household. Condos or apartments in the same building could also work. Check with your accountant.-

## Publication 17

### Considered Unmarried

To qualify for head of household status, you must be either unmarried or considered unmarried on the last day of the year. You are considered unmarried on the last day of the tax year if you meet all the following tests:

- You file a separate return. A separate return includes a return claiming married filing separately, single, or head of household filing status.
- You paid more than half the cost of keeping up your home for the tax year.
- *Your spouse did not live in your home during the last six months of the tax year.* Your spouse is considered to live in your home even if he or she is temporarily absent due to special circumstances.

### *Temporary Absences*

You and your qualifying person are considered to live together even if one or both of you are temporarily absent from your home due to special circumstances such as illness, education, business, vacation, or military service. It must be reasonable to assume the absent person will return to the home after the temporary absence. You must continue to keep up the home during the absence.

Your home was the main home of your child, stepchild, or foster child for more than half the year. (See "Home of Qualifying Person," later, for rules applying to a child's birth, death, or temporary absence during the year.)

You must be able to claim an exemption for the child. However, you meet this test if you cannot claim the exemption only because the noncustodial parent can claim the child using the rules described later in "Children of Divorced or Separated Parents (or Parents Who Live Apart)" under "Qualifying Child" or in "Support Test for Children of Divorced or Separated Parents (or Parents Who Live

Apart)" under "Qualifying Relative." The general rules for claiming an exemption for a dependent are explained later.

-When you are separated, still married, or divorced, couples should settle their differences and plan their taxes.

Example,

A couple has three children. Both parents work. They do not live together and have separate households. They are still married. She is the custodial parent and entitled to head of household. She makes $80,000, and he makes $30,100. She can take one or up to three children. She is not entitled to the earned income credit. She loses a child credit and an exemption worth about $2,000 thousand in tax for each child she allows her husband to claim. He gains the same for each child. If they were divorced, the husband would get single filing status and head of household if a child lived with him. It does not pay tax wise to drag on getting a divorce. After you are divorced, each former spouse can file as single or head of household if they have a child living with them. Filing single or head of household can possibly entitle you to the earned income credit and the credit for child and dependent care expenses if you are the custodial parent.

You cannot claim the earned income credit if you file as "Married Filing Separately."

Same facts as above except the wife earns $30,100-she would be entitled to the earned income credit.

## Tip

The custodial divorced parent can give up her child exemption(s) to her ex-spouse and still be entitled to head of household status. He cannot take head of household status because the child did not live with him.

A married couple with two children have not lived together the last six months of the year. The custodial parent can take head of household status, which would allow her to possibly claim certain credits.

Millions of taxpayers are confused with regard to who has the right to an exemption and possibly entitled to head of household status. I felt that it was very important to include these tie-breaking rules and examples from Publication 17-

## Tiebreaker Rules

To determine which person can treat the child as a qualifying child to claim the six tax benefits just listed, the following tiebreaker rules apply:

- If only one of the persons is the child's parent, the child is treated as the qualifying child of the parent.
- If the parents file a joint return together and can claim the child as a qualifying child, the child is treated as the qualifying child of the parents.
- If the parents do not file a joint return together but both parents claim the child as a qualifying child, the IRS will treat the child as the qualifying child of the parent with whom the child lived for the longer period of time during the year. If the child lived with each parent for the same amount of time, the IRS will treat the child as the qualifying child of the parent who had the higher adjusted gross income (AGI) for the year.
- If no parent can claim the child as a qualifying child, the child is treated as the qualifying child of the person who had the highest AGI for the year.
- If a parent can claim the child as a qualifying child but no parent does so claim the child, the child is treated as the qualifying child of the person who had the highest AGI for the year, but only if that person's AGI is higher than the highest AGI of any of the child's parents who can claim the child. If the child's parents file a joint return with each other, this rule can be applied by treating the parents' total AGI as divided evenly between them. See example 8.

Subject to these tiebreaker rules, you and the other person may be able to choose which of you claims the child as a qualifying child. See examples 1 through 13.

The following examples may help you in determining whether you can claim the EIC when you and someone else have the same qualifying child.

### Example 1

You and your two-year-old son, Jimmy, lived with your mother all year. You are twenty-five years old, unmarried, and your AGI is $9,000. Your only income was $9,000 from a part-time job. Your mother's only income was $20,000 from her job, and her AGI is $20,000. Jimmy's father did not live with you or Jimmy. The special rule explained later for divorced or separated parents (or parents who live apart) does not apply. Jimmy is a qualifying child of both you and your mother because he meets the relationship, age, residency, and joint return tests for both you and your mother. However, only one of you can treat him as a qualifying child to claim the EIC (and the other tax benefits listed earlier for which that person qualifies). He is not a qualifying child of anyone else, including his father. If you do not claim Jimmy as a qualifying child for the EIC or any of the other tax benefits listed earlier, your mother can treat him as a qualifying child to claim the EIC (and any of the other tax benefits listed earlier for which she qualifies).

### Example 2

The facts are the same as in example 1, except your AGI is $25,000. Because your mother's AGI is not higher than yours, she cannot claim Jimmy as a qualifying child. Only you can claim him.

### Example 3

The facts are the same as in example 1, except that you and your mother both claim Jimmy as a qualifying child. In this case, you as the child's parent will be the only one allowed to claim Jimmy as a qualifying child for the EIC and the other tax benefits listed earlier for which you qualify. The IRS will disallow your mother's claim to the EIC and any of the other tax benefits listed earlier unless she has another qualifying child.

*Example 4*

The facts are the same as in example 1, except that you also have two other young children who are qualifying children of both you and your mother. Only one of you can claim each child. However, if your mother's AGI is higher than yours, you can allow your mother to claim one or more of the children. For example, if you claim one child, your mother can claim the other two.

*Example 5*

The facts are the same as in example 1, except that you are only eighteen years old. This means you are a qualifying child of your mother. Because of rule 10, discussed next, you cannot claim the EIC and cannot claim Jimmy as a qualifying child. Only your mother may be able to treat Jimmy as a qualifying child to claim the EIC. If your mother meets all the other requirements for claiming the EIC and you do not claim Jimmy as a qualifying child for any of the other tax benefits listed earlier, your mother can claim both you and Jimmy as qualifying children for the EIC.

*Example 6*

The facts are the same as in example 1, except that your mother earned $50,000 from her job. Because your mother's earned income is too high for her to claim the EIC, only you can claim the EIC using your son.

*Example 7*

The facts are the same as in example 1, except that you earned $50,000 from your job and your AGI is $50,500. Your earned income is too high for you to claim the EIC. But your mother cannot claim the EIC either because her AGI is not higher than yours.

*Example 8*

The facts are the same as in example 1, except that you and Jimmy's father are married to each other, live with Jimmy and your mother, and have an AGI of $30,000 on a joint return. If you and your husband do not claim Jimmy as a qualifying child for the EIC or any of the other tax benefits listed earlier, your mother can claim him instead. Even though the AGI on your joint return ($30,000) is more than your mother's AGI of $20,000, for this purpose, half of the joint AGI can be treated as yours and half as your husband's. In other words, each parent's AGI can be treated as $15,000.

*Example 9*

You, your husband, and your ten-year-old son, Joey, lived together until August 1, 2014, when your husband moved out of the household. In August and September, Joey lived with you. For the rest of the year, Joey lived with your husband, who is Joey's father. Joey is a qualifying child of both you and your husband because he lived with each of you for more than half the year and because he met the relationship, age, and joint return tests for both of you. At the end of the year, you and your husband still were not divorced, legally separated, or separated under a written separation agreement, so the special rule for divorced or separated parents (or parents who live apart) does not apply. You and your husband will file separate returns. Your husband agrees to let you treat Joey as a qualifying child. This means, if your husband does not claim Joey as a qualifying child for any of the tax benefits listed earlier, you can claim him as a qualifying child for any tax benefit listed earlier for which you qualify. However, your filing status is married filing separately, so you cannot claim the EIC or the credit for child and dependent care expenses. See rule 3.

*Example 10*

The facts are the same as in example 9, except that you and your husband both claim Joey as a qualifying child. In this case, only your husband will be allowed to treat Joey as a qualifying child. This is because, during 2014, the boy lived with him longer than with you. You cannot claim the EIC (either with or without a qualifying child). However, your husband's filing status is "married filing separately," so he cannot claim the EIC or the credit for child and dependent care expenses. See rule 3.

*Example 11*

You, your five-year-old son, and your son's father lived together all year. You and your son's father are not married. Your son is a qualifying child of both you and his father because he meets the relationship, age, residency, and joint return tests for both you and his father. Your earned income and AGI is $12,000, and your son's father's earned income and AGI is $14,000. Neither of you had any other income. Your son's father agrees to let you treat the child as a qualifying child. This means, if your son's father does not claim your son as a qualifying child for the EIC or any of the other tax benefits listed earlier, you can claim him as a qualifying child for the EIC and any of the other tax benefits listed earlier for which you qualify.

*Example 12*

The facts are the same as in example 11, except that you and your son's father both claim your son as a qualifying child. In this case, only your son's father will be allowed to treat your son as a qualifying child. This is because his AGI ($14,000) is more than your AGI ($12,000). You cannot claim the EIC (either with or without a qualifying child).

*Example 13*

You and your seven-year-old niece, your sister's child, lived with your mother all year. You are twenty-five years old, and your AGI is $9,300. Your only income was from a part-time job. Your mother's AGI is $15,000. Her only income was from her job. Your niece's parents file jointly, have an AGI of less than $9,000, and do not live with you or their child. Your niece is a qualifying child of both you and your mother because she meets the relationship, age, residency, and joint return tests for both you and your mother. However, only your mother can treat her as a qualifying child. This is because your mother's AGI ($15,000) is more than your AGI ($9,300).

## Special Rule for Divorced or Separated Parents (or Parents Who Live Apart)

A child will be treated as the qualifying child of his or her noncustodial parent (for purposes of claiming an exemption and the child tax credit, but not for the EIC) if all of the following statements are true:

1.  The parents are divorced or legally separated under a decree of divorce or separate maintenance, are separated under a written separation agreement, or lived apart at all times during the last six months of 2014, whether or not they are or were married. (You only need one of the three to be true.)
2.  The child received over half of his or her support for the year from the parents.
3.  The child is in the custody of one or both parents for more than half of 2014.
4.  Either of the following statements is true.
    a.  The custodial parent signs form 8332 or a substantially similar statement that he or she will not claim

the child as a dependent for the year, and the noncus-todial parent attaches the form or statement to his or her return. If the divorce decree or separation agreement went into effect after 1984 and before 2009, the noncustodial parent may be able to attach certain pages from the decree or agreement instead of form 8332. (For the year January 1–December 31, 2014)

b.  A pre-1985 decree of divorce or separate mainte-nance or written separation agreement that applies to 2014 provides that the noncustodial parent can claim the child as a dependent, and the non-custodial parent provides at least $600 for support of the child during 2014. (Obviously, this needs to be updated and is confusing.)

-Use form 8453 to send in your form 8332 when you e-file. This will save you time and aggravation dealing with back-and-forth correspondence with the IRS. The transmittal can also be used to submit other forms not transmitted during e-file. See form 8453.-

Transmittal form 8453
U.S. Individual Income Tax Transmittal for an IRS E-file Return

➢  See instructions on back.
➢  Information about form 8453 and its instructions is avail-able at *www.irs.gov/form8453*.

If conditions 1 through 4 apply, only the noncustodial parent can claim the child for purposes of the dependency exemption (line 6c) and the child tax credits (lines 52 and 67). However, this special rule does not apply to head of household filing status, the credit for child and dependent care expenses, the exclusion for dependent care benefits, or the earned income credit. See Publication 501 for details.

**Custodial and noncustodial parents**

The custodial parent is the parent with whom the child lived for the greater number of nights in 2014. The noncustodial parent is the other parent. If the child was with each parent for an equal number of nights, the custodial parent is the parent with the higher adjusted gross income. See Publication 501 for an exception for a parent who works at night, rules for a child who is emancipated under state law, and other details.

## Post-1984 and pre-2009 decree or agreement

The decree or agreement must state all three of the following:

1. The noncustodial parent can claim the child as a dependent without regard to any condition, such as payment of support.
2. The other parent will not claim the child as a dependent.
3. The years for which the claim is released.

The noncustodial parent must include all of the following pages from the decree or agreement:

- Cover page (include the other parent's SSN on that page).
- The pages that include all the information identified in 1 through 3 above.
- Signature page with the other parent's signature and date of agreement.

You must include the required information even if you filed it with your return in an earlier year. Use form 8453 transmittal to send in if you e-file. I would consider paper filing.

## Post-2008 decree or agreement

If the divorce decree or separation agreement went into effect after 2008, the noncustodial parent cannot include pages from the decree or agreement instead of form 8332. The custodial parent must sign either form 8332 or a substantially similar statement the only purpose of which is to release the custodial parent's claim to an exemption for a child, and the noncustodial parent must include a copy with his or her return. The form or statement must release the custodial parent's claim to the dependent.

**To qualify for the earned income credit, observe the following rules:**

**Rule 1-your AGI must be less than**

$46,997 ($52,427 for married filing jointly) if you have three or more qualifying children,

$43,756 ($49,186 for married filing jointly) if you have two qualifying children,

$38,511 ($43,941 for married filing jointly) if you have one qualifying child, or

$14,590 ($20,020 for married filing jointly) if you do not have a qualifying child.

**Adjusted gross income (AGI)**

AGI is the amount on line 38 (form 1040), line 22 (form 1040A), or line 4 (form 1040EZ). If your AGI is equal to or more than the applicable limit listed above, you cannot claim the EIC.

Example,

Your AGI is $38,550, you are single, and you have one qualifying child. You cannot claim the EIC because your AGI is not less than $38,511. However, if your filing status was married filing jointly, you might be able to claim the EIC because your AGI is less than $43,941.

You must be able to claim an exemption for the child. However, you meet this test if you cannot claim the exemption only because the noncustodial parent can claim the child using the rules described in "Children of Divorced or Separated Parents (or Parents Who Live Apart)" under "Qualifying Child in chapter 3," or referred to in "Support Test for Children of Divorced or Separated Parents (or Parents Who Live Apart)" under "Qualifying Relative" in chapter 3.

The general rules for claiming an exemption for a dependent are explained under "Exemptions for Dependents" in chapter 3.

If you were considered married for part of the year and lived in a community property state (listed earlier under Married Filing Separately), special rules may apply in determining your income and expenses. See Publication 555 for more information.

**Nonresident alien spouse**-you are considered unmarried for head of household purposes if your spouse was a nonresident alien at any time during the year and you do not choose to treat your nonresident spouse as a resident alien. However, your spouse is not a qualifying person for head of household purposes. You must have another qualifying person and meet the other tests to be eligible to file as a head of household.

**Choice to treat spouse as resident**-you are considered married if you choose to treat your spouse as a resident alien. See Publication 17.

**Marital status**-in general, your filing status depends on whether you are considered unmarried or married.

**Unmarried persons**-you are considered unmarried for the whole year if, on the last day of your tax year, you are unmarried or legally separated from your spouse under a divorce or separate maintenance decree. State law governs whether you are married or legally separated under a divorce or separate maintenance decree.

**Divorced persons**-if you are divorced under a final decree by the last day of the year, you are considered unmarried for the whole year.

**Divorce and remarriage**-if you obtain a divorce for the sole purpose of filing tax returns as unmarried individuals, and at the time of divorce you intend to and do, in fact, remarry each other in the next tax year, you and your spouse must file as married individuals in both years.

**Annulled marriages**-if you obtain a court decree of annulment, which holds that no valid marriage ever existed, you are considered unmarried even if you filed joint returns for earlier years. You must file form 1040X, Amended U.S. Individual Income Tax Return, claiming single or head of household status for all tax years that are affected by the annulment and are not closed by the statute of limitations for filing a tax return. Generally, for a credit or refund, you must file form 1040X within three years (including extensions) after the date you filed your original return or within two years after the date you paid the tax, whichever is later. If you filed your original return early (for example, March 1), your return is considered filed on the due date (generally April 15). However, if you had an extension to file (for example, until October 15) and filed on September 30, use September 30 for your computation.

## Filing Joint Returns after Filing Separate Returns

You can change your filing status from a separate return to a joint return by filing an amended return using form 1040X. You generally can change to a joint return anytime within three years from the date of the separate return or returns. This does not include any extensions. A separate return includes a return filed by you or your spouse claiming married filing separately, single, or head of household filing status.

## Filing Separate Returns after Joint Return

Once you file a joint return, you cannot choose to file separate returns for that year after the due date of the return. Exception-a personal representative for a decedent can change from a joint return elected by the surviving spouse to a separate return for the decedent. The personal representatives had one year from the due date of the return (including extensions) to make the change.

If you get an annulment, you are considered as never been married. You and your husband are required to go back and file amended tax returns for all open years. You would be entitled to any refund due or may have to pay additional tax.

It is important to consider filing separate returns when you spouse has student loans, unpaid child support, or back taxes. If you filed a joint return, IRS will take any tax refund due to you. For example, the husband was not working and was not able to pay child support for his daughter from a previous relationship. His current wife filed a joint return with him, and IRS gave her very large refund to the state. The wife may be entitled to recoup her share of the refund by filing form 8379 as an injured spouse.

## Unrelated Tip

-If you have personally cosigned for a student loan, you should consider taking out term insurance on the student in case he or she dies. Recently, on the news, the parents were stuck with a $200,000 student loan when their child died. IRS will take 15 percent of your Social Security if you have cosigned for your child and the loan has not been paid.

Sometimes separate returns are filed because one of the parties does not want to divulge their personal Tax information-for example, the very rich wife of a senator or congressman.-

Publication 17

If you choose married filing separately, the following credits and deductions are reduced at levels half those for a joint return:

- The child tax credit.
- Retirement savings contribution credit.
- The deduction for personal exemption and itemized deductions.
- Capital loss deduction is limited to $1500.
- Rental activity losses are limited to $12,500.

However, if you are considered unmarried and can file a return as head of household, it appears that a reduction is not necessary. For additional information, look up married filing separately in Publication 17.

Filing separately in community property states Arizona, California, Idaho, Louisiana, Nevada, New Mexico, Texas, Washington, and Wisconsin, each spouse would normally be required to pick up 50 percent of the income and 50 percent of the expenses. See Publication 555.

-ACA (Obama Care) can affect your subsidy if you are married or single. See chapter 11. Your husband or wife's employer may only cover their employee. Your combined income may affect the employer's contribution to their health care or knock both of you out of a subsidy. If they both earned $30,000 or 40,000 and were married, they would probably not receive a subsidy if they had no children. If they were both single, both may receive a subsidy. Also, ACA overlooked the fact that some married women file their tax returns separately. The Treasury Department is preparing to take steps to allow married survivors of domestic abuse to claim subsidies for health plans, no matter how they file their taxes.

A couple is celebrating thirty-five or forty years of marriage and are retired and on Social Security.

Married seniors with both having Social Security or one working would lose the $32,000 base if they file separately. The base would be zero. Seniors would be better off getting divorced and then each get a $25,000 base when filing separately. A single person includes 50 percent of the Social Security benefit if the taxable income is between $25,000 and $34,000, and 85 percent if above 34,000. The same taxable percentages apply for married couples whose taxable income is between $32,000 and $44,000 filing a joint return. However, unmarried couples would have a higher level of $50,000 to $68,000, and 85 percent of Social Security would be taxable on income over $68,000.

A more important question is, Should you get married in the first place? Five years ago, I met the perfect woman for me. We share living expenses. We cannot get married because she would lose her Tri Care military insurance forever. The Tri Care is around $250 a year. She is only sixty-four and a military widow. Her Social Security (from her husband) would be 85 percent taxable, and my federal pension would be reduced by 10 percent, plus my pension would be reduced by the 10 percent I previously saved being single and would be spread over a period of years. We would also have to pay $200 a month to cover her under my Blue Cross Plan.

When your spouse gives you the joint return for you to sign, carefully look at the income he or she is reporting and the deductions he or she is taking on the return. If you suspect that your husband is cheating on his taxes and if it is significant, consider filing separately. Men are more likely to commit fraud than women. If you are a housewife and not working, you don't have to file a tax return. In some situations, a taxpayer may forge a spouse's signature and commit fraud. If you are getting a divorce and you feel that your husband or wife is hiding substantial income, don't file a joint return. Check with your tax preparer or another accountant.-

Under the following circumstances, you can sign a joint return for your spouse:

- *Spouse died before signing*-the executor or administrator must sign the return for the spouse. If no one has been appointed, you can send return for your spouse and enter filing as surviving spouse in the area where you signed the return.

- *Injury or disease prevents signing*-you can sign your spouse's name in the proper space followed by the words by your name (Joe Smith), husband or wife. Be sure to also sign in the space provided for your signature. Attach a statement showing the reason your spouse cannot sign and that the spouse has agreed to your signing for him or her.

- *Signing as guardian of spouse*-if you are the guardian of your spouse who is mentally incompetent, you can sign the return for your spouse as guardian.

- *Spouse in combat zone*-if you do not have a power of attorney, attach a signed statement to your return explaining that your spouse is serving in a combat zone.

- *Other reasons spouse cannot sign*-you can sign for your spouse only if you are given a valid power of attorney. Attach a copy of the power of attorney to your tax return.

CHAPTER 10

# Tax Filing Options
# for Same-Sex Couples
# Lawfully Married

The Supreme Court ruling on same-sex marriage is now the law of the land. The first part of the chapter covers the most important information regarding your income tax obligations. The second part of the chapter covers common law marriages and civil unions as well as how the law was changed.

IR-2013-72, Aug. 29, 2013

Washington-The U.S. Department of the Treasury and the Internal Revenue Service (IRS) today ruled that same-sex couples, legally married in jurisdictions that recognize their marriages, will be treated as married for federal tax purposes. The ruling applies regardless of whether the couple lives in a jurisdiction that recognizes same-sex marriage or a jurisdiction that does not recognize same-sex marriage.

Legally married same-sex couples generally must file their 2013 federal income tax return using either the married filing jointly or married filing separately filing status.

Individuals who were in same-sex marriages may, but are not required to, file original or amended returns, choosing to be treated as married for federal tax purposes for one or more prior tax years still open under the statute of limitations.

Generally, the statute of limitations for filing a refund claim is three years from the date the return was filed or two years from the date the tax was paid, whichever is later. As a result, refund claims can still be filed for tax years 2013, 2014, and 2015.

Additionally, employees who purchased same-sex spouse health insurance coverage from their employers on an after-tax basis may treat the amounts paid for that coverage as pretax and excludable from income.

## How to File a Claim for Refund

Taxpayers who wish to file a refund claim for income taxes should use form 1040X, Amended U.S. Individual Income Tax Return.

Taxpayers who wish to file a refund claim for gift or estate taxes should file form 843, Claim for Refund and Request for Abatement. For information on filing an amended return, see Tax Topic 308, Amended Returns, available on IRS.gov, or the "Instructions to Forms 1040X and 843." Information on where to file your amended returns is available in the instructions to the form.

Treasury and the IRS will begin applying the terms of Revenue Ruling 2013-17 on Sept. 16, 2013, but taxpayers who wish to rely on the terms of the Revenue Ruling for earlier periods may choose to do so, as long as the statute of limitations for the earlier period has not expired.

**Answers to Frequently Asked Questions for Individuals of the Same-Sex Who Are Married under State Law**

The following questions and answers provide information to individuals of the same sex who are lawfully married (same-sex spouses). These questions and answers reflect the holdings in Revenue Ruling 2013-17 in 2013-38 IRB 201.

**Q1. When are individuals of the same sex lawfully married for federal tax purposes?**

A1. For federal tax purposes, the IRS looks to state or foreign law to determine whether individuals are married. The IRS has a general rule recognizing a marriage of same-sex spouses that was validly entered into in a domestic or foreign jurisdiction whose laws authorize the marriage of two individuals of the same sex even if the married couple resides in a domestic or foreign jurisdiction that does not recognize the validity of same-sex marriages.

**Q2. Can same-sex spouses file federal tax returns using a married filing jointly or married filing separately status?**

A2. Yes. For tax year 2013 and going forward, same-sex spouses generally must file using a married filing separately or jointly filing status. For tax year 2012 and all prior years, same-sex spouses who file an original tax return on or after September 16, 2013 (the effective date of Rev. Rul. 2013-17), generally must file using a married filing separately or jointly filing status. For tax year 2012, same-sex spouses who filed their tax return before September 16, 2013, may choose (but are not required) to amend their federal tax returns to file using married filing separately or jointly filing status. A taxpayer generally may file a claim for refund for three years from the date the return was filed or two years from the date the tax was paid, whichever is later. For information on filing an amended return, go to Tax Topic 308, Amended Returns, at http://www.irs.gov/taxtopics/tc308.html.

**Q3. Can a taxpayer and his or her same-sex spouse file a joint return if they were married in a state that recognizes same-sex marriages but they live in a state that does not recognize their marriage?**

A3. Yes. For federal tax purposes, the IRS has a general rule recognizing a marriage of same-sex individuals that was validly entered into in a domestic or foreign jurisdiction whose laws authorize the marriage of two individuals of the same sex even if the married couple resides in a domestic or foreign jurisdiction that does not recognize the validity of same-sex marriages. The rules for using a married filing jointly or married filing separately status described in Q&A no. 2 apply to these married individuals.

**Q4. Can a taxpayer's same-sex spouse be a dependent of the taxpayer?**

A4. No. A taxpayer's spouse cannot be a dependent of the taxpayer.

**Q5. Can a same-sex spouse file using head of household filing status?**

A5. A taxpayer who is married cannot file using head of household filing status. However, a married taxpayer may be considered unmarried and may use the head of household filing status if the taxpayer lives apart from his or her spouse for the last six months of the taxable year and provides more than half the cost of maintaining a household that is the principal place of abode of the taxpayer's dependent child for more than half of the year. See Publication 501 for more details.

**Q6. If same-sex spouses (who file using the married filing separately status) have a child, which parent may claim the child as a dependent?**

A6. If a child is a qualifying child under section 152(c) of both parents who are spouses (who file using the married filing separate status), either parent, but not both, may claim a dependency deduction for the qualifying child. If both parents claim a dependency deduction for the child on their income tax returns, the IRS will treat the child as the qualifying child of the parent with whom the child resides for the longer period of time during the taxable year. If the child resides with each parent for the same amount of time during the taxable year, the IRS will treat the child as the qualifying child of the parent with the higher adjusted gross income.

**Q7. Can a taxpayer who is married to a person of the same sex claim the standard deduction if the taxpayer's spouse itemized deductions?**

A7. No. If a taxpayer's spouse itemized his or her deductions, the taxpayer cannot claim the standard deduction (section 63[c][6][A]).

**Q8. If a taxpayer adopts the child of his or her same-sex spouse as a second parent or coparent, may the taxpayer ("adopting parent") claim the adoption credit for the qualifying adoption expenses he or she pays or incurs to adopt the child?**

A8. No. The adopting parent may not claim an adoption credit. A taxpayer may not claim an adoption credit for expenses incurred in adopting the child of the taxpayer's spouse (section 23).

I will now cover common-law marriages and civil unions as well as the recent history leading up to the recent Supreme Court decision. Civil unions not covered by state law will also be covered. Before October 6, 2014, thirty-one states banned gay marriage. After the Supreme Court refused to hear a same-sex marriage case, change came rapidly.

Of the thirty-six states that allowed same-sex marriage, twenty-five were allowed by judges, eight were decided by state legislatures, and three by popular vote. Those three were Maine, Maryland, and Washington. Now, all states must recognize same-sex couples.

Eight states and the District of Columbia recognize common-law marriages. They are Alabama, Colorado, Kansas, Rhode

Island, South Carolina, Iowa, Montana, Utah, Texas, and the District of Columbia. Just because a woman and man or same-sex couple live together is not enough. The couples must appear to be a married couple in all respects except having a marriage license. Alabama, District of Columbia, and Texas are not listed above in the thirty-six states.

A common-law marriage is a union of two people created by agreement followed by cohabitation that is legally recognized by a state. Common-law marriages have three basic features: (1) a present written agreement to be married, (2) cohabitation, and (3) public representations of marriage. You have to take legal action to dissolve a common-law marriage.

The Service further concluded in Revenue Ruling 58-66 that its position with respect to a common-law marriage also applies to a couple who entered into a common-law marriage in a state that recognized such relationships and who later moved to a state in which a ceremony is required to establish the marital relationship. The Service therefore held that a taxpayer who enters into a common-law marriage in a state that recognizes such marriages shall, for purposes of federal income tax filing status and personal exemptions, be considered married.

Moreover, the IRS further clarified:

> For Federal tax purposes, the term **marriage does not include registered domestic partnerships, civil unions, or other similar formal relationships recognized under state law that are not denominated as a marriage under that state's law**, and the terms *spouse, husband and wife, husband*, and *wife* do not include individuals who have entered into such a formal relationship.

However, Illinois had a Schedule CU civil union form for the state return. Illinois now allows gay marriage.

## Civil Unions

Civil unions grant couples most of the rights of state civil marriages but provide none of the federal benefits of marriage, such as Social Security benefits. These rights include spousal support, medical decision-making privileges, access to a partner's insurance, and hospital visitation rights.

# CHAPTER 11

# ACA (Affordable Care Act) Tax and Forms 8965 and 8962

-The IRS can only collect the tax (or 1 percent for 2014, and 2 percent for 2015) plus additional amounts for your spouse and dependents, for being uninsured if you have a refund coming. You can avoid paying the tax (owe a balance due) in 2015 and a 90 percent chance in 2014 via an exemption. IRS currently cannot collect the tax unless you have a refund coming. You don't want the tax to build up because IRS may change the law in the future. I have summarized and copied parts of over thirty IRS tax tips below.-

**ACA penalties**

> 2014-the higher of $95 per person up to three people, or $285, or 1 percent.
> 2015-the higher of $325 per person up to three people, or $975, or 2 percent.
> 2016-the higher of $695 per person up to three people, or $2,085, or 2.5 percent.
> 2017-the same as 2016 plus increase to cost of living.

-However, if you earn more than projected and your credit is reduced, IRS can levy or garnish your wages for the balance due. For example, if you are single and earn more than $46.680, IRS will take back the whole credit. The less you earn, the greater the subsidy or credit. If you earn $37,000 instead of $31,000, you will have to give back part of the subsidy 86 percent who sign up for ACA will receive financial assistance.-

In tax years 2014 and later, you should keep records of your own and your family members' health-care insurance coverage, including records of employer-provided coverage or premiums paid and type of coverage for private coverage so you can show that you and your family members had and maintained required minimum essential coverage. If you are claiming the premium tax credit, you will need information about any advance credit payments you received through the Health Insurance Marketplace, the premiums you paid, and the type of coverage you obtained at the Marketplace. If you or any of your family members are exempt from minimum essential coverage, you should retain certificates of exemption you may receive from the Marketplace or any other documentation to support an exemption claimed on your tax return.

There are two new lines pertaining to the Affordable Care Act on the 2014 form 1040.

- Line 61 or line 38 on form 1040-A
- Health Care: Individual Responsibility

Beginning in 2014, individuals must have health-care coverage, qualify for a health coverage exemption, or make a shared responsibility payment with their tax return. If you had qualifying health-care coverage (called minimum essential coverage) for every month of 2014 for yourself, your spouse (if filing jointly), and anyone you could or did claim as a dependent, check the box on this line and leave the entry space blank. Otherwise, do not check the box on this line and see the instructions for form 8965.

Minimum essential coverage-most health-care coverage that people have is minimum essential coverage. Minimum essential coverage includes health-care coverage provided by your employer, health insurance coverage you buy through the Health Insurance Marketplace.

Line 69 Form 1040

**Premium Tax Credit**

If you, your spouse, or a dependent enrolled in health insurance through the Marketplace, you may be able to claim the premium tax credit. See the instructions for line 69 and form 8962. The ACA tax credits go directly to the insurance companies.

You may be eligible to claim the premium tax credit if you, your spouse, or a dependent enrolled in health insurance through the Health Insurance Marketplace. The premium tax credit helps pay for this health insurance. Complete form 8962 to determine the amount of your premium tax credit, if any. Enter the amount, if any, from form 8962, line 26. To get the credit, you must file a return and a joint return if you are married.

**Financial Assistance Availability**

You could be eligible to get help from the government to pay for your monthly health insurance premium through a tax credit (sometimes called a premium subsidy). Your coverage could even be free or just a few dollars a month depending on your household income, family size, and the plan you are interested in. The best way to find out about your eligibility is to go to our enrollment platform and answer a few simple questions. You can get a quote in less than three minutes.

**Expanding Access**

A major objective of the new health-care law is expanding access to health care. One of the ways the law does that is by making prices more affordable with financial assistance through tax credits, sometimes referred to as premium subsidies. If you make less than a certain amount per year, the government will contribute toward your payment. A good rule of thumb is, the government doesn't think you should have to pay more than 9.5 percent of your household income on it, so if your monthly premium for health insurance exceeds that, the government may cover the rest.

## Qualifying for Financial Assistance

If your household income falls within the following ranges, you'll have a good chance of qualifying for financial assistance. The lower your income is within these ranges, the more financial assistance you may receive. If your income is less than these amounts, you may be eligible for Medicaid.

| | |
|---|---|
| $11,670 to $46,680 | for individuals |
| $15,730 to $62,920 | for a household of 2 |
| $19,790 to $79,160 | for a household of 3 |
| $23,850 to $95,400 | for a household of 4 |
| $27,910 to $111,640 | for a household of 5 |
| $31,970 to $127,880 | for a household of 6 |
| $36,030 to $144,120 | for a household of 7 |
| $40,090 to $160,360 | for a household of 8 |

## Affordable Care Act Tax Provisions for Individuals and Families

The Affordable Care Act, or health-care law, contains health insurance coverage and financial assistance options for individuals and families. The IRS administers the tax provisions included in the law. Use the "Affordable Care Act and Taxes-At a Glance" chart to better understand the health-care law and how it affects you. See "What's Trending" for news on trending topics and answers to questions we are hearing. Visit HealthCare.gov for more information on coverage options and financial assistance.

## What do I need to know about the health-care law?

The Individual Shared Responsibility Provision requires you and each member of your family to have qualifying health insurance (called minimum essential coverage), have an exemption, or make a shared responsibility payment when you file your federal income tax return. If you get your insurance coverage through the Health Insurance Marketplace, you may be eligible for a Premium Tax Credit. Filing electronically is the easiest way to file a complete and accurate tax return. Electronic Filing options include free Volunteer Assistance, IRS Free File, commercial software and professional assistance.

**Coverage**

- If you are like most people, you probably already have qualifying health-care coverage and don't need to do anything more than continue your insurance.
- If you don't have or maintain coverage, you will have to get an exemption or make a payment with your federal income tax return.
- If you don't have coverage, you may be able to get it through the Health Insurance Marketplace. For more information about the marketplace, visit HealthCare.gov.

**Credits**

- If you get coverage through the health insurance marketplace, you may be eligible for the Premium Tax Credit (PTC).
- The premium tax credit can be paid in advance to your insurance company or to you when you file your federal income tax return. Find out more about the option to get it now or get it later. For more information, see Publication 5120.
- If you receive advance credit payments, you need to report changes in circumstances that will affect the credit to the Marketplace as they happen. For more information, see Publication 5152.

**Payments**

- If you don't have coverage or qualify for an exemption, you may have to make an individual shared responsibility payment when you file your income tax return.
- For 2014, generally, the payment amount is the greater of 1 percent of your household income above your filing threshold or $95 per adult ($47.50 per child) limited to a family maximum of $285.
- You will report your coverage, exemption, or payment on your federal income tax return. For more information, see questions no. 25 and 26.

Here is information about the new forms and updates to the existing forms:

### Form 8965, Health Coverage Exemptions

- Complete this form to report a Marketplace-granted coverage exemption or claim an IRS-granted coverage exemption on the return.
- Use the worksheet in the Form 8965 Instructions to calculate the shared responsibility payment.

### Form 8962, Premium Tax Credit

- Complete this form to reconcile advance payments of the premium tax credit and to claim this credit on the tax return.

Additionally, if individuals purchased coverage through the Health Insurance Marketplace, they should receive form 1095-A, Health Insurance Marketplace Statement, which will help complete form 8962.

Form 1040

- Line 46-Enter advance payments of the premium tax credit that must be repaid.
- Line 61-Report health coverage and enter individual shared responsibility payment.
- Line 69-If eligible, claim net premium tax credit, which is the excess of allowed premium tax credit over advance credit payments.

Form 1040A

- Line 29-Enter advance payments of the premium tax credit that must be repaid.

- Line 38-Report health coverage and enter individual shared responsibility payment.
- Line 45-If eligible, claim net premium tax credit, which is the excess of allowed premium tax credit over advance credit payments.

Form 1040EZ

- Line 11-Report health coverage and enter individual shared responsibility payment.
- Form 1040EZ cannot be used to report advance payments or to claim the premium tax credit.

## Reporting Requirements

Most taxpayers will simply check a box on their tax return to indicate that each member of their family had qualifying health coverage for the whole year. No further action is required. Qualifying health insurance coverage includes coverage under most, but not all, types of health-care coverage plans. Use the chart on IRS.gov/aca to find out if your insurance counts as qualifying coverage.

For a limited group of taxpayers-those who qualify for, or received advance payments of the premium tax credit-the health-care law could affect the amount of tax refund or the amount of money they may owe when they file in 2015. Visit IRS.gov/aca to learn more about the premium tax credit.

## Exemptions

You may be eligible to claim an exemption from the requirement to have coverage. If you qualify for an exemption, you will need to complete the new IRS form 8965, Health Coverage Exemptions, when you file your tax return. You must apply for some exemptions through the Health-Care Insurance Marketplace. However, most of the exemptions are easily obtained from the IRS when you file your tax return. Some of the exemptions are available from either the Marketplace or the IRS.

If you receive an exemption through the Marketplace, you'll receive an exemption certificate number to include when you file your taxes. If you have applied for an exemption through the Marketplace and are still waiting for a response, you can put "pending" on your tax return where you would normally put your exemption certificate number.

## Individual Shared Responsibility Payment

If you do not have qualifying coverage or an exemption for each month of the year, you will need to make an individual shared responsibility payment when you file your return for choosing not to purchase coverage. Examples and information about figuring the payment are available on the IRS Calculating the Payment page.

## Premium Tax Credits

If you bought coverage through the Health Insurance Marketplace, you should receive form 1095-A, Health Insurance Marketplace Statement from your Marketplace by early February. Save this form because it has important information needed to complete your tax return.

If you are expecting to receive form 1095-A and you do not receive it by early February, contact the Marketplace where you purchased coverage. Do not contact the IRS because IRS telephone assistors will not have access to this information.

If you benefited from advance payments of the premium tax credit, you must file a federal income tax return. You will need to reconcile those advance payments with the amount of premium tax credit you're entitled to based on your actual income. As a result, some people may see a smaller or larger tax refund or tax liability than they were expecting. When you file your return, you will use IRS form 8962, Premium Tax Credit (PTC), to calculate your premium tax credit and reconcile the credit with any advance payments.

**Issue Number: HCTT-2015-29**
**Inside This Issue**

### Report Changes in Circumstances That Could Affect Your 2015 Premium Tax Credit

Advance payments of the premium tax credit provide financial assistance to help you pay for the insurance you buy through the Marketplace.

However, it is important to notify the Marketplace about changes in circumstances to allow the Marketplace to adjust your advance payment amount. This adjustment will decrease the likelihood of a significant difference between your advance credit payments and your actual premium tax credit. Changes in circumstances that you should report to the Marketplace include, but are not limited to the following:

- An increase or decrease in your income
- Marriage or divorce
- The birth or adoption of a child
- Starting a job with health insurance
- Gaining or losing your eligibility for other health-care coverage
- Changing your residence

For the full list of changes you should report, visit HealthCare. gov/how-do-i-report-life-changes-to-the-marketplace.

If you report changes in your income or family size to the Marketplace when they happen in 2015, the advance payments will more closely match the credit amount on your 2015 federal tax return. This will help you avoid getting a smaller refund than you expected or even owing money that you did not expect to owe.

### Employers: Don't Overlook the Small Business Health-Care Tax Credit

Do you own or run a small business or tax-exempt group with fewer than twenty-five full-time employees? If you do, you should know that the Small Business Health Care Tax Credit can help you provide insurance to your employees. You may be able to save on your taxes if you paid for at least half of their health insurance premiums. Here are several things that you should know about this important credit:

- **Maximum Credit**
  For tax years beginning in 2014 and after, the maximum credit is 50 percent of premiums paid by small business employers. The limit is 35 percent of premiums paid by tax-exempt small employers, such as charities.
- **Number of Employees**
  You may qualify if you had fewer than twenty-five employees who work full-time, or a combination of full-time and part-time. For example, two half-time employees equal one full-time employee for purposes of the credit.
- **Qualified Health Plan**
  You must have paid premiums for your employees enrolled in a qualified health plan offered through a Small Business Health Options Program, or SHOP, Marketplace. There are limited exceptions to this requirement.
- **Average Annual Wages**
  To qualify for the credit, the average annual wages of your full-time equivalent employees must have been less than $51,000 in 2014. The IRS will adjust this amount for inflation each year.
- **Half the Premiums**
  You must have paid a uniform percentage of the cost of premiums for all employees. The amount you paid must be equal to at least 50 percent of the premium cost of the insurance coverage for each employee.
- **Two-Year Limit**
  An eligible employer may claim the credit for any two-consecutive taxable years, beginning in or after 2014. This credit can be claimed for two consecutive years, even if you claimed the credit at any point from 2010 through 2013.

- **Tax Forms to Use**

    All employers use the form 8941, Credit for Small Employer Health Insurance Premiums, to calculate the credit. For-profit businesses claim the credit on form 3800, General Business Credit. Tax-exempt organizations claim it on form 990-T, Exempt Organization Business Income Tax Return.

# CHAPTER 12

# How to Handle a Tax Audit, 70 to 80 Percent or More Are Correspondence Audits

**Chapter 100 Percent My Comments**

The first thing I learned as an R/A was the terminology "facts and circumstances." You needed all the facts to make a proper determination. For example, a tax-free exchange involving two buildings may seem proper. However, a one day over the required time limit for the transaction can make the transaction taxable. A taxpayer can give you a lot of facts but omit the facts that make the event taxable.

**How you should handle an office audit?**

An office auditor is not as skilled as a revenue agent. However, do not underestimate an office auditor. I was a coach in a revenue agent training group. One of my trainees was previously an experienced office auditor. I was amazed to see his work papers, which included a ten-page gross receipts analysis and audit report completed in one day. There were very few office auditors in the Chicago district, and therefore, the majority of these audits were handled by correspondence audits.

## Scheduling your office audit or field audit

Wait at least ten days before you respond to your IRS notice and schedule the audit four to six weeks into the future. This will give you time to accumulate the necessary records. If you need additional time, call a few days before your appointment and ask for additional time. Going on vacation, moving, weddings, divorce, and many other excuses will work. An accountant will normally try to postpone the audit until after the tax season. However, revenue agents would not put up with the postponement. I never did.

I have read many accountants' opinions on how to handle an audit. Some say not to hand a paid bill file to an agent. Every auditor handles an audit differently. I had a joint committee case (taxpayer filed a carryback loss to get a refund). I had to verify the loss, which was caused by an increase to cost of goods sold. The company had three suppliers. I learned that the invoices were in three separate folders. I asked for the folders. I spent three hours listing the invoices in my work papers in their proper order. The cost per unit purchased more than doubled over a two-year period. I verified the loss in three hours. The corporation received their refund. Every case is different. Now, if you had personal items in that folder, I can see why your accountant would not give the whole file.

If an agent wants you to verify contributions or some other expense, such as employee insurance expense, telephone, etc., be prepared and organized. For example, create a lot of work papers for the agent. Make copies of the letters from charities along with a list of the charities, amount, check number, date, and the actual contribution checks available for inspection. The more work papers I had, the less I had to write and explain. If you have a clean return, make a copy of your work papers (if you have any) for the agent. Be able to verify only the items listed in the information document request (IDR). Don't volunteer any information or records.

Some accountants like to try to waste the auditor's time by starting late or have long lunches. There are no IRS quotas on time and tax dollars. Playing games is counterproductive. If a manager sees an agent turn in twenty no-changes in a row, the manager would become very concerned. Managers do not like old cases in process a long time. The agent may have been on a detail or training. That is when the agent may cut the audit short and close the case.

The most common audit issues and some examples of adjustments are as follows:

1. Income-most auditors and agents usually always ask, "Did you report all of your income?" They will also ask you if you had any nontaxable income-for example, a discharge of indebtedness or municipal bonds. There are certain professions that are scrutinized more closely because of the possibility of receiving cash, which may not be reported. A bank deposit analysis and standard of living analysis is often prepared.

   When your noncash contributions exceed $500, attach a list of items contributed.

   |  |  | Cost | FMV |
   |---|---|---|---|
   | Bag one | eight shirts | 245 | 15 |
   | | Seven blouses, five slacks | 375 | 30 |
   | | Six men's suits | 1,350 | 135 |
   | | Total | 1,970 | 180 |

   | | | | |
   |---|---|---|---|
   | Bag two | living room draperies and curtain's | 2,105 | 145 |

   Continue on listing bags.

   I would not take more than 10 percent because you are supposed to use thrift store values. If you have furniture pickup, make sure you get a receipt showing what was picked up. There are at least five charitable charities like Salvation Army, Goodwill, Am vets, etc., who will pick up your heavy furniture, refrigerator, etc. for free. Why should you have to lift the furniture?

The IRS processes so many tax returns that it knows what to expect from all kinds of people and situations. It knows, for example, the typical range of charitable contributions for people at every income level. If your reported generosity in a given year is far above the normal amount, that may be a red flag that prompts the IRS to take a closer look. If you're being honest on your return and you really *did* donate what you said, then an audit will be a simple matter of your providing records and the IRS closing the case. When there is a large contribution deduction, my advice would be to attach a list of contributions. Show payee, amount, and check number and any letters from charities regarding large donations. Also, many people tithe 10 percent, which is not out of line.

**Is income from a garage sale taxable?** No, because most items are sold far below cost. However, if you sold an antique or collectible for more than your cost, it would be taxable.

- **Casualty losses**-raise your DIF score substantially and, therefore, your chances of audit. Whenever you have a casualty or flood damage, make sure that you take pictures ASAP. Obtain a police report for a home break in or auto accident. Any reimbursement from the insurance company will reduce your casualty loss.

- **Exemptions for dependents**-sometimes both parents claim the same exemption or a child. Only the custodial parent is entitled to the exemption unless it is given up in writing. Sometimes the law changes. For example, a full-time college student who is twenty-four and earns more than the exemption amount would disqualify him from being taken as an exemption.

- **Earned income credit**-many taxpayers are not entitled to the earned income credit. For the EIC, a valid SSN is a number issued by the Social Security Administration unless "Not Valid for Employment" is printed on your Social Security card and the number was issued solely to allow the recipient of the SSN to apply for or receive a federally funded benefit. However, if "Invalid for Work Only with DHS Authorization" is printed on your Social

Security card, your SSN is valid for the EIC purposes only as long as the DHS authorization is still valid.
- **Employee business expenses**-car, travel, tools, and entertainment expenses will be examined. The agent will check the employer reimbursement policy. A taxpayer who receives a W-2 and 1099 from the same employer is considered an employee.

## Auto Expense Tip

If you take the actual expenses, you are required to have receipts. This includes gas, oil, repairs, licenses, depreciation, insurance, tolls, parking, car washes, etc.

The law states you must keep a log or diary. District policy allows us to reconstruct mileage if it is obvious that a taxpayer's trade or business requires him to use his/her auto.

## Reconstruction of mileage examples

Use repair bills or oil change bills. Oil change bills are easy to obtain, and oil change places and car dealerships will have records.

Mileage on repair bill 4/1/2013 10,300
Mileage on oil change 9/12003 24,600
Total mileage for five-month period 14,300
12 months mileage, 14,300 divided by 5 = 2,860 per month
2,860 × 12 months = 34,320 mileage for the year

*Based on length of ownership*

Car purchased on 1/1/12009
Car now has 94,000 miles
94,000 miles ÷ 47 months (length of time owned) =
    2,000 miles a month
12 × 2,000 = 24,000 miles per year

*Gas receipts*

2013 Buick Lesabre 20 miles per gallon at $4
Gas receipts $4,610 divided by $4 = 1,152.5
× 20mpg = $23,050 miles

## Travel and Entertainment

If you do not have any substantiation, do not make up a phony diary. Just because you use a different color ink and make a diary look old doesn't mean you will get away with it. That would be criminal fraud. Some people use the wrong year diary. Instead, use your desk calendar, which may have appointments on it to show business meetings. Record all entertainment for the last two months to show what your normal entertainment expenses are. Charge card statements will show the expenses. Try to tie them in with your desk calendar. Many charge cards list all your entertainment and business expenses at year end.

See the chapter on keeping records for a great worksheet to keep track of your travel and entertainment.

The revenue agent and the representative or taxpayer are respectful to each other. This means being rude or yelling at each other should not be tolerated by either party. If the auditor or agent is rude, ask to speak to their manager and ask him/her to reassign the case. Bring in only the documents requested on the information document request (IDR). Do not bring in extra records. If the auditor requests information regarding nonlisted items, just say you are not prepared to discuss these items. If you are aware that your tax return may have problems, hire a representative.

Do not bring copies of your tax returns. The auditor already has the original return. If copies of returns are requested, tell the auditor that you will have to look for them-which is not a lie. If you have to verify a carryover item from a prior return, bring in the schedule or page.

**Bring in only receipts and cancelled checks for requested items.**

Never bring in all your canceled checks, both personal and business, not related to the tax return. These checks may cause the auditor to look in other areas and especially income. However, you may have to show your bank deposits if you have a business.

**Do not give original documents to the IRS.**

Let him/her make copies. Some representatives do not agree with this. However, I always used copies of original documents and the taxpayer's work papers to show verification of the expense. The more work papers I had, the less time I needed to spend on the case. I was working on a case with an inventory issue. The corporation purchased inventory in various stages of completion and reallocated the items to benefit the corporation tax wise. The CPA accidently gave me a work paper showing the original allocation. I said that I didn't know much about their inventory method and asked for a copy. I couldn't believe the CPA firm handed me the adjustment. I went to my office and waited a day to tell them about the adjustment. Don't volunteer any information and say as little as possible.

When I was a new agent, an agent in the group was auditing a couple at their place of business. The couple talked in Polish and discussed the issues they did not want him to find. The agent wrote up all the issues and handed the couple the report. The agent then said good-bye in Polish. The agent spoke Polish.

**Books and records-poor records can account for 60 to 70 percent of IRS audit adjustments.**

*If* you lost your records because of a flood, casualty, moving, or your dog ate them, try to reconstruct them. I will cover record keeping in another chapter. You can show current year expenses for the two most current months to show the auditor what you normally spend on expenses. If reasonable, the auditor will have justification to allow most or all of your deduction.

130

If you deducted substantial items on your tax return that you cannot substantiate because they are bogus or never paid, you may need to hire an accountant to advise you and possibly represent you. If you can substantiate every item listed in the auditors IDR, I would suggest that you handle the audit. Be prepared to substantiate each item with a bill, letter, cancelled check, etc. If you don't have a clean return, you will probably be wise to hire an accountant to represent you.

I had a friend who wanted my advice on an audit when I worked at the IRS. I told him not to lie or bullshit the auditor. I told him to be honest and to try to explain his business, which was a cash business. Most IRS auditors are fair. My friend later called me to thank me and was very happy with the audit results.

If you failed to report substantial income that would be reflected in your bank statements, I would definitely hire an accountant.

If the accountant feels there is a chance for criminal fraud and indictment, he may suggest hiring a tax lawyer. What you tell a lawyer is covered by a client lawyer privilege. See the criminal fraud chapter. Most tax lawyers want a lot of money up front and are quite expensive. That is why I said to see an accountant with a lot or some fraud experience first.

**Be organized and on time.**

Don't give in to quickly regarding auto or entertainment or other expenses regarding disallowance due to lack of substantiation. Ask for more time to verify the expenses. If the auditor test-checked your entertainment and came up with a percentage to disallow, fight for a higher percentage. Come up with reasons or an argument to allow more expenses.

**Always fight for a larger deduction.**

Don't be afraid to go unagreed. If there is a negligence penalty being asserted, threaten to go unagreed. It is quite common for the Appeals Division to drop the negligence penalty.

**Ask for tax law regarding issues that support disallowance.**

The auditor cannot say it is not allowable without a code section or law.

**Wait till audit is over before presenting any issues in your favor.**

Otherwise, the auditor may try to find adjustments to offset your issues. Ask if the auditor is through with the audit before you mention the issues.

**Don't lie to an agent.**

When you are interviewed, answer "Yes," "No," "I don't remember," "This was not listed in the IDR, and I am not prepared to answer your question," "I will have to research that," or "Is this relevant to the current tax year?" You could open up a can of worms mentioning something about your lifestyle.

# CHAPTER 13

---

# Tax Tips to Help You
# Choose a Tax Preparer

-Every CPA knows accounting, and every lawyer knows about the law. Every enrolled agent has to take a very tough test on taxes unless he/she worked at IRS. Just because they have a title behind their name, don't assume they have a lot of experience dealing with the IRS. The average lawyer doesn't do tax returns for a living, and a few prepare estate tax returns. However, a lawyer who specializes in taxes is very knowledgeable in most cases. If an IRS agent has referred you for a criminal investigation, you want a lawyer who specializes in IRS fraud cases. I often dealt with these law firms when we went after organized crime. Some attorneys also specialize in corporate or legal matters, such as tax shelters, preparing corporate minutes, patent filing, and representing taxpayers and corporations on tax matters in court. You may want to keep your regular accountant for all other matters.

The average CPA rarely handles IRS audits and may be weak in meet-and-deal ability. These accountants work alone or in small firms doing mainly simple 1040 and schedule C returns. The midsize and larger CPA firms handle more challenging issues and deal more frequently on IRS audits. The large firms may handle international issues, which require the really bright CPAs and attorneys. If you had an IRS collection problem with a revenue officer, who would you hire to represent you? I would consider not using my regular tax man/woman. I would hire a CPA, attorney, or enrolled agent who specializes in collection cases and collection matters. That also goes for businesses who are behind in their payroll taxes. You may want to keep your regular accountant for all other matters. If you need to file an offer in compromise or installment agreement, you want to hire someone who has experience in that area. The IRS personnel you will deal with are very formidable. In most cases, you will not be a match for their experience and skills.

CPAs can be very helpful with your financial situations, such as setting up your business, preparing financial reports, and when needed, certifying them. They can set up your record-keeping, do bookkeeping, set up a retirement plan, and help with life changes. Try to choose one which has experience in your type of business. Check to see what the CPAs experience is in regards to filing returns.

Larger or more complex corporations hire the larger CPA firms to prepare their returns. One 1040 return had 150 pages, and numerous carryforward adjustments from the prior year and carry-over adjustments to the subsequent years were affected by my tax adjustments. I had the CPA firm compute the tax for me. The CPA firm had to run the complete program to come up with the proper tax. I then compared their results with mine.

The average CPA and small firm can do a good job preparing your tax returns. The best way to find a good accountant is to ask other professionals, friends, and relatives about their accountant. Are they happy with their accountant and fees charged? For example, a doctor can ask other doctors about their accountant's skills and fees. There are firms that specialize handling doctors' and dentists' tax work and investments. After you are set up with all the clever tax breaks, you can always switch to another accountant that charges only $110 an hour or less.

A doctor I know had a small corporation with three employees and a part-time bookkeeper. He was paying a CPA in a very small firm $225 an hour and asked for my advice. I told him to shop around, and he found a CPA who charged him $110 an hour. He is very happy with the new accountant.

There are some firms that specialize in pension plans, and you may want to set up a defined benefit plan, profit sharing, or pension plan. There are some firms that specialize in exempt organizations. When I was auditing a new car auto dealership, the outside accountant specialized in auto dealerships.-

### Directory of Federal Tax Return Preparers Now Online

The IRS this week launched a new online public directory of tax return preparers. This searchable directory on IRS.gov will help taxpayers find a tax professional with credentials and select qualifications to help them prepare their tax returns. Practitioners can check the PTIN system to ensure their directory listings are correct.

### What Is Circular 230? Regulations Governing Practice before the Internal Revenue Service

Circular 230 is a document containing the statute and regulations detailing a tax professional's duties and obligations while practicing before the IRS; authorizing specific sanctions for violations of the duties and obligations; and describing the procedures that apply to administrative proceedings for discipline.

### What Does "Practice before the IRS" Entail?

"Practice before the IRS" comprehends all matters connected with a presentation to the IRS, or any of its officers or employees, relating to a taxpayer's rights, privileges, or liabilities under laws or regulations administered by the IRS. Such presentations include, but are not limited to, preparing documents; filing documents; corresponding and communicating with the IRS; rendering oral and written advice with respect to any entity, transaction, plan, or arrangement, or other plan or arrangement having a potential for tax avoidance or evasion; and representing a client at conferences, hearings, and meetings.

## Understanding Tax Return Preparer Credentials and Qualifications

Any tax professional with an IRS preparer tax identification number (PTIN) is authorized to prepare federal tax returns. However, tax professionals have differing levels of skills, education, and expertise.

An important difference in the types of practitioners is "representation rights." Here is guidance on each credential and qualification:

**Unlimited representation rights**-enrolled agents, certified public accountants, and attorneys have unlimited representation rights before the IRS. Tax professionals with these credentials may represent their clients on any matters including audits, payment/collection issues, and appeals.

**Limited representation rights**-preparers without one of the above credentials (also known as "unenrolled preparers") have limited practice rights. They may only represent clients whose returns they prepared and signed, but only before revenue agents, customer service representatives, and similar IRS employees-including the Taxpayer Advocate Service. They cannot represent clients whose returns they did not prepare, and they cannot represent clients regarding appeals or collection issues even if they did prepare the return in question.

**Reminder**-everyone described above must have an IRS-issued preparer tax identification number (PTIN) in order to legally prepare your tax return for compensation. Make certain your preparer has one and enters it on your return filed with the IRS. (They are not required to enter it on the copy they provide you.)

Additional guidance

- FS-2015-6, Understanding Who You Pay to Prepare Your Tax Return
- General IRS Guidance on Choosing a Tax Professional

*Page Last Reviewed or Updated: 06-Feb-2015*

**Issue Number: IRS Special Edition Tax Tip 2015-01**
**Inside This Issue**

**New IRS Tool Can Help You Find a Tax Preparer**

The IRS has launched a new online public directory of tax return preparers. Now you can use this tool to help you select a tax return preparer with the credentials and qualifications that you prefer. Here are some of the key features of the new Directory of Federal Tax Return Preparers with Credentials and Select Qualifications:

**• What types of tax preparers does the directory include?**

The directory lists enrolled agents, attorneys, CPAs, and those who have completed the requirements for the voluntary IRS Annual Filing Season Program. All preparers listed have a valid preparer tax identification number, or PTIN, for 2015.

**• What types of tax preparers does it not include?**

The directory does not include tax return preparers with PTINs who are not attorneys, CPAs, enrolled agents, or Annual Filing Season Program participants. Volunteer tax return preparers who offer free services are also not included.

**• How does the new directory work?**

You may search the directory using the preferred credentials or qualifications you seek in a preparer. You may also search by a preparer's location, including those who practice abroad.

**• What does a search result show?**

Directory listings feature the name, city, state, and zip code of included tax preparers.

You can use the directory as a tool to get help from a tax professional on the Affordable Care Act tax provisions that affect returns filed this year.

Go to IRS.gov/chooseataxpro to find out more about the different types of tax preparers. Use the new partner page on IRS.gov for links to the websites of national nonprofit tax professional groups. These groups can also help you find the type of qualified tax help that you prefer.

**IRS YouTube Videos:**

- Choose a Tax Preparer Wisely

**Make a Complaint about a Tax Return Preparer**

If you have been financially impacted by a tax return preparer's misconduct or improper tax preparation practices, you can report it to the IRS on form 14157, Complaint: Tax Return Preparer.

Most paid tax return preparers are professional, honest, and trustworthy. The IRS is committed to investigating those who act improperly. For example, observe the following:

- Embezzling a client's refund
- Altering documents
- Creating or omitting income to generate a larger refund
- Creating false exemptions or dependents to generate a larger refund
- Creating false expenses, deductions, or credits to generate a larger refund
- Failing to sign tax returns they prepare and file (Note, if electronically filed, your copy may not contain a signature.)
- Failing to enter a preparer tax identification number (PTIN) on a tax return or improperly using a PTIN belonging to another individual
- Refusing to provide clients with a copy of their tax return
- Neglecting to return a client's records or holding the records until the preparation fee is paid

- Using an incorrect filing status to generate a larger refund
- Preparing client returns using off-the-shelf tax software or IRS Free File, both of which are intended for use by individuals
- Falsely claiming to be an attorney, certified public accountant, enrolled agent, enrolled retirement plan agent, or enrolled actuary

The completed form 14157, along with all supporting information, can be mailed or faxed, but please do not do both. Mailing and faxing the form may delay the processing of your complaint.

If mailing form 14157, send to the following address:

Internal Revenue Service
Attn: Return Preparer Office
401 W. Peachtree Street NW
Mail Stop 421-D
Atlanta, GA 30308

If faxing form 14157, send to 855-889-7957

Note, if you are completing a form 14157-A, Tax Return Preparer Fraud or Misconduct Affidavit, and a form 14157, send both completed forms to the following:

Internal Revenue Service
AM–Preparer Complaints Mail Stop 58
3333 Getwell Road
Memphis, TN 38118

The IRS provides guidance for choosing a tax professional.

*Page Last Reviewed or Updated: 26-Feb-2015*

# CHAPTER 14

## The Quickest Way to Get a Transcript or Copy of Your Tax Returns

-The most common need for a transcript or copy of a return is when you apply for a mortgage or loan. Don't worry, you won't need that copy of your return to apply for a mortgage. Normally, a tax return transcript will show the same line information that is on your return. Banks normally will accept a tax return transcript if no return is available. The following IRS website information will help you get your transcript or return. A copy of a return can take sixty days. You can get a copy of your transcript on line immediately. See the second IRS website below. If you have a problem online, you can always get a copy of your transcript immediately at your local IRS office. That service has been cut back at some IRS offices.

If you need a copy of your return, I would check with your preparer first to see if he/she has a copy. I always have relatives who ask for a copy of prior year returns even though I made an extra copy for them and myself. Their prior and current years are also on my computer. I cannot e-file unless I know the adjusted gross income or five-digit code.-

**Issue Number: IRS Tax Tip 2015-17**
**Inside This Issue**

## How to Get a Copy of Your Prior Year Tax Information

There are many reasons you may need a copy of your tax return information from a prior year. You may need it when applying for a student loan, home mortgage, or for a VISA. If you don't have your copy, the IRS can help. It's easy to get a free transcript from the IRS. Here are several ways for you to get what you need:

- **Tax Return Transcript**-a return transcript shows most line items from your tax return just as you filed it. It also includes forms and schedules you filed. However, it does not reflect changes made to the return after you filed it. In most cases, your tax return transcript will have all the information a lender or other agency needs.
- **Tax Account Transcript**-this transcript shows any adjustments made by you or the IRS after you filed your return. It shows basic data, like marital status, type of return, adjusted gross income, and taxable income.

## How to Get a Transcript

You can request transcripts online, by phone, or by mail. Both types of transcripts are free of charge. They are available for the most current tax year after the IRS has processed the return. You can also get them for the past three tax years.

    **Order online**-use the "Get Transcript" tool available on IRS. gov. You can use this tool to confirm your identity and to immediately view and print copies of your transcript in a single session for free. The tool is available for five types of tax records: tax account transcript, tax return transcript, record of account, wage and income, and verification of nonfiling.

**Order by phone**-call 800-908-9946. A recorded message will guide you through the process.

**Order by mail**-the easy way to order your transcript by mail is to use the "Get Transcript by Mail" online option on IRS.gov. On the other hand, you can complete and mail form 4506T-EZ to get your tax return transcript. Use form 4506-T to request your tax account transcript by mail.

## How to Get a Tax Return Copy

Actual copies of your tax returns are generally available for the current tax year and as far back as six years. *The fee per copy is $50.* Complete and mail form 4506 to request a copy of your tax return. Mail your request to the IRS office listed on the form for your area.

Delivery times for online and phone orders typically take five to ten days from the time the IRS receives the request. You should allow thirty days to receive a transcript ordered by mail and seventy-five days for copies of your tax return. You can print tax forms online at IRS.gov/forms. To get forms in the mail, go to IRS.gov/order forms to place an order.

## Copies of Prior Year Federal Tax Returns and/or a Transcript

Most taxpayers will ask for a copy of their prior year tax return. In many cases, however, a transcript will provide the information they need more quickly. Transcripts provide taxpayers with a computer-created record of their tax return-which includes most of the line items as filed with the IRS, including any accompanying forms and schedules. The transcript does not reflect any changes the taxpayer, his/her representative, or the IRS made after the return was filed. You can download and print your transcript immediately or request the transcript be mailed to your address on record using our new online application, Get Transcript.

Get a record of your past tax returns, also referred to as transcripts. IRS transcripts are often used to validate income and tax filing status for mortgage applications, students and small business loan applications, and during tax preparation.

CHAPTER 15

# Tips for Managing and Saving Your Records: The Majority of IRS Tax Adjustments Are Due to Poor Records

**Tips for Managing Your Tax Records**

IRS Tax Tip 2011-71, April 11, 2011

After you file your taxes, you will have many records that may help document items on your tax return. You will need these documents should the IRS select your return for examination. Here are five tips from the IRS about keeping good records.

1.  Normally, tax records should be kept for three years.
2.  Some documents-such as records relating to a home purchase or sale, stock transactions, IRA, and business or rental property-should be kept longer.
3.  In most cases, the IRS does not require you to keep records in any special manner. Generally speaking, however, you

should keep any and all documents that may have an impact on your federal tax return.

4.  Records you should keep include bills; credit card and other receipts; invoices; mileage logs; canceled, imaged, or substitute checks; proofs of payment; and any other records to support deductions or credits you claim on your return.

Whether you are an individual taxpayer or a business owner, you can avoid headaches at tax time by keeping good records during the year. (The following are not my comments.)

- Keeping well-organized records helps you answer questions if your return is selected for examination or prepare a response if you're billed for additional tax.
- In most cases, the IRS does not require you to keep records in any special manner, but you should keep any and all documents that may have an impact on your federal tax return.
- You should usually keep the records supporting items on your tax returns for at least three years.
- This includes records to support deductions or credits you claim on your returns-such as invoices, receipts, mileage logs, and cancelled checks, or any other proof of payment.
- So what records should you keep if you're a small business owner?
- You must keep all employment tax records for at least four years after the tax becomes due or is paid, whichever is later.
- Other important documents you should keep include records for gross receipts-such as cash register tapes, bank deposit slips, receipt books, invoices, credit card charge slips, and forms 1099 miscellaneous.
- Proof of purchases-for instance, cancelled checks, cash register tape receipts, credit card sales slips, and invoices.

- Expense documents-which include invoices, cancelled checks, cash register tapes, account statements, credit card sales slips, and petty cash slips for small payments.
- Documents to verify your assets like purchase and sales invoices, real estate closing statements, and cancelled checks.
- Also, you should normally keep records relating to your business assets until at least three years after you sell or otherwise dispose of the property.
- Examples of these assets include building, machinery, equipment, and office furniture or fixtures purchased and used in your business.
- You need these records to determine the annual depreciation in gain or loss when you sell the assets.

For more information about record keeping, check out IRS Publication 552, Recordkeeping for Individuals; Publication 583, Starting a Business and Keeping Records; and Publication 463, Travel, Entertainment, Gift, and Car Expenses.

Everyone in business must keep records. Keeping good records is very important to your business. Good records will help you do the following:

- Monitor the progress of your business
- Prepare your financial statements
- Identify source of receipts
- Keep track of deductible expenses
- Prepare your tax returns
- Support items reported on tax returns

**Monitor the progress of your business.**

You need good records to monitor the progress of your business. Records can show whether your business is improving, which items are selling, or what changes you need to make. Good records can increase the likelihood of business success.

**Prepare your financial statements.**

You need good records to prepare accurate financial statements. These include income (profit and loss) statements and balance sheets. These statements can help you in dealing with your bank or creditors and help you manage your business.

- An *income statement* shows the income and expenses of the business for a given period.
- A *balance sheet* shows the assets, liabilities, and your equity in the business on a given date.

**Identify source of receipts.**

You will receive money or property from many sources. Your records can identify the source of your receipts. You need this information to separate business from nonbusiness receipts and taxable from non-taxable income.

The following is an easy way to keep track of your records. Attach (staple) your hotel receipts and expenses over $75 to your weekly sheet or to a diary sheet.

THIS IS NOT AN OFFICIAL INTERNAL REVENUE FORM.
(I don't remember where I got this form. I
am pretty sure it was from the IRS.)

Table 5-3. **Weekly Traveling Expense and Entertainment Record**

**From:**
**To:**
**Name:**

| Expenses | Sunday | Monday | Tuesday | Wednesday | Thursday | Friday | Saturday | Total |
|---|---|---|---|---|---|---|---|---|
| **1. Travel Expenses:** Airlines | | | | | | | | |
| Excess baggage | | | | | | | | |
| Bus, train | | | | | | | | |
| Cab and limousine | | | | | | | | |

| Expenses | Sunday | Monday | Tuesday | Wednesday | Thursday | Friday | Saturday | Total |
|---|---|---|---|---|---|---|---|---|
| Tips | | | | | | | | |
| Porter | | | | | | | | |
| **2. Meals and Lodging:** Breakfast | | | | | | | | |
| Lunch | | | | | | | | |
| Dinner | | | | | | | | |
| Hotel and motel (Detail in schedule B) | | | | | | | | |
| **3. Entertainment** (Detail in schedule C) | | | | | | | | |
| **4.Other Expenses:** Postage | | | | | | | | |
| Telephone & telegraph | | | | | | | | |
| Stationery & printing | | | | | | | | |
| Stenographer | | | | | | | | |
| Sample room | | | | | | | | |
| Advertising | | | | | | | | |
| Assistant(s) | | | | | | | | |
| Trade shows | | | | | | | | |
| **5.Car Expenses:** (List all car expenses; the division between business and personal expenses may be made at the end of the year.) (Detail mileage in schedule A.) | | | | | | | | |
| Gas, oil, lube, wash | | | | | | | | |
| Repairs, parts | | | | | | | | |
| Tires, supplies | | | | | | | | |
| Parking fees, tolls | | | | | | | | |
| **6.Other** (Identify) | | | | | | | | |
| **Total** | | | | | | | | |
| **Note:** Attach receipted bills for (1) ALL lodging and (2) any other expenses of $75 or more. | | | | | | | | |
| **Schedule A-Car** | | | | | | | | |
| **Mileage:** End | | | | | | | | |
| Start | | | | | | | | |
| Total | | | | | | | | |

| Expenses | | Sunday | Monday | Tuesday | Wednesday | Thursday | Friday | Saturday | Total |
|---|---|---|---|---|---|---|---|---|---|
| **Business mileage** | | | | | | | | | |
| **Schedule B-Lodging** | | | | | | | | | |
| Hotel or motel | Name | | | | | | | | |
| | City | | | | | | | | |
| **Schedule C-Entertainment** | | | | | | | | | |
| Date | Item | Place | | Amount | Business Purpose | | Business Relationship | | |
| | | | | | | | | | |
| | | | | | | | | | |
| | | | | | | | | | |
| | | | | Weekly Reimbursements: | | | | | |
| | | | | | Travel and transportation expenses | | | | |
| | | | | | Other reimbursements | | | | |
| | | | | | Total | | | | |

## Keep Your Records Safe In Case Disaster Strikes

IRS Special Edition Tax Tip 2014-15, June 5, 2014

Some natural disasters are more common in the summer. But major events like hurricanes, tornadoes, and fires can strike anytime. It's a good idea to plan for what to do in case of a disaster. You can help make your recovery easier by keeping your tax and financial records safe. Here are some basic steps you can take now to prepare:

1. **Back Up Records Electronically**

    Many people receive bank statements by e-mail. This is a good way to secure your records. You can always get into your bank statements on line. You can also scan tax records and insurance policies onto an electronic format. You can use an external hard drive, CD, or DVD to store important records. Be sure you back up your files and keep them in a safe place. If a disaster strikes your home, it may also affect a wide area. If that happens, you may not be able to retrieve your records.

2. **Document Valuables**

   Take photos or videos of the contents of your home or business. These visual records can help you prove the value of your lost items. They may help with insurance claims or casualty loss deductions on your tax return. You should store them with a friend or relative who lives out of the area.

3. **Update Emergency Plans**

   Review your emergency plans every year. Update them when your situation changes. Make sure you have a way to get severe weather information. Have a plan for what to do if threatening weather approaches.

4. **Get Copies of Tax Returns or Transcripts**

   Visit IRS.gov to get form 4506, Request for Copy of Tax Return, to replace lost or destroyed tax returns. If you just need information from your return, you can order a free transcript online or by calling 800-908-9946. You can also file form 4506T-EZ, Short Form Request for Individual Tax Return Transcript or form 4506-T, Request for Transcript of Tax Return.

5. **Count on the IRS**

   If you fall victim to a disaster, know that the IRS stands ready to help. You can call the IRS disaster hotline at 866-562-5227 for special help with disaster-related tax issues.

Visit IRS.gov to get more about IRS disaster assistance. Click on the "Disaster Relief" link in the lower left of the home page. You can also get forms and publications anytime on IRS.gov. To get them in the mail, call 800-TAX-FORM (800-829-3676).

# CHAPTER 16

## How to Notify IRS if Your Identity and Tax Refund Are Stolen

-The way IRS handles W-2s is very inefficient in regard to identity theft. Congress mandates that IRS sends out refunds as soon as possible rather than wait three months or more and verify that the W-2s are correct. When you are the victim of identity theft, it can take six months to a year to receive your refund. Wake up, Congress!

### Tip

I use Life Lock for $10 a month. It lets me know when I apply for credit right away by phone and e-mail. I have to reply yes or no if that was me applying for credit. Life Lock also notifies me when there are large data breaches. I also have Chase bank notify me when a check is issued for more than $100 by phone and e-mail.-

## Taxpayer's Guide to Identity Theft

The IRS does not initiate contact with taxpayers by e-mail to request personal or financial information. This includes any type of electronic communication, such as text messages and social media channels.

## Taxpayer Guide to Identity Theft

We know identity theft is a frustrating process for victims. We take this issue very seriously and continue to expand on our robust screening process in order to stop fraudulent returns.

## What is identity theft?

Identity theft may occur when someone uses your personal information such as your name, Social Security number (SSN) or other identifying information, without your permission, to commit fraud or other crimes.

How do you know if your tax records have been affected? Usually, an identity thief uses a legitimate taxpayer's identity to fraudulently file a tax return and claim a refund. Generally, the identity thief will use a stolen SSN to file a forged tax return and attempt to get a fraudulent refund early in the filing season. You may be unaware that this has happened until you file your return later in the filing season and discover that two returns have been filed using the same SSN.

Be alert to possible identity theft if you receive an IRS notice or letter that states that, "More than one tax return for you was filed," "You have a balance due, refund offset," or have had collection actions taken against you for a year you did not file a tax return, or IRS records indicate you received wages from an employer unknown to you. What to do if your tax records were affected by identity theft?

If you receive a notice from IRS, respond immediately. If you believe someone may have used your SSN fraudulently, please notify IRS immediately by responding to the name and number printed on the notice or letter. You will need to fill out the IRS Identity Theft Affidavit, form 14039. For victims of identity theft who have previously been in contact with the IRS and have not achieved a resolution, please contact the IRS Identity Protection Specialized Unit, toll-free, at 1-800-908-4490.

How can you protect your tax records? If your tax records are not currently affected by identity theft, but you believe you may be at risk due to a lost/stolen purse or wallet, questionable credit card activity or credit report, etc., contact the IRS Identity Protection Specialized Unit at 1-800-908-4490.

How can you minimize the chance of becoming a victim? Don't carry your Social Security card or any document(s) with your SSN on it. Don't give a business your SSN just because they ask. Give it only when required. Protect your personal computers by using firewalls, antispam/antivirus software, update security patches, and change passwords for Internet accounts. Don't give personal information over the phone, through the mail, or on the Internet unless you have initiated the contact or you are sure you know who you are dealing with.

ID Theft Tool Kit
Are you a victim of identity theft?
If you receive a notice from the IRS, please call the number
on that notice. If not, contact the IRS at 800-908-4490
Fill out the IRS Identity Theft Affidavit, form 14039.
(Please write legibly and follow the directions on the back
of the form that relate to your specific circumstances.)

Credit Bureaus
Equifax
www.equifax.com
1-800-525-6285Experian
www.experian.com
1-888-397-3742
TransUnion
www.transunion.com
1-800-680-7289

Other Resources
Visit the Federal Trade Commission's Identity Theft
page or use the FTC's Complaint Assistant.
Visit the Internet Crime Complaint Center (IC3) to learn
more about their Internet crime prevention tips.

Report Suspicious Emails
Report suspicious online or emailed phishing scams to
phishing@irs.gov.
For phishing scams by phone, fax or mail, call
1-800-366-4484.

For More Information
• IRS.gov/identitytheft
• IRS.gov/phishing

# CHAPTER 17

---

# Five Tips if You Changed Your Name Due to Marriage, Divorce, or Death of a Spouse

## Five Tips if You Changed Your Name Due to Marriage or Divorce

IRS Tax Tip 2011-23, February 02, 2011

If you changed your name as a result of a recent marriage or divorce, you'll want to take the necessary steps to ensure the name on your tax return matches the name registered with the Social Security Administration. A mismatch between the name shown on your tax return and the SSA records can cause problems in the processing of your return and may even delay your refund.

Here are five tips from the IRS for recently married or divorced taxpayers who have a name change:

1. If you took your spouse's last name or if both spouses hyphenate their last names, you may run into complica-

tions if you don't notify the SSA. When newlyweds file a tax return using their new last names, IRS computers can't match the new name with their Social Security number.

2. If you were recently divorced and changed back to your previous last name, you'll also need to notify the SSA of this name change.

3. Informing the SSA of a name change is easy; you'll just need to file a form SS-5, Application for a Social Security Card, at your local SSA office and provide a recently issued document as proof of your legal name change.

4. Form SS-5 is available on SSA's website at http://www. socialsecurity.gov, by calling 800-772-1213, or at local offices. Your new card will have the same number as your previous card but will show your new name.

5. If you adopted your spouse's children after getting married, you'll want to make sure the children have an SSN. Taxpayers must provide an SSN for each dependent claimed on a tax return. For adopted children without SSNs, the parents can apply for an Adoption Taxpayer Identification Number-or ATIN-by filing form W-7A, Application for Taxpayer Identification Number for Pending U.S. Adoptions with the IRS. The ATIN is a temporary number used in place of an SSN on the tax return. Form W-7A is available on the IRS website at http://www. irs.gov, or by calling 800-TAX-FORM (800-829-3676).

## Summer Weddings Mean Tax Changes

IRS Summertime Tax Tip 2014-02, July 7, 2014

Taxes may not be high on your summer wedding plan checklist. But you should be aware of the tax issues that come along with marriage. Here are some basic tips that can help keep those issues to a minimum:

- **Change tax withholding**-a change in your marital status means you must give your employer a new form W-4,

Employee's Withholding Allowance Certificate. If you and your spouse both work, your combined incomes may move you into a higher tax bracket. Use the IRS withholding calculator tool at IRS.gov to help you complete a new form W-4. See Publication 505, Tax Withholding and Estimated Tax, for more information.

- **Changes in circumstances**-if you receive advance payment of the premium tax credit in 2014, it is important that you report changes in circumstances, such as changes in your income or family size, to your Health Insurance Marketplace. You should also notify the Marketplace when you move out of the area covered by your current Marketplace plan. Advance payments of the premium tax credit provide financial assistance to help you pay for the insurance you buy through the Health Insurance Marketplace. Reporting changes will help you get the proper type and amount of financial assistance so you can avoid getting too much or too little in advance.
- **Address change**-let the IRS know if your address changes. To do that, file form 8822, Change of Address, with the IRS. You should also notify the U.S. Postal Service. You can ask them online at USPS.com to forward your mail. You may also report the change at your local post office.
- **Change in filing status**-if you're married as of December 31, that's your marital status for the whole year for tax purposes. You and your spouse can choose to file your federal income tax return either jointly or married filing separately each year. You may want to figure the tax both ways to find out which status results in the lowest tax.

# CHAPTER 18

# Moving, Let IRS Know

IRS Tax Tip 2011-37, February 22, 2011

If you've changed your home or business address, make sure you update that information with the IRS to ensure you receive any refunds or correspondence. The IRS offers five tips for taxpayers that have moved or are about to move:

1. **Change your IRS address records**-you can change your address on file with the IRS in several ways:
   - Write the new address in the appropriate boxes on your tax return.
   - Use form 8822, Change of Address, to submit an address or name change any time during the year.
   - Give the IRS written notification of your new address by writing to the IRS center where you file your return. Include your full name, old and new addresses, Social Security number, or employer identification number and signature. If you filed a joint return, be sure to include the information for both taxpayers. If you filed a joint return and have since

established separate residences, each spouse should notify the IRS of their new address.

- Should an IRS employee contact you about your account, you may be able to verbally provide a change of address.

2. **Notify your employer**-be sure to also notify your employer of your new address so you get your W-2 forms on time.

3. **Notify the post office**-if you change your address after you've filed your return, don't forget to notify the post office at your old address so your mail can be forwarded.

4. **Estimated tax payments**-if you make estimated tax payments throughout the year, you should mail a completed form 8822, change of address, or write the IRS campus where you file your return. You may continue to use your old preprinted payment vouchers until the IRS sends you new ones with your new address. However, do not correct the address on the old voucher.

5. **Postal service**-the IRS does use the postal service's change of address files to update taxpayer addresses, but it's still a good idea to notify the IRS directly.

Visit http://www.irs.gov/ for more information about changing your address. At http://www.irs.gov/, you can also find the address of the IRS center where you file your tax return or download form 8822. The form is also available by calling 800-TAX-FORM (800-829-3676).

# CHAPTER 19

# Filing Amended Returns and Tracking Their Status

-Before you consider filing an amended corporate return, consideration should be given to a possible audit by the IRS. If you have a clean return, then you don't have much to worry about. Large CPA firms like to file amended returns on particular issues. Most revenue agents have audited amended returns sent to the audit groups. The group manager and revenue agent decide to survey or audit the amended return. Sometimes a claim for $150,000 can cause a corporation millions of dollars in tax deficiencies. You may be opening Pandora's Box. If the R/A finds adjustments during his/her audit and sees that the same expenses were taken on the prior and subsequent years, they will also be picked up and adjusted.

When an individual taxpayer files an amended return, it is not likely to be audited if you attach a good explanation. If possible, attach verification or substantiation-for example, you forgot to attach a W-2 to your return, which had substantial withholding. IRS never gave you credit for the withholding. Attach all your W-2s and other forms that withheld tax, compute the correct tax, and just say in the explanation that IRS did not use the correct withholding amount. I would also attach a copy of the original and amended returns. You only need the first two pages (1040) of the return and any pertinent tax schedule you are changing. If you can't compute the tax, IRS will do it for you. However, if you're withholding is increased by $450, your tax due would decrease by $450 or your refund would increase by $450.

I recently filed an amended return for a taxpayer who did not take an energy tax credit he was entitled too. To my surprise, the refund came within a month. However, if you file during the tax season, that may delay your refund.-

**Where's My Amended Return?**

The "Where's My Amended Return?" tool provides the status of form 1040X Amended Tax Return for the current year and up to three prior years.

You can generally expect your amended return to be processed up to sixteen weeks from the date we receive it. It can take up to three weeks from the date you mailed it to show up in our system.

*Please note,* you will not be able to access certain amended returns using this application.

IRS telephone assistors will not be able to provide additional information while your amended return moves through processing.

There is no need to call our toll-free number unless "Where's My Amended Return?" specifically indicates that you should call.

| When to check… | What you need… | How… |
|---|---|---|
| • Three (3) weeks after you mailed your amended return. | • Social Security number<br>• Date of birth<br>• Zip code | • Get your Amended Return Status. |

**Topic 308-Amended Returns**

If you discover an error after your return has been filed, you may need to amend your return. The IRS may correct errors in math on a return and may accept returns with certain forms or schedules left out. In these instances, do not amend your return! However, do file an amended return if there is a change in your filing status, income, deductions, or credits. Also, if the form 8938 (PDF), Statement of Specified Foreign Financial Assets, applies to you, the form must be filed with an annual return or an amended return. See When and How to File in the Form 8938 Instructions (PDF).

Use form 1040X (PDF), Amended U.S. Individual Income Tax Return, to correct a previously filed form 1040 (PDF), form 1040A (PDF), form 1040EZ (PDF), form 1040NR (PDF), or form 1040NR-EZ (PDF). If you owe additional tax for a tax year for which the due date for filing the return has not passed, file form 1040X and pay the tax by the due date for that year (without regard to any extension of time to file) to avoid penalties and interest. If the due date falls on a Saturday, Sunday, or legal holiday, filing the form and paying the tax will be timely if filed or paid the next business day. To determine where you should file form 1040X, see Where to File in the Form 1040X Instructions (PDF).

File a separate form 1040X for each year you are amending. Mail each form in a separate envelope. Be sure to enter the year of the return you are amending at the top of form 1040X. The form has three columns. Column A shows original or adjusted figures from the original return. Column C shows the corrected figures. The difference between columns A and C is shown in column B. There is an area on the back of the form to explain the specific changes being made and the reason for each change. Attach any forms or schedules that are affected by the change. Generally, to claim a refund, form 1040X must be filed within three years after the due date of your original return (or if you filed your return under an extension of time to file, three years after the date you filed your return) or within two years after the date you paid the tax, whichever is later. Returns filed before the due date (without regard to extensions) are considered filed on the due date.

- Attach copies of any forms or schedules that are being changed as a result of the amendment, including any form(s) W-2 received after the original return was filed.
- Tax forms can be obtained by calling 800-829-3676 or visiting www.irs.gov.
- An amended tax return cannot be filed electronically under the e-file system.
- Normal processing time for forms 1040X is up to twelve weeks from the IRS receipt date.

*Please note*, your state tax liability may be affected by a change made on your federal return. For information on how to correct your state tax return, contact your state tax agency.

You can check the status of your form 1040X (PDF), Amended U.S. Individual Income Tax Return, using the "Where's My Amended Return?" (WMAR) online tool or the toll-free telephone number 866-464-2050 three weeks after you file your amended return. Both tools are available in English and Spanish and track the status of amended returns for the current year and up to three prior years.

You must enter your taxpayer identification number, usually your Social Security number, date of birth, and ZIP code in either application to prove your identity. Once authenticated, you can view the status of your amended return across three processing stages-*received*, *adjusted*, and *completed*.

The Web tool includes an illustrated graphic that visually communicates where your amended return resides within the processing stages. As a reminder, amended returns take up to twelve weeks to process and up to three weeks to show up in our system. There's no need to call the IRS unless the application specifically tells you to do so.

**Amended Tax Return Frequently Asked Questions**

**How long will it take to process my amended tax return?**

A form 1040X-Amended Tax Return can take up to twelve weeks to process once the IRS receives it. Earlier in the chapter, IRS said sixteen weeks. I go with sixteen weeks.

**Will "Where's My Amended Return?" provide me with the status of amended tax returns for multiple tax years?**

"Where's My Amended Return?" provides the status of form 1040X, Amended Tax Returns, for the current year and up to three prior years.

**What is the best and fastest way for me to get information about my amended tax return?**

Use the "Where's My Amended Return?" tool or call our automated toll-free number 866-464-2050. You can start checking on the status of your amended return three weeks after the 1040X has been mailed.

**Will calling the IRS help me get my amended tax return processed any faster?**

Calling us will not speed up the processing time of your amended tax return. Our phone and walk-in representatives can only research the status of your amended return if it has been twelve weeks or more since you mailed your return or if "Where's My Amended Return?" directs you to contact us.

If we need more information to process your amended return, we will contact you by mail. Otherwise, "Where's My Amended Return?" has the most up to date information available about your 1040X. Use the "Where's My Amended Return?" tool, or call our automated toll-free number 866-464-2050. Both are available twenty-four hours a day, seven days a week.

**How will I know if the IRS received my amended tax return and it is being processed?**

Use "Where's My Amended Return?" to follow your amended tax return from receipt until processing is completed. While your amended tax return is being processed, you can follow it through three stages: received, adjusted, and completed.

**What is happening when "Where's My Amended Return?" shows the status is, received?**

This means your form 1040X, Amended Tax Return, has been received, and it is being processed. Generally, amended tax returns take up to twelve weeks to be processed.

**What is happening when "Where's My Amended Return?" shows the status is, adjusted?**

This means the processing of your form 1040X, Amended Tax Return, resulted in an adjustment to your account. An adjustment may result in a refund, balances due, or no tax change.

**What is happening when "Where's My Amended Return?" shows the status is, completed?**

This means your form 1040X, Amended Tax Return, has completed processing resulting in a refund, balance due, or no tax change. This time frame also means all correspondence related to the processing of your amended tax return has been mailed to you.

**How often does "Where's My Amended Return?" update?**

"Where's My Amended Return?" updates are made no more than once per day, usually at night. So there is no need to check more often.

**I've accessed "Where's My Amended Return?" and it's been longer than twelve weeks since the IRS received my amended tax return, and it hasn't been processed. Why?**

We work hard to process amended tax returns within twelve weeks, but some amended tax returns take longer to process than others for many reasons, including when an amended tax return

- includes errors,
- is incomplete,

- is unsigned,
- is returned to you requesting additional information or signature(s),
- needs further review,
- is impacted by identity theft or fraud,
- needs to be routed to a specialized area,
- has to be cleared by the bankruptcy area within the IRS,
- has to be reviewed and approved by a revenue officer because your tax account is assigned to a revenue officer,
- has been filed and is appealing or requesting reconsideration of an IRS decision, and
- includes form 8379, Injured Spouse Allocation.

If we need more information to process your tax return, we will contact you by mail. IRS representatives can only research the status of your return if it has been twelve weeks or more since you mailed your amended tax return, or if "Where's My Amended Return?" directs you to contact us.

**Which type of amended tax returns cannot be accessed using the "Where's My Amended Return?"**

Status updates for the following types of amended returns are not available through the "Where's My Amended Return?" tool:

- carrybacks (applications and claims)
- Form 843 claims
- Injured Spouse claims
- a form 1040 marked as an amended or corrected return
- an amended return with a foreign address
- business amended returns

**Will "Where's My Amended Return?" provide a refund status on an original current tax year filed return?**

No, it does not provide information about an original current year filed return. Use the IRS2Go mobile app or the "Where's My

Refund?" tool. You can start checking on the status of your tax return within twenty-four hours after we have received your e-filed return or four weeks after you mail a paper return. Both are available twenty-four hours a day, seven days a week. See Tax Topic 152 for more information.

CHAPTER 20

# The Office of Appeals and Taxpayer's Appeal Rights

## About the Office of Appeals

Every year, the Office of Appeals helps over a hundred thousand taxpayers resolve their tax disputes without going to Tax Court. Appeals is an independent organization within the IRS whose mission is to help taxpayers and the government resolve tax disagreements. Appeals *does not* take sides in a dispute; rather, we offer an objective point of view on each individual case.

**Table 21 Appeals Workload, by Type of Case, Fiscal Year Ending September 30, 2014**

| From IRS Data Book. | Cases Received | Cases Closed | Cases pending Sept. 30, 2014 |
|---|---|---|---|
| Total cases | 113,608 | 115,472 | 57,373 |
| | | | |
| Collection due process | 40,355 | 41,266 | 20,545 |
| Examination | 36,919 | 37,246 | 23,025 |

| | | | |
|---|---|---|---|
| Penalty appeals | 10,213 | 9,140 | 3,689 |
| Offers in compromise | 9,231 | 8,987 | 4,442 |
| Innocent spouse | 3,012 | 4,038 | 1,714 |
| Industry cases | 1,469 | 1,843 | 1,743 |
| Coordinated indutry cases | 129 | 165 | 370 |
| Other | 12,280 | 12,787 | 1,845 |

Appeals also offers mediation services through fast track settlement, early referral, and other mediation programs. These mediation programs are designed to help you resolve your dispute at the earliest possible stage in the audit or collection process. The chart may be misleading because it doesn't show beginning inventory of cases. I just wanted to show some of the types of cases handled by Appeals.

**Getting Started with Appeals**

If you've received an IRS letter stating that your case qualifies to be reviewed with Appeals, then the following topics will help you get started:

- Is Appeals the place for you?
- Preparing an Appeals request.
- What can you expect from Appeals?

**Is Appeals the Place for You?**

Appeals is the place for you if *all* of the following apply:

- You received a letter from the IRS explaining your right to appeal the IRS's decision.
- You do not agree with the IRS's decision.
- You are not signing an agreement form sent to you.

If all of the above are true, then you may be ready to request an Appeals conference or hearing.

Appeals is not for you if *any* of the following apply:

- The correspondence you received from the IRS was a bill, and there was no mention of Appeals.
- You did not provide all information to support your position to the examiner during the audit. I don't agree with that.
- Your only concern is that you cannot afford to pay the amount you owe.

If you cannot identify the requirements or if you do not meet the conditions for having your case, enter the Appeals process as explained above, contact the IRS employee you have been working with, or call Taxpayer Service for assistance at 1-800-829-1040.

## Alternative Dispute Resolution

Appeals offers mediation programs that can expedite the resolution of disputed issues.

## Preparing a Request for Appeals

If you disagree with the IRS's determination, you may request an Appeals conference by filing a written protest. You may represent yourself or have a professional represent you. The representative must be an attorney, a certified public accountant, or an enrolled agent authorized to practice before the IRS. If you want your representative to talk to us without you, you must provide us with a copy of a completed power of attorney form 2848, *Power of Attorney and Declaration of Representative.*

To decide if you should appeal your tax dispute, consider the following:

- If you believe the IRS made an incorrect decision based on a misinterpretation of the law, check the publications discussing your issue(s), or refer to Tax Topics.

- If you believe the IRS did not properly apply the law due to a misunderstanding of the facts, be prepared to clarify and support your position.
- If you believe the IRS is taking inappropriate collection action against you, or your offer in compromise was denied and you disagree with that decision, be prepared to clarify and support your position.
- If you believe the facts used by the IRS are incorrect, then you should have records or other evidence to support your position.

## Protests

A formal written protest is required in all cases to request an Appeals conference, unless you qualify for the **Small Case Request** procedure discussed below or another special appeal procedure.

Note, if you disagree with a lien, levy, seizure, or denial or termination of an installment agreement, see Publication 1660, *Collection Appeal Rights*, for information on filing your protest.

## How to file a Formal Written Protest

Include all of the following:

1. Your name, address, and a daytime telephone number
2. A statement that you want to appeal the IRS findings to the Office of Appeals
3. A copy of the letter you received that shows the proposed change(s)
4. The tax period(s) or year(s) involved
5. A list of each proposed item with which you disagree
6. The reason(s) you disagree with each item
7. The facts that support your position on each item
8. The law or authority, if any, that supports your position on each item
9. The penalties of perjury statement as follows: "Under the penalties of perjury, I declare that the facts stated in this

protest and any accompanying documents are true, correct, and complete to the best of my knowledge and belief."

10. Your signature under the penalties of perjury statement

If your representative prepares and signs the protest for you, he or she must substitute a declaration for the penalties of perjury statement that includes

1. That he or she submitted the protest and any accompanying documents, and
2. Whether he or she knows personally that the facts stated in the protest and any accompanying documents are true and correct.

You must send your formal written protest within the time limit specified in the letter that offers you the right to appeal the proposed changes. Generally, the time limit is thirty days from the date of the letter.

*Note*, forms to use to file your appeal are available online or by calling 1-800-829-3676 (1-800-TAX-FORM).

**Time Frame for Resolving Your Case**

The time it takes to resolve your case depends on the facts and circumstances. It could take anywhere from ninety days to a year. Please contact your appeals officer or settlement officer for a more specific time frame.

*Page Last Reviewed or Updated: 16-Jan-2014*

# CHAPTER 21

# Ten Things to Know about the Taxpayer Advocate Service

The quickest way to have a problem with the IRS is to ignore their correspondence. The taxpayer had a lien put on his home, and the IRS levied on 100 percent of the taxpayer's 1099 income. The taxpayer missed the deadline for filing for a Collection Due Process hearing. I filed form 12153 (Request for a Collection Due Process or Equivalent Hearing). The reason I gave was a denial of an installment agreement, IRS taxing 100 percent of 1099 income. The completed form is sent to the address on the levy. Next, I had to contact the taxpayer advocate in the Chicago area. After a few months, the taxpayer signed an installment agreement and the garnishment of 1099 income stopped.

**The Taxpayer Advocate Service Is Here to Help You**

IRS Tax Tip 2014-24, March 3, 2014

1. The Taxpayer Advocate Service (TAS) is an independent organization within the IRS and is your voice at the IRS.

2. We help taxpayers whose problems are causing financial difficulty. This includes businesses as well as individuals.

3. You may be eligible for our help if you've tried to resolve your tax problem through normal IRS channels and have gotten nowhere, or you believe an IRS procedure just isn't working as it should.

4. As a taxpayer, you have rights that the IRS must respect. We'll help you understand those rights and ensure that they're protected in any contacts with the IRS.

5. If you qualify for our help, you'll be assigned to one advocate who will be with you at every turn. And our service is always free.

6. We have at least one local taxpayer advocate office in every state, the District of Columbia and Puerto Rico. You can call your advocate, whose number is in your local directory, in Publication 1546, Taxpayer Advocate Service-Your Voice at the IRS, and on our website at www.irs.gov/advocate. You can also call us toll-free at 1-877-777-4778.

7. Our tax toolkit at http://www.taxpayeradvocate.irs.gov/ has basic tax information, details about tax credits (for individuals and businesses), and lots more.

8. TAS also handles large-scale or systemic problems that affect many taxpayers. If you know of one of these broader issues, please report it to us at www.irs.gov/sams.

9. You can get updates at
   - www.facebook.com/YourVoiceAtIRS
   - Twitter.com/YourVoiceatIRS
   - www.youtube.com/TASNTA

10. TAS is here to help you because when you're dealing with a tax problem, *the worst thing you can do is nothing at all!*

How to Get Tax Help

You can get help with unresolved tax issues. Order free publications and forms, ask tax questions, and get information from the IRS in several ways. By selecting the method that is best for you, you will have quick and easy access to tax help.

Taxpayer Advocate Service-the Taxpayer Advocate Service (TAS) is your voice at the IRS. Our job is to ensure that every taxpayer is treated fairly and that you know and understand your rights. We offer free help to guide you through the often confusing process of resolving tax problems that you haven't been able to solve on your own. Remember, the worst thing you can do is nothing at all. TAS can help if you can't resolve your problem with the IRS and

- Your problem is causing financial difficulties for you, your family, or your business,
- You face (or your business is facing) an immediate threat of adverse action and
- You have tried repeatedly to contact the IRS but no one has responded, or the IRS has not responded to you by the date promised.

Table 20. Taxpayer Advocate Service: Post filing Taxpayer Assistance Program, by Type of Issue, Fiscal Year 2014

Taxpayer Advocate Service Cases Received by Type of Issue

Stolen identity
Pre-refund wage verification hold
Earned income tax credit
Processing amended returns
Levies
Processing original returns
Injured spouse claims
Examination reconsideration
Open examination
IRS offset to IRS tax liability
Closed automated under reporter program
Unposted and rejected returns
Other refund inquiries/issues
Installment agreements

Applications for tax exempt status

All others

The Taxpayer Advocate Service generally receives cases from any of the following sources. IRS employee referrals are based on IRS guidance; direct taxpayer requests for assistance (by phone, in person, outreach activities, or through correspondence); practitioners; and congressional office referrals. Cases may be received in one fiscal year and closed in another.

CHAPTER 22

# Penalty Abatement and First-Time Abatement

**IRM 20.1.1.3.6.1 (08-05-2014)**
**First-Time Abate (FTA)**

**The First-Time Abatement (FTA) waiver can
be used to abate three penalties:**

> Failure to File-FTF 5 percent a month for five
>     months, or 25 percent
> Failure to Pay-FTP .5 percent a month up to 25 percent
> Failure to Deposit Penalty

You must be current on the three previous years, paying all taxes and filing timely, which includes extensions. You also must be current on any installment agreement you have. An estimated tax penalty will not disqualify you. The 1120-S Corporations and Partnerships can apply for the FTA.

## How to Request a Penalty Abatement

For penalties imposed by IRS-mailed notices, start the abatement process by mail. As soon as you receive a tax bill with penalties, write back and ask for an abatement. Use IRS form 843, *Claim for Refund and Request for Abatement.* (A copy is available on the IRS's website.) Attach to your letter a copy of the IRS notice showing the penalty.

Also attach copies of substantiating documents-such as a doctor's statement, fire department report, insurance claim, or death certificate of a family member. Without supporting papers, your abatement request may not get serious consideration.

## If Your Abatement Request Is Rejected

If the IRS officially rejects your abatement request, you will get a written notice. You can *appeal.* File a protest-a letter requesting an appeal.

IRS will abate over the phone but will not go over a certain amount. Written requests for abatement should be signed and sent to your current IRS Service Center. If you received an IRS notice, send to the address on the notice. If you can show reasonable cause, include that to increase your chances of penalty abatement.

RCS 1.15.28, Item 149
Reasonable Cause Assistant
Background

## Treasury Inspector General for Tax Administration

## Penalty Abatement Procedures Should Be Applied Consistently to IRS Taxpayers and Should Encourage Voluntary Compliance

### September 19, 2012
### Reference Number: 2012-40-113

The FTA waiver is not being granted to most taxpayers who qualify for the waiver. From the IRS's individual master file, we identified 278,840 taxpayers who had been assessed an FTF penalty and 1,367,750 taxpayers who had been assessed a FTP penalty for tax year 2010 and appeared to qualify for the FTA waiver because they

- Had compliant tax histories for the three prior years, and
- Had not been granted abatements for either penalty for tax year 2010.

**Impact on Taxpayers**

Internal Revenue Code imposes a Failure to File (FTF) penalty for failing to file a tax return and a Failure to Pay (FTP) penalty for failing to pay the tax shown on any tax return by the date prescribed. The IRS can abate both penalties under certain circumstances. If the IRS does not administer these and other penalties fairly and accurately, taxpayers' confidence in the tax system will be jeopardized.

The IRS developed a tool called the Reasonable Cause Assistant to help its employees accurately process penalty abatement request; however, the reasonable cause assistant does not always provide employees with the appropriate penalty abatement determination. In these cases, IRS employees are instructed to override the reasonable cause assistant and follow Internal Revenue Manual policies and procedures. The reasonable cause assistant made incorrect determinations for 56 of 63 (89 percent) cases sampled. None of the inaccurate determinations were corrected by employees. IRS employees accepted the Reasonable Cause Assistant determination even though it conflicted with the Internal Revenue Manual penalty abatement procedures.

**IRM 20.1.1.3.6.1 (08-05-2014)**
**First Time Abate (FTA)**

1. RCA Reasonable Cause Assistant provides an option for penalty relief for the FTF-IRC 6651(a)(1), IRC 6698(a)(1), and IRC 6699(a)(1); FTP (IRC 6651(a)(2) and IRC 6651(a)(3); and/or FTD (IRC 6656) penalties if the following are true for the taxpayer:

A.   Has not previously been required to file a return or has no prior penalties (except the estimated tax penalty, TC 17X) for the preceding three years on the same MFT (except MFT 30/31, and see the exception for MFTs 01 and 14 in paragraph [5][f]), and

B.   Has filed, or filed a valid extension for, all currently required returns and paid, or arranged to pay, any tax due.

Example,

Consider the taxpayer current if he or she has an open installment agreement and are current with his or her installment payments.

2.   Note, if the taxpayer is not currently in compliance per (1) (b) but all other FTA criteria are met, provide the taxpayer an opportunity to fully comply before considering reasonable cause.

3.   First-time abate (FTA) is an administrative waiver and does not carry any oral statement authority.

4.   A penalty assessed and subsequently reversed in full will generally be considered to show compliance for that tax period unless the exception in (5) (c) applies. RCA considers fully reversed penalties in its FTA analysis.

5.   The FTA administrative waiver can only apply to a single tax period for a given MFT. For example, if a request for penalty relief is being considered for two or more tax periods on the same MFT and the earliest tax period meets FTA criteria, penalty relief based on FTA only applies to the earliest tax period, not all tax periods being considered. Penalty relief for all subsequent tax periods will be based on the showing of reasonable cause (and as applicable, an absence of willful neglect).

Correction of Service Error-to be used when it is determined that the IRS made an error that resulted in an incorrect penalty or computed the penalty incorrectly or inappropriately.

## CIVIL PENALTIES ASSESSED AND ABATED FOR FISCAL YEAR 2014 (FROM IRS DATA BOOK)

| | CIVIL PENALTIES ASSESSED NUMBER | CIVIL PENALTIES ABATED NUMBER |
|---|---|---|
| TOTAL CIVIL PENALTIES | 31,235,124 | 3,256,068 |
| | | |
| ACCURACY | 554,467 | 115,787 |
| BAD CHECK | 431,859 | 11,666 |
| DELINQUENCY | 3,223,243 | 660,474 |
| ESTIMATED TAX | 8,902,388 | 188,813 |
| FAILURE TO PAY | 18,114,683 | 2,274,073 |
| FRAUD | 3,326 | 692 |
| OTHER | 5,158 | 5,063 |

## IRM 20.1.1.3.2 (11-25-2011)
## Reasonable Cause

1.  Reasonable cause is based on all the facts and circumstances in each situation and allows the IRS to provide relief from a penalty that would otherwise be assessed. Reasonable cause relief is generally granted when the taxpayer exercised ordinary business care and prudence in determining his or her tax obligations but nevertheless failed to comply with those obligations.

2.  Taxpayers have reasonable cause when their conduct justifies the nonassertion or abatement of a penalty. Each case must be judged individually based on the facts and circumstances at hand. Consider the following in conjunction with specific criteria identified in the remainder of this subsection:

    A.  What happened and when did it happen?

    B.  During the period of time the taxpayer was noncompliant, what facts and circumstances prevented the taxpayer from filing a return, paying a tax, and/or otherwise complying with the law?

    C.  How did the facts and circumstances result in the taxpayer not complying?

      D.   How did the taxpayer handle the remainder of his or her affairs during this time?

      E.   Once the facts and circumstances changed, what attempt did the taxpayer make to comply?

3.   Reasonable cause *does not exist* if, after the facts and circumstances that explain the taxpayer's non-compliant behavior cease to exist, the taxpayer fails to comply with the tax obligation within a reasonable period of time.

## IRM 20.1.1.3.2.2 (02-22-2008)
### Ordinary Business Care and Prudence

1.   Ordinary business care and prudence includes making provisions for business obligations to be met when reasonably foreseeable events occur. A taxpayer may establish reasonable cause by providing facts and circumstances showing that he or she exercised ordinary business care and prudence (taking that degree of care that a reasonably prudent person would exercise) but nevertheless were unable to comply with the law.

2.   In determining if the taxpayer exercised ordinary business care and prudence, review available information including the following:

      A.   **Taxpayer's reason**-the taxpayer's reason should address the penalty imposed. To show reasonable cause, the dates and explanations should clearly correspond with events on which the penalties are based. If the dates and explanations do not correspond to the events on which the penalties are based, request additional information from the taxpayer that may clarify the explanation. See IRM 20.1.1.3.2, *Reasonable Cause*.

      B.   **Compliance history**-check the preceding tax years (at least three) for payment patterns and the taxpayer's overall compliance history. The same penalty, previously assessed or abated, may indicate that the taxpayer is not exercising ordinary business care. If this is the taxpayer's first incident of noncompliant behavior, weigh this factor with other reasons the taxpayer gives for reasonable cause since a first-time failure to comply does not by itself establish reasonable cause.

C. **Length of time**-consider the length of time between the event cited as a reason for the noncompliance and subsequent compliance. See IRM 20.1.1.3.2, *Reasonable Cause*. Consider (1) when the act was required by law, (2) the period of time during that the taxpayer was unable to comply with the law due to circumstances beyond the taxpayer's control, and (3) when the taxpayer complied with the law.

D. **Circumstances beyond the taxpayer's control**-consider whether or not the taxpayer could have anticipated the event that caused the noncompliance. Reasonable cause is *generally* established when the taxpayer exercises ordinary business care and prudence but, due to circumstances beyond the taxpayer's control, the taxpayer was unable to timely meet the tax obligation.

### *IRM 20.1.1.3.2.2.1 (11-25-2011)*
Death, Serious Illness, or Unavoidable Absence

1. Death, serious illness, or unavoidable absence of the taxpayer, or a death or serious illness in the taxpayer's immediate family may establish reasonable cause for filing, paying, or depositing late for the following:

   A. **Individual**-if there was a death, serious illness, or unavoidable absence of the taxpayer or a death or serious illness in the taxpayer's immediate family (i.e., spouse, sibling, parents, grandparents, children).

   B. **Corporation, estate, trust, etc.**-if there was a death, serious illness, or other unavoidable absence of the taxpayer (person responsible), or a member of such taxpayer's immediate family, and that taxpayer *had sole authority to execute the return, make the deposit, or pay the tax.*

2.  If someone other than the taxpayer, or the person responsible, is authorized to meet the obligation-consider the reasons why that person did not meet the obligation when evaluating the request for relief. In the case of a business, if only one person was authorized, determine whether this was in keeping with ordinary business care and prudence.

3.  Information to consider when evaluating a request for penalty relief based on reasonable cause due to death, serious illness, or unavoidable absence includes, but is not limited to, the following:

    A.  The relationship of the taxpayer to the other parties involved

    B.  The date of death

    C.  The dates, duration, and severity of illness

    D.  The dates and reasons for absence

    E.  How the event prevented compliance

    F.  If other business obligations were impaired

    G.  If tax duties were attended to promptly when the illness passed, or within a reasonable period of time after a death or return from an unavoidable absence

## IRM 20.1.1.3.2.2.2 (08-05-2014)
## Fire, Casualty, Natural Disaster, or Other Disturbance-Reasonable Cause

1.  Determine if the taxpayer could not comply timely because the taxpayer was an "affected person" eligible for disaster relief as provided for in IRM 25.16.1.1.

2.  For taxpayers not considered an "affected person," reasonable cause relief from a penalty may be requested if there was a failure to timely comply with a requirement to file a return or pay a tax as the result of a fire, casualty, nat-

ural disaster, or other disturbance. However, one of these circumstances by itself does not necessarily provide penalty relief.

3. Penalty relief may be appropriate if the taxpayer exercised ordinary business care and prudence, but due to circumstances beyond the taxpayer's control, he or she was unable to comply with the law.

4. Factors to consider include the following:
   - Timing
   - Effect on the taxpayer's business
   - Steps taken to attempt to comply
   - If the taxpayer complied when it became possible

## IRM 20.1.1.3.2.2.3 (12-11-2009)
### Unable to Obtain Records

1. Explanations relating to the inability to obtain the necessary records may constitute reasonable cause in some instances but may not in others.

2. Consider the facts and circumstances relevant to each case and evaluate the request for penalty relief.

## IRM 20.1.1.3.3 (11-25-2011)
### Statutory Exceptions and Administrative Waivers

This subsection addresses statutory exceptions and administrative waivers. These two very separate categories are placed together because in many instances an administrative waiver is an extension of rules that were provided for by statute.

## IRM 20.1.1.3.3.3 (08-05-2014)
### Undue Hardship

1. An undue hardship may support the granting of an extension of time for paying a tax or deficiency (i.e., form 1127, *Application for Extension of Time for Payment of Tax Due to*

*Undue Hardship*). Treas. Reg. 1.6161–1(b), provides that an undue hardship must be more than an inconvenience to the taxpayer. The taxpayer must show that he or she would sustain a substantial financial loss if *required to pay* a tax or deficiency on the due date.

2.  Undue hardship *may* also support relief from the addition to tax for failure to pay tax if the explanation for the non-compliance supports such a determination. However, the mere inability to pay *does not* ordinarily provide the basis for granting penalty relief. Under Treas. Reg. 301.6651–1(c), the taxpayer must also show that he or she exercised ordinary business care and prudence in providing for the payment of the tax liability.

    A.  The taxpayer may claim that enough funds were on hand, but as a result of unanticipated events, the taxpayer was unable to pay the taxes.

    B.  Consider an individual taxpayer's inability to pay a factor when considering penalty relief if the taxpayer shows that, had the payment been made on the payment due date, undue hardship (as defined in Treas. Reg. 1.6161–1[b]) would have resulted.

    C.  In the case where a taxpayer files bankruptcy, consider inability to pay a factor if the insolvency occurred before the tax payment due date.

## IRM 20.1.1.3.3.4 (08-05-2014)
### Advice

1.  This section discusses the following three basic types of advice that may qualify for statutory, regulatory, or administrative penalty relief:

    A.  Written advice provided by IRS

    B.  Oral advice provided by IRS

    C.  Advice provided by a tax professional

2. Information to consider when evaluating a request for abatement or nonassertion of a penalty due to reliance on advice includes, but is not limited to, the following:

   A. Was the advice in response to a specific request, and was the advice received related to the facts contained in that request?

   B. Did the taxpayer reasonably rely on the advice?

# CHAPTER 23

# How to Receive a Reward for Turning In Tax Cheats

**Per IRS**

**Reporting Suspected Tax Fraud Activity**

Tax fraud or abusive return preparers can be reported to the IRS on form 3949-A, Information Referral. This form is available as a download from the IRS website at IRS.gov or by calling (800) 829-3676 to order by mail. The completed form, or a letter detailing the alleged fraudulent activity, should be sent to Internal Revenue Service, Fresno, CA, 93888.

The mailing should contain specific information about the individual or business, the activity, when the alleged violation took place, the amount of money involved, how the reporter became aware of it, and any other information that might be helpful to an investigation. The identity of the person filing the report is not required, but it could be helpful in an investigation, and it can be kept confidential.

Rewards based on the amount of additional tax, penalties, and interest owed can be made to individuals who report fraud. Form 211, Application for Award for Original Information, can be used to claim a reward.

The IRS's Whistleblower Office will make the final decision about whether an award will be paid and for how much. Award amounts are based on the value of the information you provided compared with the amount of additional tax, penalties, and interest collected by the IRS.

-A taxpayer has just as much power as an IRS agent to initiate a taxpayer's audit. If I as an agent wanted someone audited, I would have to provide specific and credible information to the Criminal Investigation Division. You would have to do the same. If the information is general and if they use it, the reward would be 1 or 2 percent. If your facts are right on the money, you can get up to ten percent. If you have credible information, I suggest you go to your local IRS office and ask to speak with a special agent.

Informants are kept confidential. You can also inform on someone anonymously, but there would be no reward. In fact, we have audited many people with less than credible information. Taxpayers inform on people for the following reasons:

- A moral or civic duty
- A dislike or hatred for the person
- Trying to straighten out a friend or relative

You would be surprised to know how often a relative, neighbor, spouse, lover, business associate, or friends turn people in for tax evasion. Many are not aware they may be entitled to an award.

Taxpayers get into trouble when they brag about cheating on their taxes or they tell a friend, mistress, spouse, or relative. A falling-out with any of these individuals may cause them to become an informant. When a taxpayer brags about his large stash of money, relatives start asking for loans. Then they ask for another loan.

A neighbor may inform on a policeman because he put in a large in ground pool or made substantial home improvements. The neighbor may be jealous and wonder how he could afford the improvement on a policeman's salary. However, the policeman or his wife may have received an inheritance. Without additional facts, IRS will not normally follow up with an investigation-

**See Instructions for Form 211, Application for Award for Original Information**

Form 211 (Rev. 3-2014)

**Whistleblower-Informant Award**

The IRS Whistleblower Office pays money to people who blow the whistle on persons who fail to pay the tax that they owe. If the IRS uses information provided by the whistleblower, it can award the whistleblower up to 30 percent of the additional tax, penalty, and other amounts it collects.

**Information about Submitting a Whistleblower Claim**

*Who can get an award?*

The IRS may pay awards to people who provide specific and credible information to the IRS if the information results in the collection of taxes, penalties, interest, or other amounts from the noncompliant taxpayer.

The IRS is looking for solid information, not an "educated guess" or unsupported speculation. We are also looking for a significant federal tax issue-this is not a program for resolving personal problems or disputes about a business relationship.

*What are the rules for getting an award?*

The law provides for two types of awards. If the taxes, penalties, interest, and other amounts in dispute exceed $2 million, and a few other qualifications are met, the IRS will pay 15 percent to 30 percent of the amount collected. If the case deals with an individual, his or her annual gross income must be more than $200,000. If the whistleblower disagrees with the outcome of the claim, he or she can appeal to the Tax Court. These rules are found at Internal Revenue Code IRC Section 7623(b) Whistleblower Rules.

The IRS also has an award program for other whistleblowers-generally those who do not meet the dollar thresholds of $2 million in dispute or cases involving individual taxpayers with gross income of less than $200,000. The awards through this program are less, with a maximum award of 15 percent up to $10 million. In addition, the awards are discretionary and the informant cannot dispute the outcome of the claim in Tax Court.

If you decide to submit information and seek an award for doing so, use IRS form 211. The same form is used for both award programs.

## Whistleblower Internal Revenue Manual
IRM 25.2.2, Whistleblower Awards

This chapter provides procedures and guidance for all Service personnel to follow when dealing with payment of whistleblowers' claims for award.

*Page Last Reviewed or Updated: 06-Mar-2015*

## How Do You Report Suspected Tax Fraud Activity?

| If You... | Then | And |
|---|---|---|
| Suspect or know of an individual or a business that is not complying with the tax laws on issues, such as,<br><br>• False exemptions or deductions<br>• Kickbacks<br>• False/altered document<br>• Failure to pay tax<br>• Unreported income<br>• Organized crime<br>• Failure to withhold | Use form 3949-A, Information Referral.<br><br>*Caution: Do not use form 3949-A to report the issues below:* | Print the form and mail to<br><br>• Internal Revenue Service<br>• Fresno, CA 93888<br><br>or order the form by mail or by calling the Tax Fraud Hotline recording at 1-800-829-0433. *Note*, we don't accept alleged tax law violation referrals over the phone. You may also send a letter to the address above instead of using form 3949-A. Please include as much information as possible, such as these important points:<br><br>1. Name and address of person or business you are reporting<br>2. The individual's Social Security number or the business' employer identification number<br>3. A brief description of the alleged violation(s), including how you became aware or obtained information about the violation(s)<br>4. The years involved<br>5. The estimated dollar amount of any unreported income<br>6. Your name, address, and telephone number<br><br>Although you are not required to identify yourself, it is helpful to do so. Your identity will be kept confidential. |

| Suspect someone *stole your identity and used your SSN* for employment purposes or could use your SSN to file a tax return | Use form 14039. Spanish version, Form 14039SP | Complete the form online, print it, and mail or fax to the appropriate office using the options listed on page 2 of the form. Include photocopies of at least one of the documents listed on the form to verify your identity. For additional information, refer to the Taxpayer Guide to Identity Theft |
|---|---|---|
| Suspect *fraudulent activity* or an abusive tax scheme by a *tax return preparer* or tax preparation company | Use form 14157A. Form 14157-A (see below) may also be required. | You may complete the form online, print it, and mail it to the IRS address on the form. |
| Suspect *a tax return preparer* filed a return or altered your return without your consent and you are seeking a change to your account | Use form 14157 and form 14157-A. | Send *both* forms (form 14157 and form 14157-A) to the address shown in the Instructions for Form 14157-A. |
| Suspect an *abusive tax promotion* or promoter | Use form 14242 | The form can be mailed or faxed to the IRS address or fax number on the form. |
| Suspect misconduct or wrongdoing by an *exempt organization* or employee plan | Use form 13909. | Mail it to the address provided on the form. |
| Have information and want to *claim a reward* | Use form 211. | Mail it to the address in the instructions for the form. |
| Suspect you received or are aware of *fraudulent IRS e-mails and websites* | Please let us know! See our Phishing Web page. | |

*Page Last Reviewed or Updated: 16-Apr-2015*

# CHAPTER 24

# How to Deal with the Collection Division

-The revenue officer (R/O) has the most difficult job at the IRS. He/ she may have forty-five cases in their inventory. A taxpayer can get violent over a $700 bill. Their job is to collect the tax, which was made more difficult after the Restructuring and Reform Act of 1998. The law was passed because of the many complaints of abuse by IRS employees. The IRS Inspection Service later said that many of the complaints were false. Included in this law was Section 1203, the "10 Deadly Sins," which mandated termination of IRS employees. It was no wonder that collections dropped by 80 percent after the law passed. The R/Os became afraid to do his/her job. One missed required signature on a seizure could result in termination. As long as I can remember, R/Os have had unmanageable inventories. You will not receive any sympathy from an R/O because you ignored all the IRS letters sent to you. However, most will treat you fairly. I have been told by R/Os that having a good manager was important to liking the job. However, not all R/Os liked their boss.

In one dealing with collection, a client was treated better than expected. His account was treated as a closed case and currently uncollectible. IRS also stopped taking 15 percent of his Social Security. However, form 433-F would have to be filed on a yearly basis in the future. If there is an increase in income, IRS may again initiate collection procedures.

Let us now look at how you got into trouble.-

- The first letter is a request for payment.
- The second notice is CP 501/502, which is a reminder.
- Next comes notice 503, "Urgent, Request Immediate Action Is Required."
- Five weeks after the first notice, you will receive IRS Notice CP 504-Final Request Letter, Balance Due. A levy will be issued by the automated collection system.
- If the taxpayer fails to pay, the case is referred to automated collection system (ACS). If ACS cannot resolve payment, the IRS will issue letter 1058-Final Notice, Notice of Intent to Levy and Your Right to a Hearing. Please respond immediately.

## LT 11 (Letter 1058) Frequently Asked Questions (FAQs)

### What is the notice telling me?

This notice is telling you that we intend to issue a levy against your bank accounts, wages, or other assets because you still have a balance due on one of your tax accounts. It is also telling you that we will begin searching for other assets on which to issue a levy and that we may also file a federal tax lien, if we have not already done so.

### What do I have to do?

Pay the amount due as shown on the notice. Mail us your payment in the envelope we sent you. Include the bottom part of the notice to make sure we correctly credit your account.

If you can't pay the whole amount now, call us at the number printed at the top of the notice to see if you qualify for an installment agreement.

## How much time do I have?

You should contact us or pay your balance due immediately. Enforcement action may be taken to collect that balance due thirty days after the date of this letter.

## What happens if I don't pay?

If you don't pay or make arrangements to pay, we have several options available that we may use to collect the money. One option is to issue a levy against your state tax refund, wages, other income sources, or bank accounts. Another option is for us to file a Notice of Federal Tax Lien. The lien gives us a legal claim to your property as security or payment for your tax debt.

## Who should I contact?

If you have any questions about the notice or wish to resolve your outstanding balance, call us at the number printed at the top of the notice. The person who answers the phone will assist you.

## What if I don't agree or have already taken corrective action?

If you do not agree with this notice, you have the right to an appeal. Call us immediately at the number printed at the top of the notice. We will do our best to help you. If you called us about this matter before, but we did not correct the problem, you may want to contact the Office of the Taxpayer Advocate.

If you have already paid or arranged for an installment agreement, you should still call us at the number printed at the top of the notice to make sure your account reflects this.

*Page Last Reviewed or Updated: 28-Jan-2015*

-Ignoring IRS notices will always cause you a lot of problems of your own making. Sometimes the taxpayers have never received the notices because the IRS did not have their current address. The R/O found out where you worked and issued a levy and garnished 100 percent of your wages or 1099 income. By law, your employer cannot fire you because of garnishment but probably could find some other reason to fire you. Many taxpayers quit working because their income goes to the IRS. Some taxpayers quit work and then work for cash.

This is the time to hire a representative who is a lawyer, CPA, or enrolled agent who has experience dealing with the Collection Division. Your best option is to apply for an installment agreement, offer in compromise, or try to have the R/O 53 (currently uncollectible) your account. The last two require filling out form 433-A. Form 433-A is not required on a streamlined installment agreement (under $50,000).

If the taxpayer has retired and living on Social Security, lost their job, or has an illness preventing work now or in the future, your best bet is to fill out form 433-A. If you can show that the taxpayer does not have enough income to pay for current living expenses, there is a good chance the R/O will be considering the account currently uncollectable. If 15 percent was being taken out of Social Security, that too may also be deemed uncollectible.

How to correctly fill out form 433-A and receive all the deductions you are entitled to is very important to help get the best settlement possible. I prepared a check sheet to make it easy for you in chapter one. I also have a form 433-A in chapter one and an explanation of all the expenses near the end of that chapter.

Since R/Os have too many cases in their inventory, they can't spend too much time on each case. So be prepared to give them all necessary information ASAP. The R/O will be quite happy to resolve your case as quickly as possible. Giving information piecemeal and dragging on your case will not help your case. That means having your monthly wages or income verified and using the expenses from the National Standards as your expenses. If you or a family member has an illness that needs to be considered, come in with a letter from your doctor and any pertinent medical bills. You will have to also verify any expenses exceeding the National Standards. See chapter 1.

What to do if you have unfiled returns-file them as soon as possible because you can't resolve your problems until the returns are filed. See chapter 6 on how to proceed.-

## IRM 5.1.10.3 (06-07-2013)
## Initial Contact

1. If the initial contact with a taxpayer is not in the field and such field contact is required (see the table below), the reason why it is not must be documented in the case history. The following table contains the criteria for valid initial contact:

| If | Then the following will be considered a valid initial contact |
|---|---|
| Taxpayer has no representative on record | Field visit to taxpayer's address of record, regardless of whether actual contact is made. |
| Taxpayer has a representative | A. Telephone contact with representative.<br>B. Field visit to representative's address of record, regardless of whether actual contact is made. |
| Telephone message left for representative to call back | A second telephone call within initial contact time frame. (See *IRM 5.1.10.3.1*.) |
| Representative's telephone number of record out of service, incorrect, or does not pick up | Field visit to taxpayer address of record, regardless of whether actual contact is made. |

2. The above actions will be considered reasonable efforts to contact the taxpayer directly.
3. If the taxpayer has a representative with a valid power of attorney, then contact will be made with the representative. When

contacting the POA, follow guidelines for effective initial contact (IRM 5.1.10.3.2). For BMF taxpayers, if initial contact is
not at the taxpayer's place of business, a field visit to the taxpayer's place of business must still take place, when practical.
Visiting the taxpayer's business, assessing the operation, and
viewing the assets will contribute to an informed collectability determination. For IMF taxpayers with a representative, the
initial contact does not have to be at the individual's residence;
however, a field call to view the property or other assets may be
necessary at a later date.

## IRM 5.1.10.5 (04-20-2010)
### Contact Letters

Some of the preprinted letters available to correspond with taxpayers
include the following:

| Letter | Purpose of Letter |
| --- | --- |
| Letter 725 (DO) | To set up an appointment with a taxpayer |
| Letter 729 | To address unfiled returns |
| Letter 728 | To provide the current balance due |
| Letter 3220 | To provide the balance due after receipt of payment |
| Letter 3221 | To respond to an inquiry regarding the balance due |
| Letter 3586 (CG) | To schedule an appointment to conduct a Trust Fund Recovery Penalty interview |
| Letter 4222 | To notify taxpayer of case resolution |
| Letter 4223 | To notify taxpayer of case closed as currently uncollectible |

1. Any letter required by statute (letters 1058, 2975, 3164, 3172,
   2439[P], etc.) relating to a joint return under IRC 6013 must
   be sent separately to each individual who filed the joint return.

**Contacting Taxpayers**

Some contacts cannot be made without the prior consent of the taxpayer or the permission of a court of competent jurisdiction. These include the following:

A.  Contacting the taxpayer at any unusual time or place, or at a time or place an employee knows, or should know, is inconvenient to the taxpayer.
B.  Contacting the taxpayer at work if there is reason to believe the employer does not allow such contact.
C.  Directly contacting a taxpayer if the Service knows the taxpayer has an authorized representative and knows or can readily ascertain the representative's name and address.

**Exception**

- The representative consents to the employee directly contacting the taxpayer.
- The representative does not respond in a reasonable time. (See IRM 5.1.23.5, *Bypassing Taxpayer's Representative*.)

Employees can generally assume that it is convenient to contact the taxpayer after 8:00 a.m. and before 9:00 p.m. local time Monday through Friday at the taxpayer's location, unless there is reason to know otherwise.

## 5.1.10.7.1 (06-07-2013)
### Rights During Interviews

Generally, if a taxpayer states during any interview that he or she wishes to consult with an authorized representative, the employee will suspend the interview to permit such consultation. If the interview is suspended, allow up to ten business days for the consultation with an authorized representative. The employee should inform the taxpayer of the consequences if the representative fails to contact the employee within ten business days.

Note-unenrolled return preparers are not permitted and should not be allowed to act as a taxpayer representative before collection.

## 5.1.10.7.3 (03-20-2009)
### Other Taxpayer Rights

- Taxpayers generally have the right to designate the application of voluntary payments to their accounts.
- Taxpayers are entitled to request and receive receipts for any payments made on their accounts, whether in current or delinquent status.
- Taxpayers have the right to submit an offer to compromise a tax liability. See IRM 5.8, Offer in Compromise.
- A taxpayer may have a right to an installment agreement. See IRM 5.14, Installment Agreements.
- Taxpayers may request that their case be transferred to another IRS office. Generally, such requests will be honored if the taxpayer has a valid reason.
- Taxpayers have the right to contact Taxpayer Advocate Service at any time during the collection process, especially if they are experiencing, or will experience, a financial hardship as a result of the Service's actions. Revenue officers must provide form 911 and explain a taxpayer's right to seek help from TAS.

# CHAPTER 25

# What if There Is a Federal Lien on My Home or Other Personal Property

**IRS Tax Tip**

If there is a federal tax lien on your home, you must satisfy the lien before you can sell or refinance your home. There are a number of options to satisfy the tax lien. Normally, if you have equity in your property, the tax lien is paid (in part or in whole depending on the equity) out of the sales proceeds at the time of closing. If the home is being sold for less than the lien amount, the taxpayer can request the IRS discharge the lien to allow for the completion of the sale. Taxpayers or lenders also can ask that a federal tax lien be made secondary to the lending institution's lien to allow for the refinancing or restructuring of a mortgage.

Also, the IRS is making other fundamental changes to liens in cases where taxpayers enter into a direct debit installment agreement (DDIA).

Additionally, the IRS will modify procedures that will make it easier for taxpayers to obtain lien withdrawals. Liens will now be withdrawn once full payment of taxes is made if the taxpayer requests it.

For more information, see IR-2011-20, IRS "Announces New Effort to Help Struggling Taxpayers Get a Fresh Start; Major Changes Made to Lien Process"; IR-2008-141, "IRS Speeds Lien Relief for Homeowners Trying to Refinance, Sell"; and "Understanding a Federal Tax Lien."

## IRS Announces New Effort to Help Struggling Taxpayers Get a Fresh Start; Major Changes Made to Lien Process.

IR-2011-20, February 24, 2011

Washington-In its latest effort to help struggling taxpayers, the Internal Revenue Service today announced a series of new steps to help people get a fresh start with their tax liabilities.

The goal is to help individuals and small businesses meet their tax obligations, without adding unnecessary burden to taxpayers. Specifically, the IRS is announcing new policies and programs to help taxpayers pay back taxes and avoid tax liens.

"Today's announcement centers on the IRS making important changes to its lien filing practices that will lessen the negative impact on taxpayers. The changes include:

- Significantly increasing the dollar threshold when liens are generally issued, resulting in fewer tax liens;
- Making it easier for taxpayers to obtain lien withdrawals after paying a tax bill;
- Withdrawing liens in most cases where a taxpayer enters into a direct debit installment agreement;

- Creating easier access to installment agreements for more struggling small businesses; and
- Expanding a streamlined offer in compromise program to cover more taxpayers.

## Tax Lien Thresholds

The IRS will significantly increase the dollar thresholds when liens are generally filed. The new dollar amount is in keeping with inflationary changes since the number was last revised. Currently, liens are automatically filed at certain dollar levels for people with past-due balances.

The IRS plans to review the results and impact of the lien threshold change in about a year.

A federal tax lien gives the IRS a legal claim to a taxpayer's property for the amount of an unpaid tax debt. Filing a Notice of Federal Tax Lien is necessary to establish priority rights against certain other creditors. Usually, the government is not the only creditor to whom the taxpayer owes money.

"Raising the lien threshold keeps pace with inflation and makes sense for the tax system," Shulman said. "These changes mean tens of thousands of people won't be burdened by liens, and this step will take place without significantly increasing the financial risk to the government."

## Tax Lien Withdrawals

The IRS will also modify procedures that will make it easier for taxpayers to obtain lien withdrawals.

Liens will now be withdrawn once full payment of taxes is made if the taxpayer requests it. The IRS has determined that this approach is in the best interest of the government.

## Direct Debit Installment Agreements and Liens

The IRS is making other fundamental changes to liens in cases where taxpayers enter into a direct debit installment agreement (DDIA). For taxpayers with unpaid assessments of $25,000 or less, the IRS will now allow lien withdrawals under several scenarios:

- Lien withdrawals for taxpayers entering into a direct debit installment agreement.
- The IRS will withdraw a lien if a taxpayer on a regular installment agreement converts to a direct debit installment agreement.
- The IRS will also withdraw liens on existing direct debit installment agreements upon taxpayer request.

Liens will be withdrawn after a probationary period demonstrating that direct debit payments will be honored.

CHAPTER 26

# What if a Levy on Your Wages Is Causing a Hardship or You Can't Pay Your Installment Agreement

Contact the IRS at the telephone number on the levy or correspondence immediately and explain your financial situation. Service is available from 8 a.m. to 8 p.m. local time, Monday through Friday. If the levy is creating an immediate economic hardship, the levy may be released. A levy release does not mean you are exempt from paying the balance. The IRS will work with you to establish payment plans or take other steps to help you pay off the balance. To help ensure quick action, please have the fax number available for the bank or employer office that is processing the levy.

## Levy

A levy is a legal seizure of your property to satisfy a tax debt. Levies are different from liens. A lien is a claim used as security for the tax debt, while a levy actually takes the property to satisfy the tax debt.

## IRS Data Book

| Enforcement activity | 2013 | 2014 |
|---|---|---|
| Number of notices of federal tax liens filed (7) | 602,005 | 535,580 |
| Number of notices of levy requested on third parties (8) | 1,855,095 | 1,995,987 |
| Number of seizures (9) | 547 | 432 |

[7] Represents the number of lien requests entered into the IRS Automated Lien System.

[8] Represents the number of levies requested upon third parties by the Automated Collection System and Field Collection programs.

[9] Represents the number of seizures conducted by the Field Collection program.

*Notes*, this table reflects delinquent collection activities for all return types.

*Source*-Small Business/Self-Employed, Collection, Performance Planning and Analysis, Reports, Collection Data Assurance.

If you do not pay your taxes (or make arrangements to settle your debt), the IRS may seize and sell any type of real or personal property that you own or have an interest in. For instance:

- We could seize and sell property that you hold (such as your car, boat, or house), or
- We could levy property that is yours but is held by someone else (such as your wages, retirement accounts, dividends, bank accounts, licenses, rental income, accounts receivables, the cash loan value of your life insurance, or commissions).

We usually levy only after these three requirements are met:

- We assessed the tax and sent you a Notice and Demand for Payment.
- You neglected or refused to pay the tax.
- We sent you a *Final Notice of Intent to Levy and Notice of Your Right to a Hearing* (levy notice) at least thirty days before the levy. We may give you this notice in person, leave it at your home or your usual place of business, or

send it to your last known address by certified or registered mail, return receipt requested. Please note, if we levy your state tax refund, you may receive a Notice of Levy on Your State Tax Refund, Notice of Your Right to Hearing after the levy.

Employers generally have at least one full pay period after receiving a form 668-W, Notice of Levy on Wages, Salary, and Other Income before they are required to send any funds from their employee's wages. Encourage your employees that have a levy placed on their wages to contact the IRS as soon as possible to discuss a release of levy and resolution of their tax liability.

You may ask an IRS manager to review your case, or you may request a Collection Due Process hearing with the Office of Appeals by filing a request for a Collection Due Process hearing with the IRS office listed on your notice. You must file your request within thirty days of the date on your notice. Some of the issues you may discuss include:

- You paid all you owed before we sent the levy notice.
- We assessed the tax and sent the levy notice when you were in bankruptcy and subject to the automatic stay during bankruptcy.
- We made a procedural error in an assessment.
- The time to collect the tax (called the statute of limitations) expired before we sent the levy notice.
- You did not have an opportunity to dispute the assessed liability.
- You wish to discuss the collection options.
- You wish to make a spousal defense.

At the conclusion of your hearing, the Office of Appeals will issue a determination. You will have thirty days after the determination date to bring a suit to contest the determination. Refer to Publication 1660 (PDF), for more information. If your property is levied or seized, contact the employee who took the action. You also may ask the manager to review your case. If the matter is still unresolved, the manager can explain your rights to appeal to the Office of Appeals.

## Levying Your Wages, Federal Payments, State Refunds, or Your Bank Account

If we levy your wages, salary, federal payments, or state refunds, the levy will end when

- The levy is released,
- You pay your tax debt, or
- The time expires for legally collecting the tax.

If we levy your bank account, your bank must hold funds you have on deposit, up to the amount you owe, for twenty-one days. This holding period allows time to resolve any issues about account ownership. After twenty-one days, the bank must send the money plus interest, if it applies, to the IRS. To discuss your case, call the IRS employee whose name is shown on the Notice of Levy.

*Page Last Reviewed or Updated: 31-Mar-2014*

# CHAPTER 27

# What if My Debt Is Forgiven?

**What If My Debt Is Forgiven?**

The tax impact of debt forgiveness or cancellation depends on your individual facts and circumstances. Generally, if you borrow money from a commercial lender and the lender later cancels or forgives the debt, you may have to include the cancelled amount in income for tax purposes. The lender is usually required to report the amount of the canceled debt to you and the IRS on a form 1099-C, Cancellation of Debt. There are several exceptions to the taxability of cancelled debt, such as insolvency or bankruptcy. For more information, see the Mortgage Forgiveness Debt Relief Act and Debt Cancellation.

**Top 10 Tax Tips about Home Mortgage Debt Cancellation**

IRS Tax Tip 2015-32, March 5, 2015

If your lender cancels part or all of your debt, you normally must pay tax on that amount. However, the law provides for an exclusion that may apply to homeowners who had their mortgage debt cancelled in 2014. In most cases where the exclusion applies, the amount of the cancelled debt is not taxable. Here are the top 10 tax tips about mortgage debt cancellation:

1. **Main home**-if the cancelled debt was a loan on your main home, you may be able to exclude the cancelled amount from your income. You must have used the loan to buy, build, or substantially improve your main home to qualify. Your main home must also secure the mortgage.

2. **Loan modification**-if your lender cancelled part of your mortgage through a loan modification or "workout," you may be able to exclude that amount from your income. You may also be able to exclude debt discharged as part of the Home Affordable Modification Program (HARP) or HAMP. The exclusion may also apply to the amount of debt cancelled in a foreclosure.

3. **Refinanced mortgage**-the exclusion may apply to amounts cancelled on a refinanced mortgage. This applies only if you used proceeds from the refinancing to buy, build, or substantially improve your main home. Amounts used for other purposes don't qualify.

4. **Other cancelled debt**-other types of cancelled debt such as second homes, rental, and business property, credit card debt, or car loans do not qualify for this special exclusion. On the other hand, there are other rules that may allow those types of cancelled debts to be nontaxable.

5. **Form 1099-C**-if your lender reduced or cancelled at least $600 of your debt, you should receive Form 1099-C, Cancellation of Debt, in January of the next year. This form shows the amount of cancelled debt and other information.

6. **Form 982**-if you qualify, report the excluded debt on form 982, Reduction of Tax Attributes Due to Discharge of Indebtedness. File the form with your federal income tax return.

7. **IRS Free File**-IRS e-file is fastest, safest, and easiest way to file. You can use IRS Free File to e-file your tax return for free. If you earned $60,000 or less, you can use brand

name tax software. The software does the math and completes the right forms for you. If you earned more than $60,000, use Free File Fillable Forms. This option uses electronic versions of IRS paper forms. It is best for people who are used to doing their own taxes. Free File is available only on IRS.gov/freefile.

8. **IRS.gov tool**-the IRS has several free tools on its website to help you file your tax return. Use the Interactive Tax Assistant tool on IRS.gov to find out if your cancelled mortgage debt is taxable.

9. **Exclusion extended**-the law that authorized this exclusion had expired at the end of 2013. The Tax Increase Prevention Act extended it to apply for one year, through December 31, 2014.

10. **More information**-for more on this topic, see Publication 4681, Canceled Debts, Foreclosures, Repossessions, and Abandonments.

## Insolvency Worksheet

Date debt was canceled (mm/dd/yy)

_____|_____

Part I. Total liabilities immediately before the cancelation (do not include the same liability in more than one category)

_____

**Amount owed**
**immediately before**
**The cancellation**

1.  Credit card debt $_____
2.  Mortgage(s) on real property (including first and second mortgages and home equity loans (mortgage(s) can be on personal residence, any additional residence, or property held for investment or used in a trade or business $_____

3. Car and other vehicle loans $_____
4. Medical bills owed $_____
5. Student loans $_____
6. Accrued or past-due mortgage interest $_____
7. Accrued or past-due real estate taxes $_____
8. Accrued or past-due utilities (water, gas, electric) $_____
9. Accrued or past-due childcare costs $_____
10. Federal or state income taxes remaining due for prior tax years) $_____
11. Judgements $_____
12. Business debts (including those owed as a sole proprietor or partner) $_____
13. Margin debt on stocks and other debt or purchase or secured by investment assets other than real property $_____
14. Other liabilities (debt) not included above $_____
15. Total liabilities immediately before the cancelation. Add lines 1 through 14. $_____

## Part II. Fair Market Value (FMV) of Assets Owned Immediately before the Cancellation (Do Not Include the FMV of the Same Asset in More Than One Category)

**FMV immediately**

16. Cash and bank account balances $_____
17. Real property, including the value of land (can be main home, any additional home, or property held for investment or used in a trade or business) $_____
18. Cars and other vehicles $_____
19. Computers $_____
20. Household goods and furnishings (for example, appliances, electronics, furniture, etc.) $_____
21. Tools $_____
22. Jewelry $_____
23. Clothing $_____

24. Books $_____
25. Stocks and bonds $_____
26. Investments in coins, stamps, paintings, or other collectibles $_____
27. Firearms, sports, photographic, and other hobby equipment $_____
28. Interest in retirement accounts (IRA accounts, 401 (k) accounts, and other retirement accounts) $_____
29. Interest in a pension plan $_____
30. Interest in Education accounts $_____
31. Cash value of life insurance $_____
32. Security deposits with landlords, utilities, and others $_____
33. Interest in partnerships $_____
34. Value of investment in a business $_____
35. Other investments (for example, annuity contracts, guaranteed investment contracts, mutual funds, commodity accounts, interests in hedge funds, and options) $_____
36. Other assets not included above $_____
37. FMV of total assets immediately before the cancellation. Add lines 16 through 36. $_____

## Part III Insolvency

38. **Amount of insolvency**-subtract line 37 from line 15. If zero or less, you are not insolvent. $_____

# CHAPTER 28

# The Mortgage Forgiveness Debt Relief Act

*If you owe a debt to someone else, and they cancel or forgive that debt, the canceled amount may be taxable.*

**Home Foreclosure and Debt Cancellation**

Update January 5, 2015-the Mortgage Forgiveness Debt Relief Act of 2007 generally allows taxpayers to exclude income from the discharge of debt on their principal residence. Debt reduced through mortgage restructuring, as well as mortgage debt forgiven in connection with a foreclosure, qualifies for this relief.

This provision applies to debt forgiven in calendar years 2007 through 2014. Up to $2 million of forgiven debt is eligible for this exclusion ($1 million if married filing separately). The exclusion doesn't apply if the discharge is due to services performed for the lender or any other reason not directly related to a decline in the home's value or the taxpayer's financial condition.

The amount excluded reduces the taxpayer's cost basis in the home. Further information, including detailed examples, can also be found in Publication 4681, Canceled Debts, Foreclosures, Repossessions, and Abandonments.

The questions and answers below are based on the law prior to the passage of the Mortgage Forgiveness Debt Relief Act of 2007.

## What is Cancellation of Debt?

If you borrow money from a commercial lender and the lender later cancels or forgives the debt, you may have to include the cancelled amount in income for tax purposes, depending on the circumstances. When you borrowed the money, you were not required to include the loan proceeds in income because you had an obligation to repay the lender. When that obligation is subsequently forgiven, the amount you received as loan proceeds is reportable as income because you no longer have an obligation to repay the lender. The lender is usually required to report the amount of the canceled debt to you and the IRS on a form 1099-C, Cancellation of Debt.

Here's a very simplified example. You borrow $10,000 and default on the loan after paying back $2,000. If the lender is unable to collect the remaining debt from you, there is a cancellation of debt of $8,000, which generally is taxable income to you.

## Is Cancellation of Debt income always taxable?

Not always. There are some exceptions. The most common situations when cancellation of debt income is not taxable involve:

- Bankruptcy-debts discharged through bankruptcy are not considered taxable income;
- Insolvency-if you are insolvent when the debt is cancelled, some or all of the cancelled debt may not be taxable to you. You are insolvent when your total debts are more than the fair market value of your total assets. Insolvency can be fairly complex to determine and the assistance of a tax professional is recommended if you believe you qualify for this exception;

- Certain farm debts-if you incurred the debt directly in operation of a farm, more than half your income from the prior three years was from farming, and the loan was owed to a person or agency regularly engaged in lending, your cancelled debt is generally not considered taxable income. The rules applicable to farmers are complex, and the assistance of a tax professional is recommended if you believe you qualify for this exception;
- Nonrecourse loans-a nonrecourse loan is a loan for which the lenders only remedy in case of default is to repossess the property being financed or used as collateral. That is, the lender cannot pursue you personally in case of default. Forgiveness of a nonrecourse loan resulting from a foreclosure does not result in cancellation of debt income. However, it may result in other tax consequences, as discussed in question 3 below.

**I lost my home through foreclosure. Are there tax consequences?**

There are two possible consequences you must consider:

- Taxable cancellation of debt income. (Note, as stated above, cancellation of debt income is not taxable in the case of non-recourse loans.)
- A reportable gain from the disposition of the home (because foreclosures are treated like sales for tax purposes). (Note, often some or all of the gain from the sale of a personal residence qualifies for exclusion from income.)

Use the following steps to compute the income to be reported from a foreclosure:

**Step 1-Figuring Cancellation of Debt Income** *(Note, for nonrecourse loans, skip this section. You have no income from cancellation of debt.)*

1. Enter the total amount of the debt immediately prior to the foreclosure: _____

2.  Enter the fair market value of the property from form 1099-C, box 7: _____

3.  Subtract line 2 from line 1. If less than zero, enter zero: _____

The amount on line 3 will generally equal the amount shown in box 2 of form 1099-C. This amount is taxable unless you meet one of the exceptions in question 2. Enter it on line 21, Other Income, of your form 1040.

**Step 2-Figuring Gain from Foreclosure**

4.  Enter the fair market value of the property foreclosed. For nonrecourse loans, enter the amount of the debt immediately prior to the foreclosure: _____

5.  Enter your adjusted basis in the property, usually your purchase price plus the cost of any major improvements: _____

6.  Subtract line 5 from line 4. If less than zero, enter zero:

The amount on line 6 is your gain from the foreclosure of your home. If you have owned and used the home as your principal residence for periods totaling at least two years during the five-year period ending on the date of the foreclosure, you may exclude up to $250,000 (up to $500,000 for married couples filing a joint return) from income. If you do not qualify for this exclusion, or your gain exceeds $250,000 ($500,000 for married couples filing a joint return), report the taxable amount on schedule D, Capital Gains and Losses.

**I lost money on the foreclosure of my home.**
**Can I claim a loss on my tax return?**

No. Losses from the sale or foreclosure of personal property are not deductible.

**I don't agree with the information on the form 1099-C. What should I do?**

Contact the lender. The lender should issue a corrected form if the information is determined to be incorrect. Retain all records related to the purchase of your home and all related debt.

**I received a notice from the IRS on this. What should I do?**

The IRS urges borrowers with questions to call the phone number shown on the notice. The IRS also urges borrowers who wind up owing additional tax and are unable to pay it in full to use the installment agreement form, normally included with the notice, to request a payment agreement with the agency.

The Mortgage Debt Relief Act of 2007 generally allows taxpayers to exclude income from the discharge of debt on their principal residence. Debt reduced through mortgage restructuring, as well as mortgage debt forgiven in connection with a foreclosure, qualifies for the relief.

More information, including detailed examples can be found in Publication 4681, Canceled Debts, Foreclosures, Repossessions, and Abandonments. Also see IRS news release IR-2008-17.

The following are the most commonly asked questions and answers about the Mortgage Forgiveness Debt Relief Act and debt cancellation:

**What does exclusion of income mean?**

Normally, debt that is forgiven or cancelled by a lender must be included as income on your tax return and is taxable. But the Mortgage Forgiveness Debt Relief Act allows you to exclude certain cancelled debt on your principal residence from income. Debt reduced through mortgage restructuring, as well as mortgage debt forgiven in connection with a foreclosure, qualifies for the relief.

## Does the Mortgage Forgiveness Debt Relief Act apply to all forgiven or cancelled debts?

No. The act applies only to forgiven or cancelled debt used to buy, build, or substantially improve your principal residence or to refinance debt incurred for those purposes. In addition, the debt must be secured by the home. This is known as qualified principal residence indebtedness. The maximum amount you can treat as qualified principal residence indebtedness is $2 million or $1 million if married filing separately.

## Does the Mortgage Forgiveness Debt Relief Act apply to debt incurred to refinance a home?

Debt used to refinance your home qualifies for this exclusion, but only to the extent that the principal balance of the old mortgage, immediately before the refinancing, would have qualified. For more information, including an example, see Publication 4681.

## How long is this special relief in effect?

It applies to qualified principal residence indebtedness forgiven in calendar years 2007 through 2013. *It was extended for 2014. It may be extended again by Congress?*

## If the forgiven debt is excluded from income, do I have to report it on my tax return?

Yes. The amount of debt forgiven must be reported on form 982, and this form must be attached to your tax return.

## Do I have to complete the entire form 982?

No. Form 982, Reduction of Tax Attributes Due to Discharge of Indebtedness (and Section 1082 Adjustment), is used for other purposes in addition to reporting the exclusion of forgiveness of qualified principal residence indebtedness. If you are using the form only to report the exclusion of forgiveness of qualified principal residence indebtedness as the result of foreclosure on your principal residence, you only need to complete lines 1e and 2. If you kept ownership of your home and modification of the terms of your mortgage resulted in the forgiveness of qualified principal residence indebtedness, complete lines 1e, 2, and 10b. Attach the form 982 to your tax return.

**Where can I get this form?**

If you use a computer to fill out your return, check your tax preparation software. You can also download the form at IRS.gov, or call 1-800-829-3676. If you call to order, please allow seven to ten days for delivery.

**How do I know or find out how much debt was forgiven?**

Your lender should send a form 1099-C, Cancellation of Debt. The amount of debt forgiven or cancelled will be shown in box 2. If this debt is all qualified principal residence indebtedness, the amount shown in box 2 will generally be the amount that you enter on lines 2 and 10b, if applicable, on form 982.

**Can I exclude debt forgiven on my second home,
credit card or car loans?**

Not under this provision. Only cancelled debt used to buy, build, or improve your principal residence or refinance debt incurred for those purposes qualifies for this exclusion. See Publication 4681 for further details.

**If part of the forgiven debt doesn't qualify for exclusion from
income under this provision, is it possible that it may
qualify for exclusion under a different provision?**

Yes. The forgiven debt may qualify under the insolvency exclusion. Normally, you are not required to include forgiven debts in income to the extent that you are insolvent. You are insolvent when your total liabilities exceed your total assets. The forgiven debt may also qualify for exclusion if the debt was discharged in a title 11 bankruptcy proceeding or if the debt is qualified farm indebtedness or qualified real property business indebtedness. If you believe you qualify for any of these exceptions, see the instructions for form 982. Publication 4681 discusses each of these exceptions and includes examples.

**If I sold my home at a loss and the remaining loan is forgiven, does this constitute a cancellation of debt?**

Yes. To the extent that a loan from a lender is not fully satisfied and a lender cancels the unsatisfied debt, you have cancellation of indebtedness income. If the amount forgiven or canceled is $600 or more, the lender must generally issue form 1099-C, Cancellation of Debt, showing the amount of debt canceled. However, you may be able to exclude part or all of this income if the debt was qualified principal residence indebtedness; you were insolvent immediately before the discharge, or if the debt was canceled in a title eleven bankruptcy case. See form 982 for details.

**If the remaining balance owed on my mortgage loan that I was personally liable for was canceled after my foreclosure, may I still exclude the canceled debt from income under the qualified principal residence exclusion, even though I no longer own my residence?**

Yes, as long as the canceled debt was qualified principal residence indebtedness. See Publication 4681, Canceled Debts, Foreclosures, Repossessions, and Abandonments.

**Will I receive notification of cancellation of debt from my lender?**

Yes. Lenders are generally required to send form 1099-C, Cancellation of Debt, when they cancel any debt of $600 or more. The amount cancelled or deemed discharged will be in box 2 of the form.

**What if I disagree with the amount in box 2?**

Contact your lender to work out any discrepancies and have the lender issue a corrected form 1099-C.

**How do I report the forgiveness of debt that is excluded from gross income?**

1.   Check the appropriate box under line 1 on form 982, Reduction of Tax Attributes Due to Discharge of Indebtedness (and Section 1082 Basis Adjustment), to indicate the type of discharge of indebtedness and enter the amount of the discharged debt excluded from gross income on line 2. Any remaining canceled debt must be included as income on your tax return.
2.   File form 982 with your tax return.

**Can I exclude cancellation of credit card debt?**

In some cases, yes. Nonbusiness credit card debt cancellation can be excluded from income if the cancellation occurred in a title 11 bankruptcy case, or to the extent you were insolvent just before the cancellation. See the examples in Publication 4681. See page 8.

**How do I know if I was insolvent?**

You are insolvent when your total debts exceed the total fair market value of all of your assets. Assets include everything you own, e.g., your car, house, condominium, furniture, life insurance policies, stocks, other investments, or your pension and other retirement accounts.

**How should I report the information and items needed to prove insolvency?**

Use form 982, Reduction of Tax Attributes Due to Discharge of Indebtedness (and Section 1082 Basis Adjustment) to exclude canceled debt from income to the extent you were insolvent immediately before the cancellation. You were insolvent to the extent that your liabilities exceeded the fair market value of your assets immediately before the cancellation.

To claim this exclusion, you must attach form 982 to your federal income tax return. Check box 1b on form 982, and on line 2, include the smaller of the amount of the debt canceled or the amount by which you were insolvent immediately prior to the cancellation. You must also reduce your tax attributes in Part II of form 982.

**My car was repossessed, and I received a 1099-C; can I exclude this amount on my tax return?**

Only if the cancellation happened in a title 11 bankruptcy case or to the extent you were insolvent just before the cancellation. See Publication 4681 for examples.

**Are there any publications I can read for more information?**

Yes.

1.  Publication 4681, Canceled Debts, Foreclosures, Repossessions, and Abandonments (for Individuals) addresses in a single document the tax consequences of cancellation of debt issues.
2.  See the IRS news release IR-2008-17 with additional questions and answers on IRS.gov.

# CHAPTER 29

# How to Contact the IRS

**IRS Tax Tip**
**Telephone Assistance**
**Live Telephone Assistance**

When calling, you may ask questions to help you prepare your tax return or ask about a notice you have received. Please be aware that when you conclude your discussion, our system will not permit you to return to your original responder.

Telephone wait times may be lengthy, and the topics we handle over the phone are limited. Keep in mind, many questions can be resolved online without waiting. On IRS.gov, you can:

- Set up a payment plan
- Get a transcript of your tax return.
- Make a payment
- Check on your refund.
- Find answers to most of your tax questions

**Telephone Assistance for Individuals-Toll-Free, 800-829-1040**
Hours of operation: Monday–Friday, 7 a.m.–7 p.m. your local time (Alaska and Hawaii follow Pacific Time)

**Telephone Assistance for Businesses-Toll-Free, 800-829-4933**
Hours of operation: Monday–Friday, 7 a.m.–7 p.m. your local time
(Alaska and Hawaii follow Pacific Time)

**Telephone Assistance for Exempt Organizations, Retirement
Plan Administrators, and Government Entities-Toll-Free,
877-829-5500**
Hours of operation: Monday–Friday, 8 a.m. to 5 p.m. local time

**Telephone Assistance for People with Hearing Impairments-Toll-
Free, 800-829-4059 (TDD)**
Hours of operation: Monday–Friday, 7 a.m.–7 p.m. your local time
(Alaska and Hawaii follow Pacific Time)
For further information, see Tax Topic 102.

**Telephone Assistance for Individuals Who Believe They May
Be a Victim of Identity Theft, No Tax Administration Impact-
Did Not Receive a Notice from the IRS-Toll-Free, 800-908-4490**
(Automated and Live Assistance)
Hours of operation: Monday–Friday, 7 a.m.–7 p.m. your local time
(Alaska and Hawaii follow Pacific Time). For additional informa-
tion, refer to our Identity Theft and Your Tax Records page.

**Telephone Assistance for People Who Live Outside the United States**
Hours of availability vary by location. Please see our International
Services page.

**Face-to-Face Assistance**-in certain areas, IRS also has local offices
you may visit to receive assistance.


Where's My Refund? will give you personalized
refund information.

The IRS issues more than nine out of ten refunds in less than twenty-one days. Where's My Refund? has the most up to date information available about your refund. The tool is updated once a day, so
you don't need to check more often. IRS representatives can research
the status of your refund only if you've already checked Where's My

Refund? and it's been twenty-one days or more since you filed electronically, more than six weeks since you mailed your paper return, or if Where's My Refund? directs you to contact us.

Suspicious e-Mails, Phishing, and Identity Theft

The IRS does not send out unsolicited e-mails asking for personal information. An electronic mailbox has been established for you to report suspicious e-mails claiming to have been sent by the IRS.

CHAPTER 30

# How and Where to Get Free Tax Help

**Issue Number: IRS Tax Tip 2015-55**
**Inside This Issue**

## IRS.gov: Simply the Best Place to Get Tax Help

If you need help with your taxes, the IRS website is the place for you. There is no waiting for service, and it has tax tools that are easy to use. You can even prepare and e-file your tax return for free with IRS Free File. If you have questions, you can get the answers you need, when you need them. Here are the best reasons to make IRS.gov your one stop shop for tax help from the IRS.

- **Use IRS Free File**-you can prepare and e-file your federal taxes for free with IRS Free File. Free File does the hard work for you. If you made $60,000 or less, you can use free name brand tax software. If you earned more, you can use Free File fillable forms, the electronic version of IRS paper forms. Either way, you have a free e-file option, and the only way you can access it is on IRS.gov.

- **Options to file electronically**-you should file electronically whether you qualify for free volunteer help, do your own taxes or hire a tax preparer. IRS e-file is the easiest, safest, and most popular way to file a complete and accurate tax return. The fastest way to get your refund is to combine e-file with direct deposit. You get your refund in less than twenty-one days in most cases. If you owe taxes, e-file has easy pay options so you can file early and pay by the April 15 deadline.

- **Help at any time**-IRS.gov is always available. Use the "Filing" link from our home page for all your federal tax needs. Just about everything you need is right at the tip of your fingers. The Interactive Tax Assistant tool and the IRS Tax Map can answer with many of your tax law questions. You can view, download, or print tax products right away. Many IRS tools and products are also available in Spanish.

- **Find a tax preparer**-the IRS has a new tool that you can use to help you find a tax return preparer. The Directory of Tax Return Preparers tool will search and sort for a list of tax preparers in your area with the credentials and qualifications that you prefer.

- **Check your refund**-you can track your refund using the "Where's My Refund?" tool. It's quick, easy, and secure. You can check the status of your return within twenty-four hours after the IRS has received your e-filed return. If you file a paper return, you can check your refund status four weeks after you mail it. Once IRS approves your refund, the tool will give you a date to expect it. The IRS updates refund status for the tool no more than once a day.

- **Pay tax online**-electronic payments are a convenient and safe way to pay taxes. The IRS Direct Pay tool is the fastest and easiest way to pay the tax you owe. Visit IRS.gov/directpay to use this free and secure way to pay directly from your checking or savings account. If you can't pay all your taxes in full, use the Online Payment Agreement to apply for an installment agreement.

The official IRS website is IRS.gov. Don't be fooled by other sites that claim to be the IRS but end in *.com*, *.net*, or *.org*. Some scams use phony websites to get your personal and financial information. Thieves also use the information to commit identity theft or steal your money. Visit only IRS.gov for tax help from the IRS.

**Updated IRS Smartphone App Now Available**

IRS Special Edition Tax Tip 2014-05, February 5, 2014

Are you on the go but need the latest tax information at your fingertips? There's an app for that. The latest version of the innovative IRS2Go app is now available.

Here's what you can do with the redesigned IRS Smartphone app IRS2Go, version 4.0, available in English and Spanish:

- **Check the status of your refund**-the new version of IRS2Go includes an easy-to-use refund status tracker so taxpayers can follow their tax return step-by-step throughout the IRS process. Just enter your Social Security number, filing status, and your expected refund amount. You can start checking on the status of your refund twenty-four hours after the IRS confirms receipt of an e-filed return or four weeks after you mail a paper return. Since the IRS posts refund updates on a daily basis, there's no need to check the status more than once each day.

- **Find free tax preparation**-you may qualify for free tax help through the IRS Volunteer Income Tax Assistance or Tax Counseling for the Elderly programs. A new tool on IRS2Go will help you find a VITA location. Just enter your zip code and select a mileage range to see a listing of VITA/TCE sites near you. Select one of the sites, and your smartphone will show an address and map to help you navigate.

- **Get tax records**-you can request a copy of your tax bill or a transcript of your tax return using IRS2Go. The post office will deliver to your address on record.
- **Stay connected**-you can interact with the IRS by following the IRS on Twitter @IRSnews, @IRStaxpros, and @ IRSenEspanol. You can also watch IRS videos on YouTube, register for e-mail updates, or contact the IRS using the "Contact Us" feature.

For more information on IRS2Go and other IRS social media products, visit IRS.gov.

**IRS: Four Ways to Get Free Tax Help**

IRS Tax Tip 2013-30, March 11, 2013

Many of us need information when preparing our federal income tax returns, like which form to use or how to claim a credit. The IRS offers free information and services to help taxpayers online, by phone, and in person. Here are four ways to get the help you need.

1. **On the Web**-the IRS.gov website is your one-stop federal tax shop. Start here to find tips and information at "1040 Central." You'll find information about filing options, the latest news, special topics like identity theft, frequently asked questions and tax forms. You'll also find a sample of online tools like the Interactive Tax Assistant and Where's My Refund?

2. **On the Phone**-you can get free personal tax help by calling 800-829-1040. To order free tax forms and publications, call 800-TAX FORM (829-3676). Check the status of your refund 24-7 by calling 800-829-4477. Call the same number to hear taped messages on more than 150 tax topics. These phone services are available Monday through Friday, 7:00 a.m. to 7:00 p.m. local time. Hours of service in Alaska and Hawaii follow Pacific Time.

3. **In your community**-the Volunteer Income Tax Assistance Program helps people who make $51,000 or less prepare and file their tax returns. The Tax Counseling for the Elderly Program is a similar service for seniors. Both are free and offered in many local areas. Between January and April, visit IRS.gov or call 800-906-9887 for a list of VITA sites near you. To find a TCE or AARP Tax-Aide site during this same period, go to AARP.org or call 888-227-7669 (888-AARPNOW).

4. **In IRS offices**-IRS Taxpayer Assistance Centers are located in many major cities. IRS employees offer personal assistance with a variety of tax issues. Before you visit, check the IRS website for a list of office locations and the location-specific business hours and services offered. Visit IRS.gov, click on the "Help & Resources" tab, and then click "Contact Your Local IRS Office."

Publication 910, IRS Guide to Free Tax Services, offers more information about free tax help. It is available at IRS.gov.

**Additional IRS Resources**

- 1040 Central
- Free Tax Return Preparation for You by Volunteers
- Find a VITA Site Near You
- Contact Your Local IRS Office
- Publication 910, IRS Guide to Free Tax Services

**Free Tax Return Preparation for Qualifying Taxpayers**

The Volunteer Income Tax Assistance (VITA) Program offers free tax help to people who generally make $52,000 or less, persons with disabilities, the elderly, and limited English-speaking taxpayers who need assistance in preparing their own tax returns. IRS-certified volunteers provide free basic income tax return preparation with electronic filing to qualified individuals.

In addition to VITA, the Tax Counseling for the Elderly (TCE) Program offers free tax help for all taxpayers, particularly those who are sixty years of age and older, specializing in questions about pensions and retirement-related issues unique to seniors. The IRS-certified volunteers who provide tax counseling are often retired individuals associated with nonprofit organizations that receive grants from the IRS.

**Before going to a VITA or TCE site**, see Publication 3676-B for services provided and check out the What to Bring page to ensure you have all the required documents and information our volunteers will need to help you. Note, available services can vary at each site due to the availability of volunteers certified with the tax law expertise required for your return and a VITA or TCE site near you.

VITA and TCE sites are generally located at community and neighborhood centers, libraries, schools, shopping malls, and other convenient locations across the country. To locate the nearest VITA or TCE site near you, use the VITA Locator Tool or call 800-906-9887.

At select tax sites, taxpayers also have an option to prepare their own basic federal and state tax return for free using Web-based tax preparation software with an IRS-certified volunteer to help guide you through the process. This option is only available at locations that list *"Self-Prep"* in the site listing.

*Please note that when using the locator tool, you will exit IRS.gov and open Google Maps if you need directions to a specific location.*

**Find an AARP TCE Tax-Aide Site Near You**

A majority of the TCE sites are operated by the AARP Foundation's Tax Aide Program. To locate the nearest AARP TCE Tax-Aide site between January and April, use the AARP Site Locator Tool or call 888-227-7669.

Page last reviewed or updated, June 11, 2014

**Issue Number: IRS Tax Tip 2015-18**
**Inside This Issue**

**Best Ways to Get IRS Tax Help "en Español"**

Tax rules can be difficult to understand, especially if they're not in your first language. The IRS offers many free products that are easy to use for people who speak Spanish. Here are the best ways to get federal tax help in Spanish.

- **Get answers 24-7**-IRS.gov/espanol has a wealth of tax information in Spanish. You can check the status of your tax refund with the online tool "¿Dónde está mi reembolso?" Use the "Asistente EITC" tool to check if you qualify for the Earned Income Tax Credit. You may qualify for the credit if you earned less than $52,427 in 2014.
- **Try IRS e-file**-whether you do your own taxes or pay a tax preparer, you should e-file your tax return. IRS e-file is safe, easy, and the most accurate way to file. If you owe taxes, you can e-file early and pay by the April 15 tax deadline. Visit IRS.gov and enter "Presentación e-file" in the search box to learn more.
- **Get health-care law tax information**-the IRS website has information about the Affordable Care Act tax provisions in both English and Spanish. The pages explain the shared responsibility provision and the premium tax credit and their effect on the tax return you're filing in 2015. You can find information about the law, the latest news, frequently asked questions, and links to additional resources on these pages.
- **Free tax preparation by a volunteer**-you may qualify to have your taxes filed through the IRS VITA or TCE programs. The IRS certifies VITA and TCE volunteers. In most cases, VITA offers free tax preparation and e-file if you earned $53,000 or less. TCE offers help if you're age sixty or older. Visit *Voluntarios proveen ayuda gratuita con la preparación de su declaración de impuestos.*

- **Get up-to-date at the multimedia center**-watch YouTube video tax tips and listen to IRS podcasts. Both types of new media are available in Spanish. Enter the keywords "Centro Multimediático" in the search box at IRS.gov.
- **Call TeleTax for refund and tax information**-TeleTax is a toll-free, automated phone service. It's available 24-7. Use it to track your refund or listen to helpful recorded messages on more than 130 tax topics. All topics are available in Spanish. If you call to check on your refund, have a copy of your tax return handy. You can find the list of TeleTax topics in the instructions for form 1040, 1040A, or 1040EZ. The TeleTax number is 800-829-4477.
- **Get tax forms and publications**-visit IRS.gov/espanol to get several tax forms and publications in Spanish.
- Visit the IRS Spanish newsroom. You'll see the IRS's most recent news releases, tax tips, and information in the Spanish newsroom. Just type "Noticias en Espanol" in the search box on IRS.gov.
- **Stay connected through Twitter en Español**-get the latest tax information and helpful tax tips in Spanish on Twitter. Follow the national IRS Spanish Twitter account @IRSenEspanol.

# CHAPTER 31

# A List of Fourteen Free E-file Companies on IRS. Gov: Easy Steps to Get There

**Fourteen Free E-file Tax Sites**

Go to irs.gov. and click on Internal Revenue Service.

Next, click on free file in blue.

Next, click on Free File, and read Use IRS Free File. If your AGI was $60,000 or less, fillable forms are available.

Next, click on free file now.

Next, choose and click on company you want to use.

On the next screen, click on Leave IRS Site, and you will go straight to the e-file company of your choice.

Free File: I Will Choose a Free File Software

**Before You Begin...**

- Free Federal returns are only available through Free File at IRS.gov.

- Each company sets its own eligibility criteria, generally based on income, age, state residency, eligibility for the Earned Income Tax Credit, and military status.
- If your adjusted gross income was $60,000 or less, you will find one or more free software options.
- Once at the company's website, review their information to ensure it meets your needs. For example, some offer free state tax returns, and some charge a fee.
- You may either browse the list of software offers below or use our tool, Help Me Find Free File Software.

| Free File Software | | |
|---|---|---|
| FreeTaxUSA® IRS Free File Edition<br>• Adjusted Gross Income-$60,000 or less, and<br>• Age-between 17 and 75, and<br>• Live in any state, except: AK, FL, NV, NH, SD, TN, TX, WA, and WY for a free federal tax return<br>• Free extensions | 1040.com Free File Edition<br>• Adjusted Gross Income-$33,000 or less, and<br>• Live in any state or U.S. Citizens and resident aliens with foreign addresses for a free federal tax return<br>• Free extensions | H&R Block's Free File<br>• Adjusted Gross Income-$53,500 or less, and<br>• Age-53 or younger, or<br>• Eligible for the Earned Income Tax Credit, and<br>• Live in any state for a free federal tax return |
| TurboTax ® All Free(SM)<br>• Adjusted Gross Income-$31,000 or less, or<br>• $60,000 or less for active military, or<br>• Eligible for the Earned Income Tax Credit, and<br>• Live in any state for a free federal tax return<br>• Free extensions | Online Taxes at OLT.com<br>• Adjusted Gross Income-between $13,000 and $60,000, and<br>• U.S. Citizens and resident aliens with foreign addresses for a free federal tax return<br>• Free extensions | • eSmartTax By Liberty Tax Service<br>• Adjusted Gross Income-$60,000 or less, and<br>• Age-between 18 and 54, and<br>• Live in any state for a free federal tax return<br>• Free extensions |

| Free File Software | | |
|---|---|---|
| **1040NOW.NET**<br>• Adjusted Gross Income-$60,000 or less, and<br>• Live in any of these states: AL, AZ, AR, CA, GA, IA, ID, IN, KY, MI, MN, MO, MS, NC, ND, NY, OK, or, RI, SC, VA, VT, or WV for a free federal tax return<br>• U.S. citizens and resident aliens with foreign addresses *or*<br>• Adjusted Gross Income-$60,000 or less, and<br>• Age-60 or younger, and<br>• Live in any of these states: CO, CT, DC, DE, HI, IL, KS, LA, MA, MD, ME, MT, NE, NJ, NM, OH, PA, UT, or WI for a free federal tax return | **Jackson Hewitt Tax Service**<br>• Adjusted Gross Income-$60,000 or less, and<br>• Age-49 or younger, or<br>• Eligible for the Earned Income Tax Credit, and<br>• Live in any state or U.S. citizens and resident aliens with foreign addresses for a free federal tax return<br>• Free extensions | **TaxSlayer**<br>• Adjusted Gross Income-$33,000 or less, or<br>• $60,000 or less for active military, and<br>• Live in any state or U.S. citizens and resident aliens with foreign addresses for a free federal tax return<br>• Free extensions |
| **FileYourTaxes.com**<br>• Adjusted Gross Income-between $8,000 and $60,000, and<br>• Age-between 15 and 65 and<br>• Live in any state or U.S. citizens and resident aliens with foreign addresses for a free federal tax return<br>• Free extensions | **Tax ACT Free File Edition**<br>• Adjusted Gross Income-$52,000 or less, and<br>• Age-between 18 and 58, and<br>• Live in any state or U.S. citizens and resident aliens with foreign addresses for a free federal tax return<br>• Free extensions | **ezTaxReturn.com**<br>• Adjusted Gross Income-$60,000 or less, and<br>• Live in any of these states: AL, AR, AZ, CA, CO, GA, IL, LA, MA, MD, MI, MS, NC, NJ, NY, OH, PA, VA, and WI for a free federal tax return |

| Free File Software | | |
|---|---|---|
| Tax Simple <br> • Adjusted Gross Income-$60,000 or less, and <br> • Age-50 or younger, and <br> • Live in any state for a free federal tax return <br> • Free extensions | Free1040TaxReturn.com <br> • Adjusted Gross Income-$60,000 or less, and <br> • Age-70 or younger, and <br> • Live in any state, except: FL, TN, TX, WA, and WY for a free federal tax return <br> • Free extensions | |

## Ten IRS Tips about Free Tax Preparation

Each year, millions of people have their taxes prepared for free. The IRS's Volunteer Income Tax Assistance and Tax Counseling for the Elderly programs have helped people for more than forty years. Many people know these programs by their initials. Here are ten tips from the IRS about VITA and TCE:

1. **Trained and certified**-the IRS works with local community groups to train and certify VITA and TCE volunteers.
2. **VITA Program**-VITA generally offers free tax return preparation to people who earn $53,000 or less.
3. **TCE Program**-TCE is mainly for people age sixty or older. The program specializes in tax issues unique to seniors. AARP participates in the TCE program and helps people with low to moderate incomes.
4. **Free e-file**-VITA and TCE provide free electronic filing. E-filing is the safest, most accurate way to file your tax return. Combining e-file with direct deposit is the fastest way to get your refund.
5. **Tax benefits**-using VITA and TCE can help you get all the tax benefits for which you are eligible. For example, you may qualify for the Earned Income Tax Credit or the Credit for the Elderly. You can also get help with the new Health Care Law tax provisions.

6. **Bilingual help**-some VITA and TCE sites provide bilingual help for people who speak limited English.

7. **Help for military**-VITA offers free tax assistance to members of the military and their families. Volunteers help with many military tax issues. These may include the special rules and tax benefits that apply to those serving in combat zones.

8. **"Self-Prep" option**-at some VITA sites, you can prepare your own federal and state tax returns using free Web-based software. This is an option if you don't have a home computer or need much help. Volunteers are on-site to guide you if you need help. In most cases, this option offers free tax return preparation software and e-filing to people who earn $60,000 or less.

9. **Local Sites**-the IRS partners with community organizations to offer free tax services at thousands of sites around the nation. Sites start to open in late January and early February.

10. **Visit IRS.gov**-you can visit IRS.gov to find a VITA site near you. Search the word "VITA" and click on "Free Tax Return Preparation for You by Volunteers." Site information is also available by calling the IRS at 800-906-9887. To locate the nearest AARP Tax-Aide site, visit aarp.org, or call 888-227-7669.

CHAPTER 32

---

# What if I Need Legal Representation to Help with My Tax Problem but Can't Afford It?

Low-Income Taxpayer Clinics (LITCs) represent low-income taxpayers before the Internal Revenue Service, assist taxpayers in audits, appeals and collection disputes, and can help taxpayers respond to IRS notices and to correct account problems. If you are a low-income taxpayer who cannot afford professional tax assistance or if you speak English as a second language (ESL) and need help understanding your taxpayer rights and responsibilities, you may qualify for help from an LITC that provides assistance for free or for a nominal charge. Although LITCs receive partial funding from the IRS, LITCs, their employees, and their volunteers are completely independent of, and are not associated with, the federal government. The LITCs are generally operated by nonprofit organizations or academic institutions.

Each LITC independently decides if you meet the income guidelines and other criteria before it agrees to represent you. There is at least one LITC in each of the fifty states, the District of Columbia, and Puerto Rico. You can find an LITC located in or near your area by using Publication 4134, Low-Income Taxpayer Clinic List. This publication identifies all LITCs who represent low-income taxpayers before the IRS or provide ESL services and is available at www.irs. gov/advocate or your local IRS office.

Low income taxpayers also may be able to receive assistance from a referral system operated by state bar associations, state or local societies of accountants, and other nonprofit tax professional organizations.

Page last reviewed or updated, Mar 10, 2014

# CHAPTER 33

---

# Where's My Refund

**Issue Number: IR-2015-45**
**Inside This Issue**

**Tax Time Guide: IRS Reminds Taxpayers about "Where's My Refund?"**

WASHINGTON—The Internal Revenue Service today reminded taxpayers that they can quickly check the status of their tax return and refund through "Where's My Refund?"

This is the fifth in a series of ten daily IRS tips called the Tax Time Guide. These tips are designed to help taxpayers navigate common tax issues as the April 15 deadline approaches.

Taxpayers who have not yet received their refunds can use "Where's My Refund?" on IRS.gov or on the smartphone application IRS2Go 5.0 to find out about the status of their income tax refunds.

Initial information will normally be available within twenty-four hours after the IRS receives the taxpayer's e-filed return or four weeks after the taxpayer mails a paper return to the IRS. The system updates only once every twenty-four hours, usually overnight, so there's no need to check more often.

"Where's My Refund? is the quickest and easiest way for tax-payers to get important information about their tax refund," said IRS Commissioner John Koskinen. So far this year, "Where's My Refund?" has received more than 179 million hits on IRS.gov.

Taxpayers should have their Social Security number, filing status, and exact refund amount when accessing "Where's My Refund?"

Other tips in the Tax Time Guide series are available on IRS.gov.

# W-2 Missing? What if My Employer Goes Bankrupt or Out of Business?

Your employer must provide you with a form W-2 showing your wages and withholdings for the year by January 31 of the following year. For example, if you were employed during 2013, your employer should provide you with a W-2 for 2013 by January 31, 2014. You should keep up-to-date records or pay stubs until you receive your form W-2. If your employer or its representatives fails to provide you with a form W-2, contact the IRS, and we can help by providing you with a substitute form W-2. If your employer is liquidating your 401(k) plan, you have sixty days to roll it over to another qualified retirement plan or IRA. For more information, see Publication 4128, Tax Impact of Job Loss.

Change the years to current year 2015 to be filed by April 15, 2016.

**IRS Tax Tip 2014-17, February 20, 2014**

If you worked as an employee last year, your employer must give you a form W-2, Wage and Tax Statement. This form shows the amount of wages you received for the year and the taxes withheld from those wages. It's important that you use this form to help make sure you file a complete and accurate tax return.

Most employers give forms W-2 to their workers by January 31. If you haven't received yours by mid-February, here's what you should do:

1.  **Contact your employer**-you should first ask your employer to give you a copy of your W-2. You'll also need this form from any former employer you worked for during the year. If employers send the form to you, be sure they have your correct address.

2.  **Contact the IRS**-if you exhaust your options with your employer and you have not received your W-2, call the IRS at 800-829-1040. You'll need the following when you call:
    *   Your name, address, Social Security number, and phone number
    *   Your employer's name, address, and phone number
    *   The dates you worked for the employer
    *   An estimate of the amount of wages you were paid and federal income tax withheld in 2013. If possible, you can use your final pay stub to figure these amounts.

3.  **File on time**-your tax return is due by April 15, 2014. If you don't get your W-2 in time to file, use form 4852, Substitute for form W-2, Wage and Tax Statement. Estimate your wages and withheld taxes as accurately as you can. The IRS may delay processing your return while it verifies your information.

You may need to correct your tax return if you get your missing W-2 after you file. If the tax information on the W-2 is different from what you originally reported, you may need to file an amended tax return. Use form 1040X, Amended U.S. Individual Income Tax Return to make the change.

# CHAPTER 35

# Extensions

**Topic 304-Extensions of Time to File Your Tax Return**

There are three ways you can request an automatic extension of time to file a U.S. individual income tax return: (1) you can electronically file form 4868 (PDF), Application for Automatic Extension of Time to File U.S. Individual Tax Return; (2) you can pay all or part of your estimated income tax due using a credit or debit card or by using the Electronic Federal Tax Payment System (EFTPS); or (3) you can file a paper form 4868 by mail.

If you file your form 4868 electronically, you will receive an acknowledgment or confirmation number for your records, and you do not need to mail in form 4868. If you need to pay additional taxes when filing form 4868 electronically, you may do so through the outside service provider or through e-file. You can refer to your tax software or tax professional for ways to file electronically using e-file services. Several companies offer free filing of form 4868 through the Free File program that you can access on the IRS.gov website. If you wish to file electronically, be sure to have a copy of last year's tax return. You will be asked to provide the adjusted gross income (AGI) from the return for taxpayer verification.

A second way of requesting an automatic extension of time to file your individual income tax return is to pay part or your entire estimated income tax due by credit card or debit card or by using EFTPS. You may pay by phone or Internet through one of the service providers listed on form 4868. Each service provider will charge a convenience fee based on the amount of the tax payment. At the completion of the transaction, you will receive a confirmation number for your records.

Finally, you can request an automatic extension of time to file your individual income tax return by completing paper form 4868 and mailing it to the appropriate address provided on the form.

File <u>form 4868</u> (PDF) by the regular due date of your return. Also, please be aware that an extension of time to file is *not* an extension of time to pay.

For information regarding state government filing, visit state government websites.

# CHAPTER 36

# My Job as a Revenue Agent

During my last years at IRS, we hired a lot of CPAs with master's degrees. Ninety Eight % of the revenue agents are quite bright. Many are CPAs or lawyers. When there was limited hiring, IRS could raise their hiring standards. In my training class, four of the thirteen trainees had both CPA and law degrees.

First, I will answer some of the questions many people have asked me: Do I have any pull at IRS or Appeals to help friends or taxpayers?

Hell no. CPA firms hired former high IRS officials for $250,000 a year. Many clients would be impressed and may have thought these officials had pull at the IRS. They did not. In fact, it would have the opposite effect. We would go out of our way to avoid favoritism. The only way to effect a tax audit is from the very top through a congressman or National Office. On one case, a former high official tried to push through a claim. The corporation was audited, and it cost the corporation millions of dollars.

Friends asked me if I could check on a relative's tax return. A husband or wife going through a divorce wanted to know their spouse's income. It would be illegal. Whenever I requested a transcript, I would need my group manager's written approval. If I looked up information not related to my case inventory, it would be a serious IRS violation.

Will IRS agents treat me fairly?

Yes. I have audited over a thousand tax returns and have never treated anyone unfairly.

Revenue agents have some leeway in regard to how they deal with taxpayers. I would obviously give a poor widow a little break when I had some factual justification. However, we could not be Santa Claus and must justify the basis for our actions.

On two of my audits, the prior agent treated the corporate officers poorly. I knew right away that the corporate officers were very upset with how they were treated. You could cut the tension with a knife. It took me a while to earn the trust of the corporate officers and to promote a favorable opinion of IRS. I would say that the chances of being treated fairly by a revenue agent are about 98 percent or 99 percent. It is just a guess.

There were a few arrogant IRS agents who worked on large cases. However, the corporations were well represented by a team of accountants and lawyers.

I started IRS on June 19, 1967, earning $6,387. I started a thirteen-week training course in the morning and graduated that night in the auditorium theatre at Roosevelt University. I had a BSBA and thirty-three hours of accounting. Tuition was $22 an hour. I started working at the old Boston Store building at State and Madison, which is downtown Chicago. The office had no air conditioning, and there were salt tablet dispensers on the wall. We opened the windows to cool off.

I got married on February 3, 1967, and bought a 1956 Pontiac for $85. I flunked my army physical in April 1967. My rent was $75. I had the new suit I wore at my wedding and a couple of hand-me-down suits from my brother. My father was disabled, and I had to work two jobs (fifty-five hours) to help support my family and put myself through college. I worked in the Chicago Park District as a recreational leader and in a snack shop. I made $1.20 or less per hour in the snack shop. Roosevelt University would not give me any student aid or a student loan. In 1968, I bought a new Pontiac Catalina for $3,755. In 1971, I bought an all-brick two-story townhome for $17,000. In 1975, I bought a 2,200–square-foot home for $58,500. That's enough trivia.

I remember a group meeting I attended as a new agent. My boss asked me how I would handle a certain tax issue. I said it could go either way. Later, I realized I made my first mistake. My boss wanted me to make a decision one way or the other. He didn't care if I was right or wrong. That's when I realized that we were being paid to make decisions. The R/A job requires four skills. He/she must be an accountant, lawyer, detective, and salesman and have meet-and-deal skills.

*Accounting and auditing skills* are important because you have to understand how an accounting system works. Every large company handles their books differently. I soon learned that it was important to ask someone to show me how the books work rather than waste a lot of time trying to figure it out. I audited a company you have all heard of and found it difficult to follow the books. A woman had set up the records around 1930. I decided to audit the most current year first because a new modern accounting system was just installed. I then easily backed into the prior year. Every R/A has their own way of handling an audit. That way, accountants had no way to predict what an agent would look at. My life partner thought that the tax law required the same results on an audit. I told her that ten different agents would come up with different results on a large company. Each agent has to choose which accounts to audit out of hundreds or thousands of accounts. Therefore, each audit plan selects many of the same items (inventory, payroll taxes, etc.), which are required, plus other items the R/A will select. When I was a newer agent, I helped a senior agent on a large controlled case, which had 150 sets of books. I asked him where to start. He said he did comparatives on each set of books.

When I was a new agent, I spent too much time figuring which items to audit and too much time researching issues. I later learned to quickly choose items to audit and only do a little research before the audit. I could always add items I felt were appropriate during the audit.

When I was a new agent, I enjoyed my job after becoming comfortable on the job. Most revenue agents are a little nervous when they go through four office audits a day during training. The same goes for their first field audit. I worked in downtown Chicago for twenty-one years. Many of my audits were near my home on the north side (Albany Park) of Chicago. When I got off the elevated train, I walked three blocks to my parent's home. I had some dinner and then walked three more blocks to my wife and dinner.

I have classified returns for audit and have traveled to Ogden Utah and Kansas City to flag returns for audit. I can look at a corporate return and know how to reclassify items to make a corporate return look clean. I have never used this skill.

**Lawyer skills**-it was not unusual for me to be in a room with seven accountants and lawyers, citing tax law and court cases. On the larger tax audits, you are up against the brightest and the best representatives. Most senior R/As can hold their own against these representatives. The most important skill is to be prepared. I had no problem dealing with lawyers. However, a few IRS lawyers were harder to convince. On one case involving a reverse merger (the smaller company took over the larger company) the consolidated returns expert in Washington fought me on a joint committee case. On my own, I came up with an IRS tax regulation that was on point. I decided to give back $3,000,000 to the company, which saved 150 jobs. When I told my boss, he concurred with my decision. On another case (tax shelter), the Washington expert said I blew the statute involving $9 million in additional tax. She said that the work papers mentioned an LLC that affected the statute of limitations. The representative never mentioned or brought up a problem. I pointed out to her a specific IRS tax regulation that treated the 1120-S treatment was binding. No LLC was shown as a shareholder on the 1120-S.

*Meet-and-deal skills* are the most important skill. When I was hired, dealing with taxpayers and representatives was the most important skill stressed by my three interviewers. I had them laughing. Meet-and-deal skills came easy to me because I am an open person who can start a conversation with strangers anytime and anywhere. I used to enjoy going to lunch with taxpayers or representatives. I learned a lot about the taxpayer and the company. It was a useful tool because taxpayers usual said too much. The longer the lunch, the more information I received.

After some years of experience, you can, in many cases, tell if a taxpayer is lying. I always could tell if a taxpayer or representative was handing me a lot of bull. Just because a taxpayer gives you a sweaty handshake, it doesn't necessarily mean he is lying. He may be nervous. There was one big 8 firm, which was very aggressive in regard to their tax determinations. When I saw their name as preparer, I knew I would come up with a lot of tax because of previous audits with that firm.

You can also put salesman under meet-and-deal skills. An R/A has to be a salesman to convince a taxpayer that he owes a million in tax. That means showing the facts and law and that it would be futile to fight the tax determination.

*Detective*-when I went out to a large company, I would pretend to be a detective and made a game out of the audit. Prior to the opening meeting, I would send out a letter requiring certain records for my opening meeting. I first learned where the bathroom and coffee were. At that meeting, I would interview the CEO and try to set the parameters for the audit. I would answer any concerns from the CPA firm handling the audit. Next, I would tour the factory or facilities and have the business operation explained to me. I enjoyed the tour the most. You can also see the assets and machinery, which are being depreciated. I then would normally receive an office to work in and a desk to lock up records. The most guarded secrets are the officer and employee salaries on the payroll tax returns.

The first thing I would do is make a three-year comparative analysis of the corporate returns. I also made a comparative of cost of goods sold and other expenses. A balance sheet analysis including Sch. M and adjusting entries is very important-where there are bad debts, change in stock ownership, etc. The work papers tying in the return are also helpful. Included in the request for records are all adjustments carried over from a prior year. On one audit, I looked at a $318.00 schedule M item. I found out it was made up of forty debits and credits. Needless to say, the corporation tried to bury these items, which resulted in tax adjustments in the millions.

The SEC report, CPA report, inventory records, corporate record books, payroll tax returns, cancelled checks, bank statements, and corporate minutes are also important records that could alert you to possible adjustments. Possible additional IRS personnel could include the following:

- **International agent** looking at foreign transactions or transfer pricing involving foreign subsidiaries.
- **Engineer** to compute value of assets.
- **Computer audit specialist** to stratify accounts. A company may spread an expense over 5,000 accounts. A CAS can pick items such as repairs, bad debts, travel and entertainment, and asset credit balances over a certain dollar amount.
- **A payroll tax specialist**
- **An economist** to help with valuations and transfer pricing.
- **Financial products agent**-this can include commodities, stock, hedge funds, and financial transactions.

When I was a new agent, I noticed that people would avoid me at parties because I was a revenue agent. Twenty years later, things drastically changed. I became popular. People would come up to me at parties and ask all types of tax questions. Some ask me what could happen if they hadn't filed. I felt like a doctor answering a lot of questions.

On September 11, 2001, the Twin Towers had a horrible effect on corporations. Many corporations saw sales drop off sharply. Congress increased the three-year carryback loss to five years to help corporations. During the next two years, revenue agents gave corporations back large amounts of money on audits designated as joint committee cases. The corporation could carryback a loss to the fourth and fifth year, which had profits, and then receive a refund of tax. I read a Reuter's article dated August 31, 2005, that Lucent received $902 million. I estimate that it cost the government $250 billion a year in tax refunds. This obviously had an effect on George Bush's deficits.

# CHAPTER 37

# How I Effectively Dealt
# With Representatives

Almost all the representatives I have dealt with acted in a very professional manner.

When you are a new revenue agent, some representatives will try to take advantage of the agent. As agents get more experienced, their meet-and-deal skills increase substantially. I have argued issues on over a thousand cases and have had only four unagreed cases. On three cases, the representative received a worse deal in Appeals.

Here are a few examples:

When I was a new agent, I was sitting outside my supervisor's office, and a representative was giving me a hard time. He wanted to know why the taxpayer's return was selected for audit and would not let up. My boss said to mention Circular 230 (Right to Practice before the IRS), and when I did, the representative shut up.

When I was a coordinator agent, I helped senior agents with technical and auditing skills. I had a revenue agent approach me with a problem. The lawyer had copies of the taxpayers' prior and subsequent year returns but refused to show them for inspection. The lawyer was very arrogant and cited a former treasury official's book, saying he did not have to show me the returns and that we could get copies from Kansas City. I told the attorney that he was correct in that we could requisition the returns, but that could take three or four months. I dropped a copy of Circular 230 (Right to Practice before the IRS) and told him he was purposely delaying the audit, which is in violation of Circular 230 rules. The lawyer huddled in another room with a group of people and finally gave us the returns to inspect. If we had to requisition the returns, it is likely they would be audited. It is not wise to purposely upset a revenue agent.

When I was in Special Enforcement (going after organized crime), I took over a case because the R/A (a woman) felt intimidated by a representative. The representative demanded to know how much time she would spend on the case. When I started my audit, that same representative started to talk to me. I asked if he had a power of attorney. He said no. I then told him I could not talk to him without a power. The CEO called me into his office, and he was very upset. I dropped a copy of Circular 230 on his desk and explained that it was for the corporation's protection, and I could get into trouble giving information to an unauthorized person. The CEO asked if the representative would be needed. There was a corporate officer to give me the requested records, so I said I didn't think he would be needed until the audit was completed, also, that it was up to the CEO to decide. The CEO appeared happy the representative was not needed because of the cost saving.

I took over a case from a revenue agent who transferred to Florida. The rep and I resolved all the issues except unexplained bank deposits. The business and personal bank accounts were comingled. It is my job to prove income and the representative and I had no idea what amount was taxable. We felt the taxpayer also had no idea. The taxpayer provided important work to the community. The rep offered 60 percent of the unexplained deposits as income. I would have accepted less because IRS has to prove income, which would have been difficult. I told the representative that since he was fair on all the other issues, I would try to get my boss's approval. I went back to the office and later called with the good news that his offer was accepted. I never talked to my boss. Why didn't I accept the offer right away? The representative walked away very happy, thinking he got the best deal.

I was auditing a billion-dollar corporation and noticed that the accountant was acting strangely. When he brought me records, he would turn and walk away. One time, he gave me the records and stood there and watched me. I knew something was wrong but could not figure out what it was. I said loudly, "Uh huh."

He said, "You found it?"

I said, "Yes, you better tell me all about it." He then told me what issue was handled incorrectly.

I was auditing a corporation, and the taxpayer was hit with preferential dividends in the previous year. The accountants from a large auditing firm had come to an agreement on the issues. At the meeting with the taxpayer, the accountants changed their positions and took a much tougher stance on the issues. The meeting became heated. I then told the taxpayer what the issues were and that there would not be any preferential dividends-mainly because there was no current personal trip deducted by the corporation. The taxpayer agreed and was happy. The taxpayer asked me why I didn't get upset. I said, "That's easy. It's not my money."

I was discussing an issue with an accountant from a big 8 accounting firm. I had told the representative that he handled a depreciation issue incorrectly. The representative was quite upset and said, "Are you calling us liars? We certified that the CPA report was done in accordance with GAAP." After yelling at me for five minutes, I asked if he was through yelling. I then told him that I wasn't calling him a liar and that I was just saying that it was handled wrong. I then said if he could show me any APBO, ARB, accounting text-book, Journal of Taxation, IRS Regulations, or court cases that I was wrong, I would apologize. Otherwise, don't insult my intelligence. The representative later agreed to the issue.

When I was a group manager, I went on a field visit on one of my senior agents. There were seven representatives in the room, and it appeared that the revenue agent might agree with the representatives. I asked to see the research on the case that was cited. They cited the minority opinion in a case the government won. They agreed to the issue.

I was auditing a large corporation and was dealing with an aggressive big 8 firm. The CEO was getting very upset with the tone in the room. One of the representatives gave an impressive speech. I then asked what has it got to do with the issues. I proposed my issues, and the CEO could see that I was being very fair. The CEO agreed to the issues. Then we had a personal talk for forty-five minutes after hours. When you are nice to people and treat them fairly, they do appreciate it.

# CHAPTER 38

---

# Retirement Savers Credit

**Issue Number: IRS Tax Tip 2015-56**
**Inside This Issue**

**Save on Your Taxes and for Retirement with the Saver's Credit**

If you contribute to a retirement plan, like a 401(k) or an IRA, you may be able to claim the Saver's Credit. This credit can help you save for retirement and reduce the tax you owe. Here are some key facts that you should know about this important tax credit:

- **Formal name**-the formal name of the Saver's Credit is the Retirement Savings Contribution Credit. The Saver's Credit is in addition to other tax savings you get if you set aside money for retirement. For example, you may be able to deduct your contributions to a traditional IRA.

- **Maximum credit**-the Saver's Credit is worth up to $2,000 if you are married and file a joint return. The credit is worth up to $1,000 if you are single. The credit you receive is often much less than the maximum. This is due in part because of the deductions and other credits you may claim.

- **Income limits**-you may be able to claim the credit depending on your filing status and the amount of your yearly income. You may be eligible for the credit on your 2014 tax return if you are
  - ◦ Married filing jointly with income up to $60,000
  - ◦ Head of household with income up to $45,000
  - ◦ Married filing separately or a single taxpayer with income up to $30,000
- **Other rules**-other rules that apply to the credit include the following:
  - ◦ You must be at least eighteen years of age.
  - ◦ You can't have been a full-time student in 2014.
  - ◦ No other person can claim you as a dependent on their tax return.
- **Contribution date**-you must have contributed to a 401(k) plan or similar workplace plan by the end of the year to claim this credit. However, you can contribute to an IRA by the due date of your tax return and still have it count for 2014. The due date for most people is April 15, 2015.
- **Form 8880**-file form 8880, Credit for Qualified Retirement Savings Contributions, to claim the credit.
- **Free File**-if you can claim the credit, you can prepare and e-file your tax return for free using IRS Free File. The tax software will do the hard work for you. It will do the math and complete the right forms. Free File is available only through the IRS.gov website.

The following applies to 2015 tax returns:

- The AGI limit for the saver's credit (also known as the retirement savings contribution credit) for low- and moderate-income workers is $61,000 for married couples filing jointly, up from $60,000 in 2014; $45,750 for heads of household, up from $45,000; and $30,500 for married individuals filing separately and for singles, up from $30,000.

# CHAPTER 39

---

# What You Need to Know about Capital Gains

-A taxpayer had a contribution of stock issue that resulted in a disallowance of over $700,000. The taxpayer held one of his stocks for 363 days, two days short of the required one year. He had bought stock on different dates. Therefore, he could only deduct the cost of the stock as a contribution, instead of the increased fair market value.

**Tax Tip**

When you have bought different blocks of the same stock, keep track of cost and dividends. When you sell a block of stock, instruct the broker to sell the stock, which had the highest cost and the date purchased. Request a written receipt from the broker identifying the stock.-

**Issue Number: IRS Tax Tip 2 015-21**
**Inside This Issue**

## Ten Facts That You Should Know about Capital Gains and Losses

When you sell a capital asset, the sale results in a capital gain or loss. A capital asset includes most property you own for personal use or own as an investment. Here are ten facts that you should know about capital gains and losses:

1. **Capital assets**-capital assets include property, such as your home or car, as well as investment property, such as stocks and bonds.

2. **Gains and losses**-a capital gain or loss is the difference between your basis and the amount you get when you sell an asset. Your basis is usually what you paid for the asset.

3. **Net Investment Income Tax**-you must include all capital gains in your income, and you may be subject to the Net Investment Income Tax. This tax applies to certain net investment income of individuals, estates, and trusts that have income above statutory threshold amounts. The rate of this tax is 3.8 percent. For details visit IRS.gov.

4. **Deductible losses**-you can deduct capital losses on the sale of investment property. You cannot deduct losses on the sale of property that you hold for personal use.

5. **Long and short term**-capital gains and losses are either long term or short term, depending on how long you held the property. If you held the property for more than one year, your gain or loss is long term. If you held it one year or less, the gain or loss is short term.

6. **Net capital gain**-if your long-term gains are more than your long-term losses, the difference between the two is a net long-term capital gain. If your net long-term capital gain is more than your net short-term capital loss, you have a net capital gain.

7. **Tax rate**-the capital gains tax rate usually depends on your income. The maximum net capital gain tax rate is 20 percent. However, for most taxpayers, a 0 or 15 percent rate will apply. A 25 or 28 percent tax rate can also apply to certain types of net capital gains.

8. **Limit on losses**-if your capital losses are more than your capital gains, you can deduct the difference as a loss on your tax return. This loss is limited to $3,000 per year, or $1,500 if you are married and file a separate return.

9. **Carryover losses**-if your total net capital loss is more than the limit you can deduct, you can carry over the losses you are not able to deduct to next year's tax return. You will treat those losses as if they happened in that next year.

10. **Forms to file**-you often will need to file form 8949, Sales and Other Dispositions of Capital Assets, with your federal tax return to report your gains and losses. You also need to file schedule D, Capital Gains and Losses, with your tax return.

For more information about this topic, see the schedule D instructions and Publication 550, Investment Income and Expenses. You can visit IRS.gov to view, download, or print any tax product you need right away.

# CHAPTER 40

# Does Net Investment Income Apply to You

**Issue Number: IRS Tax Tip 2015-27**
**Inside This Issue**

**How to Determine if the Net Investment**
**Income Tax Applies to You**

If you have income from investments, you may be subject to the Net Investment Income Tax. You may owe this tax if you receive investment income and your income for the year is more than certain limits. Here are some key tips you should know about this tax:

- **Net investment income tax**-the law requires a tax of 3.8 percent on the lesser of either your net investment income or the amount by which your modified adjusted gross income exceeds a threshold amount based on your filing status.
- **Income threshold amounts**-you may owe this tax if your modified adjusted gross income is more than the following amount for your filing status:

| Filing Status | Threshold Amount |
|---|---|
| Single or head of household | $200,000 |
| Married filing jointly | $250,000 |
| Married filing separately | $125,000 |
| Qualifying widow(er) with a child | $250,000 |

- **Net investment income**-this amount generally includes income such as, interest, dividends, capital gains, rental and royalty income, and nonqualified annuities.

    This list is not all-inclusive. Net investment income normally does not include wages and most self-employment income. It does not include unemployment compensation, Social Security benefits, or alimony. It also does not include any gain from the sale of your main home that you exclude from your income.

    Refer to form 8960, Net Investment Income Tax, to see if this tax applies to you. You can check the form's instructions for the details on how to figure the tax.

- **How to report**-if you owe the tax, you must file form 8960 with your federal tax return. If you had too little tax withheld or did not pay enough estimated taxes, you may have to pay an estimated tax penalty.

For more on this topic, visit IRS.gov/aca.

# CHAPTER 41

# Early Retirement Distributions

-The most important exception to remember is the exception for first-time home buyer, which is only available on traditional and Roth IRAs. It is limited to the first $10,000. You can qualify as a first time home buyer:

- If you haven't owned a home in the last three years,
- You owned a home with a former spouse, and
- You owned a trailer, which did not have a permanent foundation.

It is never wise to take out retirement savings because of the tax. You are probably better off getting a home equity loan or borrowing money from your pension plan-

**Issue Number: IRS Tax Tip 2015-28**
**Inside This Issue**

**Key Points to Know about Early Retirement Distributions**

Some people take an early withdrawal from their IRA or retirement plan. Doing so in many cases triggers an added tax on top of the income tax you may have to pay. Here are some key points you should know about taking an early distribution:

1. **Early withdrawals**-an early withdrawal normally means taking the money out of your retirement plan before you reach age fifty-nine and a half.

2. **Additional tax**-if you took an early withdrawal from a plan last year, you must report it to the IRS. You may have to pay income tax on the amount you took out. If it was an early withdrawal, you may have to pay an added 10 percent tax.

3. **Nontaxable withdrawals**-the added 10 percent tax does not apply to nontaxable withdrawals. They include withdrawals of your cost to participate in the plan. Your cost includes contributions that you paid tax on before you put them into the plan.

A rollover is a type of nontaxable withdrawal. A rollover occurs when you take cash or other assets from one plan and contribute the amount to another plan. You normally have sixty days to complete a rollover to make it tax-free.

4. **Check exceptions**-there are many exceptions to the additional 10 percent tax. Some of the rules for retirement plans are different from the rules for IRAs. See IRS.gov for details about these rules.

5. **File form 5329**-if you made an early withdrawal last year, you may need to file a form with your federal tax return. See form 5329, Additional Taxes on Qualified Plans (Including IRAs) and Other Tax-Favored Accounts, for details.

## Topic 558-Additional Tax on Early Distributions from Retirement Plans Other Then IRAs

To discourage the use of retirement funds for purposes other than normal retirement, the law imposes a 10 percent additional tax on certain early distributions from certain retirement plans. The additional tax is equal to 10 percent of the portion of the distribution that is includible in income. Generally, early distributions are those you receive from a qualified retirement plan or deferred annuity contract before reaching age fifty-nine and a half. The term qualified retirement plan means:

- A qualified employee plan under section 401(a), such as a section 401(k) plan;
- A qualified employee annuity plan under section 403(a);
- A tax-sheltered annuity plan under section 403(b) for employees of public schools or tax-exempt organizations; or
- An individual retirement account under section 408(a) or an individual retirement annuity under section 408(b) (IRAs).

In general, an eligible state or local government section 457 deferred compensation plan is not a qualified retirement plan, and any distribution from such plan is not subject to the 10 percent additional tax on early distributions. However, any distribution attributable to amounts the section 457 plan received in a direct transfer or rollover from one of the qualified retirement plans listed above would be subject to the 10 percent additional tax.

Distributions that are not taxable, such as distributions that you roll over to another qualified retirement plan, are not subject to this 10 percent additional tax. For more information on rollovers, refer to Topic 413.

There are certain exceptions to this 10 percent additional tax. The following six exceptions apply to distributions from any qualified retirement plan:

- Distributions made to your beneficiary or estate on or after your death.
- Distributions made because you are totally and permanently disabled.

- Distributions made as part of a series of substantially equal periodic payments over your life expectancy or the life expectancies of you and your designated beneficiary. If these distributions are from a qualified plan other than an IRA, you must separate from service with this employer before the payments begin for this exception to apply.
- Distributions to the extent you have deductible medical expenses that exceed 10 percent of your adjusted gross income (7.5 percent if you or your spouse is age sixty-five or over) whether or not you itemize your deductions for the year. The 7.5 percent limitation is a temporary exemption from January 1, 2013, to December 31, 2016, for individuals age sixty-five and older and their spouses. For additional information, see Questions and Answers: Changes to the Itemized Deduction for 2014 Medical Expenses on IRS.gov. For more information on medical expenses, refer to Topic 502.
- Distributions made due to an IRS levy of the plan under section 6331.
- Distributions that are qualified reservist distributions. Generally, these are distributions made to individuals called to active duty for at least 180 days after September 11, 2001.

## Topic 557-Additional Tax on Early Distributions from Traditional and Roth IRAs

To discourage the use of IRAs for purposes other than retirement, the law imposes a 10 percent additional tax on early distributions from traditional and Roth IRAs unless an exception applies. Generally, early distributions are those you receive from an IRA before reaching age fifty-nine and a half. The 10 percent additional tax applies to the part of the distribution that you have to include in gross income. It is in addition to any regular income tax on that amount.

Distributions that you roll over or transfer to another IRA or qualified retirement plan are not subject to this 10 percent additional tax. For more information on rollovers, refer to Topic 413.

There are exceptions to this 10 percent additional tax for early distributions that are:

- Made to a beneficiary or estate on account of the IRA owner's death
- Made on account of disability
- Made as part of a series of substantially equal periodic payments for your life (or life expectancy) or the joint lives (or joint life expectancies) of you and your designated beneficiary
- Qualified first-time home buyer distributions
- Not in excess of your qualified higher education expenses
- Not in excess of certain medical insurance premiums paid while unemployed
- Not in excess of your unreimbursed medical expenses that are more than a certain percentage of your adjusted gross income
- Due to an IRS levy, or
- A qualified reservist distribution

**Retirement Topics-Exceptions to Tax on Early Distributions**

Most retirement plan distributions are subject to income tax and may be subject to an additional 10 percent tax.

Generally, the amounts an individual withdraws from an IRA or retirement plan before reaching age fifty-nine and a half are called "early" or "premature" distributions. Individuals must pay an additional 10 percent early withdrawal tax and report the amount to the IRS for any early distributions, unless an exception applies.

| The distribution will *not* be subject to the 10% additional early distribution tax in the following circumstances: | Exception to 10% Additional Tax | | |
|---|---|---|---|
| | Qualified Plans (401k, etc.) | IRA, SEP, SIMPLE IRA and SARSEP Plans | Internal Revenue Code Section(s) |
| **Age** | | | |
| After participant/IRA owner reaches age 59½ | Yes | Yes | 72(t)(2)(A)(i) |
| **Automatic Enrollment** | | | |
| Permissive withdrawals from a plan with auto enrollment features | Yes | Yes for SIMPLE IRAs and SARSEPs | 414(w)(1)(B) |
| **Corrective Distributions** | | | |
| Corrective distributions (and associated earnings) of excess contributions, excess aggregate contributions and excess deferrals, made timely | Yes | N/A | 401(k)(8)(D), 401(m)(7)(A), 402(g)(2)(C) |
| **Death** | | | |
| After death of the participant/IRA owner | Yes | Yes | 72(t)(2)(A)(ii) |
| **Disability** | | | |
| Total and permanent disability of the participant/IRA owner | Yes | Yes | 72(t)(2)(A)(iii) |
| **Domestic Relations** | | | |
| To an alternate payee under a Qualified Domestic Relations Order | Yes | N/A | 72(t)(2)(C) |
| **Education** | | | |
| Qualified higher education expenses | No | Yes | 72(t)(2)(E) |
| **Equal Payments** | | | |
| Series of substantially equal payments | Yes | Yes | 72(t)(2)(A)(iv) |
| **ESOP** | | | |
| Dividend pass through from an ESOP | Yes | N/A | 72(t)(2)(A)(vi) |
| **Homebuyers** | | | |
| Qualified first-time homebuyers, up to $10,000 | No | Yes | 72(t)(2)(F) |

| Levy | | | |
|---|---|---|---|
| Because of an IRS levy of the plan | Yes | Yes | 72(t)(2)(A)(vii) |
| **Medical** | | | |
| Amount of unreimbursed medical expenses (>7.5% AGI; after 2012, 10% if under age 65) | Yes | Yes | 72(t)(2)(B) |
| Health insurance premiums paid while unemployed | No | Yes | 72(t)(2)(D) |
| **Military** | | | |
| Certain distributions to qualified military reservists called to active duty | Yes | Yes | 72(t)(2)(G) |
| **Returned IRA Contributions** | | | |
| If withdrawn by extended due date of return | N/A | Yes | 408(d)(4) |
| Earnings on these returned contributions | N/A | No | 408(d)(4) |
| **Rollovers** | | | |
| In-plan Roth rollovers or eligible distributions contributed to another retirement plan or IRA within sixty days | Yes | Yes | 402(c), 402A(d) (3), 403(a) (4), 403(b) (8), 408(d)(3), 408A(d)(3) |
| **Separation from Service** | | | |
| The employee separates from service during or after the year the employee reaches age 55 (age 50 for public safety employees in a governmental defined benefit plan) | Yes | No | 72(t)(2)(A)(v), 72(t)(10) |

Note-governmental 457(b) distributions are not subject to the 10 percent additional tax except for distributions attributable to rollovers from another type of plan or IRA.

It should be 25 percent instead of 10 percent if made within the first two years of participation.

*Page Last Reviewed or Updated: 30-Mar-2015*

# CHAPTER 42

# When to Move an IRA to a Roth IRA

-There are differences if you have a 401(k) or a traditional IRA. But let's first look at my problem. I am seventy-two and have been taking out some of my federal thrift savings and paying taxes on the distributions. My federal pension is almost $89,000, and I am able to save my required distribution. At seventy and a half years, you are required to take distribution and can spread it over twenty six and a half years or less. Since I am paying tax on the distributions and I am putting the money in the bank, I am considering putting the money in a Roth IRA to save and pay the tax. As a retired federal employee, I cannot have monthly payments to an IRA because I am over seventy and one half years. If a federal employee is receiving payments from his thrift (TSP) account and "will be receiving fewer than 120 payments, the IRS will categorize your monthly payments as eligible rollover contributions. For federal income tax purposes, the IRS will treat them the same way it treats a final payment. Alternatively, if you will be receiving 120 payments or more, the IRS will categorize your payments as 'periodic payments.' You cannot transfer or roll over periodic payments into an IRA or an eligible employer plan."

If I decide to set up an IRA, I will have to file a form 79 and distribute all my funds from my thrift money directly to the IRA. A representative (e.g. Edward Jones) will have to fill out the form 5498 and send it to the IRS. Since my required minimum distribution will be paid before the end of the 2015 year, and I file before the IRS TSP closing date which is December 15, 100 percent of my thrift will be transferred. In Illinois, my pension or Social Security is not taxable for state income tax.

I will have to distribute the required minimum distribution from the IRA and can distribute an additional amount to a Roth IRA. You cannot roll over a required minimum distribution. If I leave my money in the thrift plan, I will have less than half of my funds left when I am around ninety. I am currently earning 2.07 percent. If funds are going directly to an IRA, the 20 percent withholding does not have to be withheld. If the funds go directly to you, 20 percent will be withheld, and you have sixty days to roll it over or be taxed.

Form 5498 reports your total annual contributions to an IRA account and identifies the type of retirement account you have, such as a traditional IRA, Roth IRA, SEP IRA, or SIMPLE IRA. Form 5498 will also report amounts that you roll over or transfer from other types of retirement accounts into this IRA.

If you decide to transfer to a Roth IRA, be aware that Roth IRAs accept only after-tax dollars. As a result, you must pay tax on the amount you transfer, and the tax liability is incurred for the year of the transfer. We strongly encourage you to consult with a tax advisor regarding your eligibility for, and the tax consequences of, making the transfer.

The above information will be useful to federal employees.

The following information is important when you transfer funds to a Roth IRA. Two important things you and I should be aware of are tax brackets and adjusted gross income for Medicare part B.

| Your Annual Income | | 2015 Monthly Premium |
|---|---|---|
| Amount | | |
| Individual Tax Return | Joint Tax Return | You Pay |
| $85,000 or less | $170,000 or less | $104.50 |
| $85,001 up to $107,000 | $170,001 up to $214,001 | $146.90 |
| $107,001 up to $160,000 | $214,001 up to $320,000 | $209.80 |
| $160,001 up to $214,000 | $320,001 up to $428,000 | $272.70 |
| Over $214,000 | Over $428,000 | $335.70 |

Those individuals who do not receive Social Security will pay $121.80 instead of $104.50.

If you go on Medicare for the first time in 2016, you will also pay $121.80 for part B.

If you are married and in the 15 percent tax bracket, you can have taxable income up to $74,900.

If you are single, your 15 percent tax bracket ends $37,451. Single taxpayer's brackets are one half of married brackets.

Married
25 percent up to $151,200
28 percent up to $230,450
33 percent up to $411,500
35 percent up to $464,850
39.6 over $464,850

If you were married and had taxable income of $51,800, you can contribute up to $23,100 into a Roth IRA and stay in the 15 percent bracket. If you converted a $500,000 IRA to a Roth IRA, that would put you in a 39.6 percent tax bracket. That would not be wise. If this book is a big success, I could be paying $335.70 a month for my Medicare part B.

Now let's talk about putting IRA funds into a Roth IRA. In my situation, my funds are not going down at retirement. However, many taxpayers are in a lower tax bracket when they retire. When you are over sixty, you may want to move some of your money to a

Roth IRA. Once you hit seventy and one half, you will have to make the minimum required distribution.

When you are in a period of low income, it may be a good time to convert some of your IRA to a Roth IRA. You will be in a lower tax bracket. Being out of work, going back to school or a short-term disability may be a good time to make a Roth conversion. You can choose to make a small conversion every year.

If you expect your income to go up, it may also be a good time to convert some of your money to a Roth IRA.

It may be beneficial to convert to a Roth when you are estate planning.

My reason for wanting a Roth is possible stock market gains. In the last market crash, you could have bought Ford stock at $1.66. If you had put $40,000 in Ford stock, you would have earned ten times your money. Now you would have $400,000 to invest in dividend paying stock and no tax on your gains.

Two other important considerations are Social Security and Obama Care (ACA). The tax on your conversion of some payments to a Roth can affect the taxing of your Social Security or affect Obama care premiums.-

## Distributions after Owner's Death

When your spouse is your Roth IRA beneficiary, the spouse will have the same Roth IRA rights as the spouse that died. Different rules apply if the beneficiary is not your spouse and are governed by the following:

If a Roth IRA owner dies, the minimum distribution rules that apply to traditional IRAs apply to Roth IRAs as though the Roth IRA owner died before his or her required beginning date, distributions to beneficiaries. Generally, the entire interest in the Roth IRA must be distributed by the end of the fifth calendar year after the year of the owner's death unless the interest is payable to a designated beneficiary over the life or life expectancy of the designated beneficiary.

If paid as an annuity, the entire interest must be payable over a period not greater than the designated beneficiary's life expectancy, and distributions must begin before the end of the calendar year following the year of death. Distributions from another Roth IRA cannot be substituted for these distributions unless the other Roth IRA was inherited from the same decedent. If the sole beneficiary is the spouse, he or she can either delay distributions until the decedent would have reached age 7012 or treat the Roth IRA as his or her own.

Use form 8606 to report conversion to or withdrawal from a Roth IRA. Your annual Roth IRA contributions are not reported on your form 1040.

There is no exception to the estimated tax penalty because of a Roth Conversion.

The Internal Revenue Service announced cost of living adjustments affecting dollar limitations for pension plans and other retirement-related items for tax year 2015. Many of the pension plan limitations will change for 2015 because the increase in the cost-of-living index met the statutory thresholds that trigger their adjustment. However, other limitations will remain unchanged because the increase in the index did not meet the statutory thresholds that trigger their adjustment. Highlights include the following:

- The elective deferral (contribution) limit for employees who participate in 401(k), 403(b), most 457 plans, and the federal government's Thrift Savings Plan is increased from $17,500 to $18,000.

- The catch-up contribution limit for employees aged fifty and over who participate in 401(k), 403(b), most 457 plans, and the federal government's Thrift Savings Plan is increased from $5,500 to $6,000.

- The limit on annual contributions to an Individual Retirement Arrangement (IRA) remains unchanged at $5,500. The additional catch-up contribution limit for individuals aged fifty and over is not subject to an annual cost-of-living adjustment and remains $1,000.

- The deduction for taxpayers making contributions to a traditional IRA is phased out for singles and heads of household who are covered by a workplace retirement plan and have modified adjusted gross incomes (AGI) between

$61,000 and $71,000, up from $60,000 and $70,000 in 2014. For married couples filing jointly, in which the spouse who makes the IRA contribution is covered by a workplace retirement plan, the income phase out range is $98,000 to $118,000, up from $96,000 to $116,000. For an IRA contributor who is not covered by a workplace retirement plan and is married to someone who is covered, the deduction is phased out if the couple's income is between $183,000 and $193,000, up from $181,000 and $191,000. For a married individual filing a separate return who is covered by a workplace retirement plan, the phase-out range is not subject to an annual cost-of-living adjustment and remains $0 to $10,000.

- The AGI phase-out range for taxpayers making contributions to a Roth IRA is $183,000 to $193,000 for married couples filing jointly, up from $181,000 to $191,000 in 2014. For singles and heads of household, the income phase-out range is $116,000 to $131,000, up from $114,000 to $129,000. For a married individual filing a separate return, the phase-out range is not subject to an annual cost-of-living adjustment and remains $0 to $10,000.

## Amount of Roth IRA Contributions That You Can Make for 2016

This table shows whether your contribution to a Roth IRA is affected by the amount of your modified AGI as computed for Roth IRA purpose.

| If your filing status is... | And your modified AGI is... | Then you can contribute... |
| --- | --- | --- |
| **married filing jointly** or **qualifying widow(er)** | < $184,000 | up to the limit |
| | ≥ $184,000 but < $194,000 | a reduced amount |
| | ≥ $194,000 | zero |

| married filing separately and you lived with your spouse at any time during the year | < $10,000 | a reduced amount |
|---|---|---|
| | ≥ $10,000 | zero |
| single, head of household, or married filing separately and you did not live with your spouse at any time during the year | < $117,000 | up to the limit |
| | ≥ $117,000 but < $132,000 | a reduced amount |
| | ≥ $132,000 | zero |

## Amount of Your Reduced Roth IRA Contribution

If the amount you can contribute must be reduced, figure your reduced contribution limit as follows:

1. Start with your modified AGI.
2. Subtract from the amount in 1:
   a. $184,000 if filing a joint return or qualifying widow(er),
   b. $0 if married filing a separate return, and you lived with your spouse at any time during the year, or
   c. $117,000 for all other individuals.
3. Divide the result in 2 by $15,000 ($10,000 if filing a joint return, qualifying widow[er]), or married filing a separate return and you lived with your spouse at any time during the year).
4. Multiply the maximum contribution limit (before reduction by this adjustment and before reduction for any contributions to traditional IRAs) by the result in 3.
5. Subtract the result in 4 from the maximum contribution limit before this reduction. The result is your reduced contribution limit.

CHAPTER 43

# Child Care Credit

**Top Frequently Asked Questions for Childcare Credit, Other Credits**

### Question

My spouse and I both work and are eligible for the child and dependent care credit. Can I include the expense of my five-year-old son's private kindergarten tuition as a qualified expense on form 2441, Child and Dependent Care Expenses?

### Answer

No, the expense of tuition for kindergarten does not qualify for the child and dependent care credit because kindergarten is primarily educational in nature.

However, the expense for a before- or after-school care program may qualify even though the expense of school tuition does not qualify.

## Additional Information

However, the expense for a before- or after-school care program may qualify, even though the expense of school tuition does not qualify my five-year-old son's private kindergarten tuition as a qualified expense on form 2441, Child and Dependent Care Expenses.

## Question

My babysitter refused to provide me with her Social Security number. Can I still claim the amount I paid her for childcare while I worked? If so, how do I claim these childcare expenses on my tax return?

## Answer:

Yes, if you meet the other requirements to claim the child and dependent care credit but are missing the Social Security number or other taxpayer identifying number of your provider, you can still claim the credit by demonstrating due diligence in attempting to secure this information.

- Provide whatever information you have available for your provider (such as name and address) on form 2441 (.pdf), *Child and Dependent Care Expenses.*
- Write "See Attached Statement" in the columns requesting the missing information. Explain on the attached statement that you requested the provider's identifying number, but the provider did not give it to you. This statement supports a claim of the use of due diligence in trying to secure the identifying information.

## Question

Can I claim both the child tax credit and the child and dependent care credit?

**Answer**

You can claim both the child tax credit and the child and dependent care credit on the same return if you qualify for both credits.

- If you qualify for one or both credits, you can claim the credits on form 1040 (.pdf) or form 1040A (.pdf), *U.S. Individual Income Tax Return*. In addition, to claim the dependent care credit, you must complete form 2441 (.pdf), *Child and Dependent Care Expenses*.
- Search "Child Tax Credits" in the index to the Instructions for Form 1040 or the Instructions for Form 1040A. The instructions explain who qualifies for the child tax credit and how to calculate it.
- If you are claiming the child tax credit for a dependent child who has an ITIN, complete part 1 of schedule 8812 (form 1040A or 1040) (.pdf), *Child Tax Credit*, and attach it to your form 1040, 1040A or 1040NR (.pdf), *U.S. Nonresident Alien Income Tax Return*.
- The Instructions for Form 2441 (.pdf) explain who qualifies for the dependent care credit and how to calculate it.

**Credit for the Elderly or the Disabled**

**Question**

Can I claim the credit for the elderly or the permanently and totally disabled?

**Answer**

If you are a U.S. citizen or resident alien, you may qualify for this credit if before the end of 2014,

- you were age sixty-five or older, or
- you retired on permanent and total disability *and* have taxable disability income.

Even if you meet the above tests, you cannot claim the credit if either of the following exceed certain amounts:

- your adjusted gross income, or
- the total of your nontaxable Social Security, nontaxable pensions, nontaxable annuities, and nontaxable disability income.

**Issue Number: SETT -2015-12**
**Inside This Issue**

**Don't Overlook the Child and Dependent Care Tax Credit This Summer**
IRS Special Edition Tax Tip 2015-12

Day camps are common during the summer months. Many parents pay for them for their children while they work or look for work. If this applies to you, your costs may qualify for a federal tax credit that can lower your taxes. Here are the top ten tips to know about the Child and Dependent Care Credit:

1. **Care for qualifying persons**-your expenses must be for the care of one or more qualifying persons. Your dependent child or children under age thirteen usually qualify. For more about this rule, see Publication 503, Child and Dependent Care Expenses.
2. **Work-related expenses**-your expenses for care must be work related. This means that you must pay for the care so you can work or look for work. This rule also applies to your spouse if you file a joint return. Your spouse meets this rule during any month they are a full-time student. They also meet it if they're physically or mentally incapable of self-care.
3. **Earned income required**-you must have earned income, such as from wages, salaries, and tips. It also includes net earnings from self-employment. Your spouse must

also have earned income if you file jointly. Your spouse is treated as having earned income for any month that they are a full-time student or incapable of self-care. This rule also applies to you if you file a joint return. Refer to Publication 503 for more details.

4.  **Joint return if married**-generally, married couples must file a joint return. You can still take the credit, however, if you are legally separated or living apart from your spouse.

5.  **Type of care**-you may qualify for it whether you pay for care at home, at a day care facility, or at a day camp.

6.  **Credit amount**-the credit is worth between 20 and 35 percent of your allowable expenses. The percentage depends on the amount of your income.

7.  **Expense limits**-the total expense that you can use in a year is limited. The limit is $3,000 for one qualifying person or $6,000 for two or more.

8.  **Certain care does not qualify**-you may not include the cost of certain types of care for the tax credit, including

    •   Overnight camps or summer school tutoring costs,
    •   Care provided by your spouse or your child who is under age nineteen at the end of the year, and
    •   Care given by a person you can claim as your dependent.

9.  **Keep records and receipts**-keep all your receipts and records for when you file your tax return next year. You will need the name, address, and taxpayer identification number of the care provider. You must report this information when you claim the credit on form 2441, Child and Dependent Care Expenses.

10. **Dependent care benefits**-special rules apply if you get dependent care benefits from your employer. See Publication 503 for more on this topic.

Remember that this credit is not just a summer tax benefit. You may be able to claim it for qualifying care that you pay for at any time during the year.

## Additional IRS Resources

1.  Tax Topic 602-Child and Dependent Care Credit
2.  Frequently Asked Questions-Childcare Credit
3.  Publication 926, Household Employer's Tax Guide
4.  Publication 907, Tax Highlights for Persons with Disabilities

## Topic 602-Child and Dependent Care Credit

You may be able to claim the child and dependent care credit if you paid expenses for the care of a qualifying individual to enable you and your spouse filing a joint return to work or actively look for work. You may not take this credit if your filing status is married filing separately. The credit amount is a percentage of the amount of work-related expenses you paid to a care provider for the care of a qualifying individual. The percentage depends on your adjusted gross income.

The total expenses that you may use to calculate the credit should not be more than $3,000 (one qualifying individual) or $6,000 (two or more qualifying individuals). Expenses paid for the care of a qualifying individual are eligible expenses if the primary reason is to assure the individual's well-being and protection.

A *qualifying individual* for the child and dependent care credit is:

*   Your dependent qualifying child who is under age thirteen when the care is provided,
*   Your spouse who is physically or mentally incapable of self-care and lived with you for more than half the year, or
*   A person who is *physically* or *mentally incapable* of self-care, lived with you for more than half the year, and either (i) is your dependent or (ii) could have been your dependent except that he or she is over the gross income limit or files a joint return, or you (or your spouse, if filing jointly) could have been claimed on another taxpayer's 2014 return.

An individual is *physically* or *mentally incapable* of self-care if, as a result of a physical or mental defect, the individual is incapable of caring for his or her hygiene or nutritional needs or requires the full-time attention of another person for the individual's own safety or the safety of others.

A noncustodial parent who is claiming a child as a dependent should review the rules in the topic Child of Divorced or Separated Parents or Parents Living Apart in Publication 503, Child and Dependent Care Expenses, as the rules for claiming dependency exemptions are different from the rules for a qualifying person for the child and dependent care credit. If a person is a qualifying individual for only a part of the tax year, only those expenses paid during that part of the year are included in calculating the credit. You must provide the taxpayer identification number (usually the Social Security number) of each qualifying individual.

The provided care may be in the household or outside the household; however, do not include any amounts that are not primarily for the well-being of the person. You should divide the expenses between amounts for care and the amounts that are not for care. You must reduce the remaining qualifying expenses by the amount of any dependent care benefits provided by your employer that you exclude from gross income. In general, you can exclude up to $5,000 for dependent care benefits received from your employer. Additionally, in general, the expenses claimed may not exceed the smaller of your earned income or your spouse's earned income; however, a special rule applies if your spouse is a full-time student or incapable of self-care.

*Page Last Reviewed or Updated: February 04, 2015*

# CHAPTER 44

---

# Vacation Home Rentals

**Issue Number: IRS Summertime Tax Tip 2015-03**
**Inside This Issue**

### IRS Tips about Vacation Home Rentals

If you rent a home to others, you usually must report the rental income on your tax return. However, you may not have to report the rent you get if the rental period is short and you also use the property as your home. In most cases, you can deduct your rental expenses. When you also use the rental as your home, your deduction may be limited. Here are some basic tax tips that you should know if you rent out a vacation home:

- **Vacation home**-a vacation home can be a house, apartment, condominium, mobile home, boat or similar property.
- **Schedule E**-you usually report rental income and rental expenses on schedule E, Supplemental Income and Loss. Your rental income may also be subject to net investment income tax.

- **Used as a home**-if the property is "used as a home," your rental expense deduction is limited. This means your deduction for rental expenses can't be more than the rent you received. For more about these rules, see Publication 527, Residential Rental Property (Including Rental of Vacation Homes).

- **Divide expenses**-if you personally use your property and also rent it to others, special rules apply. You must divide your expenses between the rental use and the personal use. To figure how to divide your costs, you must compare the number of days for each type of use with the total days of use.

- **Personal use**-personal use may include use by your family. It may also include use by any other property owners or their family. Use by anyone who pays less than a fair rental price is also personal use.

- **Schedule A**-report deductible expenses for personal use on schedule A, Itemized Deductions. These may include costs such as mortgage interest, property taxes, and casualty losses rented less than fifteen days. If the property is "used as a home" and you rent it out fewer than fifteen days per year, you do not have to report the rental income. In this case, you deduct your qualified expenses on schedule A.

**Additional IRS Resources**

- Tax Topic 415-Renting Residential and Vacation Property
- Rental Income and Expenses-Real Estate Tax Tips

CHAPTER 45

# CPE for 25 Percent the Price

I used to spend $360 for twenty-four hours spent at a three-day seminar and $34 for an online two-hour ethics course. That is $394 for the required twenty-six hours for an enrolled agent. The E/A must have seventy-two hours of CPE credit over three years and a minimum of sixteen hours in any year. If you need twenty-six hours a year, I recommend the Tax School, www.thetaxschool.com. I pay $88 plus $8 shipping. The twenty-six hours includes two hours of ethics training. "The Tax School offers five quality courses that can be completed in the comfort and convenience of your office or home. No all-day lectures to attend." The Tax School also requests your PTIN so it can forward your completion to the IRS. I have also used PES, which costs more ($159 for twenty-six hours) but has a better variety of courses. If you need more than twenty-six hours, you may want to use both CPE firms. APLusCPE charges $54.95 for twenty-four hours of EA CPE and $9.95 for E/A ethics. I have not checked them out.

CPAs and attorneys require more hours of CPE. Each state has its own requirements. There are some firms that advertise $139 and $149 for unlimited on line CPE credit. I recommend that you check with your state to see if they will accept the CPE.

CHAPTER 46

# When Emotional Distress and Physical Illness Awards Are Not Taxable

A taxpayer received a 1099 from a company that polluted the air. Everyone who lived within a mile of the company received a cash award. The taxpayer reported the award as taxable.

Since the taxpayer was not injured, I thought it was taxable. I was not aware of all the facts.

I later learned that the company had released friable asbestos into the air. Inhaling asbestos or asbestos fibers landing on food or drinks can cause mesothelioma. The high school is four blocks from the taxpayer's home. Two dozen students had to be taken to the hospital after breathing polluted air. When I brought up this information, the taxpayer told me that she also had become quite ill. Everyone living within a mile of the company may have the strong possibility of future health problems. I would have moved. I filed a claim for refund, and she received her refund in twenty weeks.

## IRS Publication 4345
### Personal physical injuries or physical sickness

If you received a settlement for personal physical injuries or physical sickness and did not take an itemized deduction for medical expenses related to the injury or sickness in prior years, the full amount is nontaxable. Do not include the settlement proceeds in your income.

*But*

If you received a settlement for personal physical injuries or physical sickness, you must include in income that portion of the settlement that is for medical expenses you deducted in any prior year(s) to the extent the deduction(s) provided a tax benefit. If part of the proceeds is for medical expenses you paid in more than one year, you must allocate on a pro rata basis the part of the proceeds for medical expenses to each of the years you paid medical expenses. See recoveries in Publication 525 for details on how to calculate the amount to report. The tax benefit amount should be reported as "Other Income" on line 21 of form 1040.

Emotional distress. Emotional distress itself is not a physical injury or physical sickness, but damages you receive for emotional distress due to a physical injury or sickness are treated as received for the physical injury or sickness. Do not include them in your income.

If the emotional distress is due to a personal injury that is not due to a physical injury or sickness (for example, unlawful discrimination or injury to reputation), you must include the damages in your income, except for any damages you receive for medical care due to emotional distress. Emotional distress includes physical symptoms that result from emotional distress, such as headaches, insomnia, and stomach disorders.

CHAPTER 47

# How to Avoid an Audit if Previous Audit of Your Return(s) Resulted in a No-Change Letter or a Small Tax Deficiency

-If you received a no-change report in a previous year (last year or two), you may be able to avoid a current audit. This is especially true if the IRS is auditing you for the same issues as in prior years. Before your first appointment, fax a copy of the no-change report and the prior and current information document requests (if available) to the group manager. Then talk to the group manager and explain why it would be a waste of your time and their time to audit the return.

There are some taxpayers who are audited almost every year because of the nature of their expenses-for example, very large travel and entertainment expenses. If there are very small adjustments or no-change reports after each audit, this could justify skipping the audit. If not, maybe the group manager may agree to limit the scope of the audit.-

# ABOUT THE AUTHOR

The following are some of the author's qualifications:

- The Chicago District civil fraud coordinator for five years
- Group manager and the information gathering project group manager
- Taught and audited reorganizations, mergers, and consolidations
- Taught all required revenue agent courses, fraud CPE, special agents, special enforcement, and taught instructors how to teach
- The Coordinated Agent Program for three years where he helped senior revenue agents with their technical and auditing skills
- Special enforcement group, which went after organized crime
- Review staff, twice reviewing revenue agent cases
- The Exempt Organization Group (E/O) and the
- E/O reviewer
- Audited hundreds of corporations and many large tax shelters

CPSIA information can be obtained
at www.ICGtesting.com
Printed in the USA
LSOW02n0421160317
34124FS

9 781683 486879